HOW TO THINK ABOUT WAR AND PEACE

How to Think About WAR and PEACE

by

MORTIMER J. ADLER

Introduction by John J. Logue

FORDHAM UNIVERSITY PRESS
NEW YORK

Library of Congress Cataloging-in-Publication Data

Adler, Mortimer Jerome, 1902–
    How to think about war and peace / by Mortimer J. Adler :
introduction to the 1995 edition by John J. Logue.
        p.   cm.
    Originally published: New York : Simon and Schuster, 1944.
    Includes bibliographical references.
    ISBN 0-8232-1642-X (hardcover).—ISBN 0-8232-1643-8 (pbk.)
    1. Peace. I. Title.
JX1952.A35   1996
327.1'72—dc20   95-49502
                                                      CIP

Printed in the United States of America

TO MY SONS
AND THEIRS

Table of Contents

Introduction to the 1995 Edition

BY JOHN J. LOGUE

I AM overjoyed that Fordham University Press is republishing Mortimer Adler's classic book *How to Think About War and Peace*. It is an honor to write an introduction to this 1944 book in 1995, the fiftieth-anniversary year of the weak and troubled United Nations. For, although it was written a year before the U.N.'s Founding Conference in San Francisco, Mr. Adler's book has a great deal to say to the world of 1995 and the U.N. of 1995. It is a careful and reasoned brief for replacing the existing system of sovereign nation-states with a world federation of limited but adequate power.

During the long Cold War, world government seemed a utopian idea to most people. The U.N. coalition's victory in the 1990–91 Gulf War made it seem unnecessary. But recent events in Bosnia, Rwanda, and elsewhere may persuade policy elites to take it much more seriously than they have in the past. So may recent developments in the arms race.

I first read *How to Think About War and Peace* in 1944 at Camp Hale, Colorado. It had a profound effect on me and on what I did with my life. At Camp Hale we were training in what would soon become the Tenth Mountain Infantry Division. Needless to say, I was thinking a lot about war and peace in 1944. So were my three brothers, each about to go overseas.

Early in 1943 my widowed mother had had quite a shock. Her four sons had joined the Army within a month. Ed, 21, would soon be a bombardier with the 15th Air Force in Italy. Gordon, 20, would be a navigator with the same Air Force. John, 19, would be training with the Tenth Mountain, high in the Rockies. And Frank, 18, would soon be in France, with the 44th Infantry Division. Fortunately, the Logue brothers all came back—and resumed their studies at Yale. Ed, Gordon, and Frank had all been in combat. I had not. Rheumatic arthritis—or so I understood—put me in Camp Hale's hospital for sixteen weeks. I was put on limited service and eventually became an archivist at the Command and General Staff School.

The Basic Cause of War

Like most of my generation, I wondered why World War II had happened. The proximate causes were reasonably clear. Britain and France had entered the war in September 1939 because Germany had invaded Poland. The Soviet Union had entered in June 1941 because Germany had invaded her territory. The U.S. had entered in December 1941 because the Japanese had bombed Pearl Harbor.

But what was the basic cause of World War II, a six-year war that killed twenty million people? And why had World War I happened, that bloody war that killed more than thirteen million people between August 1914 and November 1918? And what, if any, strategy could prevent a World War III? These were the kinds of questions I asked myself in the mountains of Colorado.

As a political science major I was familiar with the traditional explanations for the coming of war. The conventional catalogue was a long one. It included human nature, nationalism, ideology, greed, ambition, treachery, appeasement, fear, weakness, subversion, militarism, pacifism, propaganda, economic deprivation, armament, disarmament, economic and political imperialism, imbalance of power, and poor leadership.

For most thinking people, "What is the basic cause of war?"

seems to be an insoluble problem. It certainly was for me, until I read *How to Think About War and Peace*. With this book Mortimer Adler persuaded me that anarchy was and is the basic cause of war and that the necessary remedy for it is government. It is not love or saintliness or national character which provides civil peace in our towns and cities and states and nations. It is government, world government. I became and remain an ardent world federalist. Like Mortimer Adler, I know that it will be very difficult to achieve a world government. But it will be far easier than trying to keep the peace without one.

In *How to Think About War and Peace* Adler says that anarchy is the appropriate name for the existing international system. It is an unworkable system that will lead to world war unless it is replaced by a world government of limited but adequate power which can make and enforce world law. It must be democratic, and so must its member nations. That world federation must be a constitutional democracy, i.e., it must have a constitution which not only empowers the federation's government but also limits its powers and balances its institutions. Needless to say, the federation must have substantial and dependable funding. It must also be able to make and enforce laws on arms reduction.*

Professor Adler was not content with merely stating the goal of world government and arguing that it was necessary and desirable. He was also deeply concerned with how to reach it. In this book he patiently and lucidly examines the many obstacles to reaching a world government and the many forces and developments which might help achieve it. He discusses the mental blocks that persuade most people that war is inevitable and that it is quixotic to try to get rid of it. He reminds us that for centuries physical afflictions

---

*A postscript to this Introduction will discuss how that world federation might come into existence.

like infantile paralysis were thought to be inevitable, or incurable, or both, but they have almost been abolished. He reminds us that despicable social institutions like slavery were also thought to be inevitable, but they too have been abolished or almost abolished. Then why can't we abolish war?

Adler concludes that we can abolish war if we propose and effectively promote the only possible cure for war, i.e., a world government. How long would it take to get world government? Mortimer Adler's answer indicates that he is a prudent man. In this 1944 book he concludes that it will take about five hundred years and that there will probably be several world wars along the way.

Hiroshima and the Rise of the World Federalist Movement

But less than two years after Adler's book was published atom bombs exploded over Hiroshima and Nagasaki, causing a tremendous loss of life. They brought World War II to an abrupt end and had a profound effect on human thought. The massive destruction persuaded Adler that the human race could not afford another world war and that world government must be and could be achieved in fifty years. He said so in a letter to the editors of *Commonweal* which appeared in the August 31, 1945, issue of that magazine. It said, in part:

> The atomic bomb had no less drastic effect on my thinking than it did on yours. I sincerely thought that the obstacles to world federation were so great that we couldn't expect to achieve this goal for centuries. But even a century is now too long. The so-called "United Nations", merely confederated under the San Francisco Charter, are not united enough to prevent another world war in the next fifty years. With the atomic bomb

vastly improved in efficiency and magnitude, another world war will do more than postpone the beginning of world peace. We can no longer wait through several more world wars for the world to overcome the moral and spiritual, the economic and political, obstacles to world federation. Instead of 500 years, we have less than fifty to save "the last best hope of earth." We are called upon to do that, not out of nobility of purpose, but from sheer necessity in the interest of self-preservation.

World federalism caught on quickly after the bombing of Hiroshima and Nagasaki. Federalist organizations sprang up in many countries. For a brief period it seemed possible that a world federation would be established before, perhaps well before, Mortimer Adler's deadline. In the United States many World War II veterans joined the movement. So did many young people who had been too young for military service. Prominent conservative Republicans and prominent liberal Democrats also signed up. In February 1947, in Asheville, North Carolina, six federalist organizations merged to form United World Federalists (UWF). By far the largest U.S. federalist organization, UWF soon had 47,000 members and active chapters in many, if not most, U.S. states.

UWF was frequently in the news, with demonstrations, dinners, petition campaigns, and testimony before congressional committees. The organization had considerable influence on Capitol Hill. In 1947 a world federalist resolution was introduced in both houses of Congress. It called on President Truman to immediately take the initiative in calling a General Conference of the United Nations pursuant to Article 109 for the purpose of making the United Nations capable of enacting, interpreting, and enforcing world law to prevent war.

Seven senators and ten congressmen, some of them Democrats, some Republicans, co-sponsored these concurrent resolutions. Three of those House members would soon be senators and then become prominent national figures: Estes Kefauver, the Democratic vice presidential candidate in 1956; Mike Mansfield, soon to become the Democratic majority leader in the Senate; and Richard Nixon, soon to be Vice President and then President of the United States.

Prominent federalists of that time included physicist Albert Einstein, Supreme Court Justice William O. Douglas, Cass Canfield, chairman of the board of Harper & Brothers, W. T. Holiday, president of Standard Oil of Ohio, and Norman Cousins, editor of *The Saturday Review.* A world federalist article by Holiday appeared in *Reader's Digest.* A condensation of federalist Emery Reves's book *The Anatomy of Peace* appeared in the same publication.

In the early 1950s the Cold War, McCarthyism, and the Korean War helped to lessen the numbers and the enthusiasm of the world federalists. So did divisions within the movement. The world survived Adler's fifty-year deadline, but the dangers increase. The United Nations certainly deserves some of the credit for keeping the peace. So does the universal fear of nuclear war. So do the superpowers who, during the Cold War, restrained and, in some cases, disciplined nations in their respective spheres of influence.

The arms race continued, however. So did the slaughter. There have been more than a hundred wars since World War II, and some twenty million people were killed in them. Although the U.N. Charter required the U.N. to stop many of those wars, it intervened with force in only three or four of them. The past half-century has demonstrated how weak the United Nations is, how inadequate its Charter is, and how unwilling the Great Powers are to restructure and empower it so that it can do its job. While U.N. peacekeeping forces have saved a great many lives, twenty million dead is a terrible indictment, not of the leadership of the U.N., but of the national political leaders who refuse to give the organization the means to do its job.

Broadening the Concept of World Federalism

Although the U.N. remains weak and poor, there was some progress toward world federation during its first fifty years. Perhaps the most important part of it was a broadening of the concept of world federation. The U.N. played an important role in that progress. So did the efforts of the Brandt, Palme, Brundtland, Nyerere, and other Commissions and study groups. So did the founding and growth of what is now called the European Union. One of the most important developments of those years was the almost complete abolition of colonialism. Another was a significant increase in the proportion of democratic nations in the U.N. A third was humanity's increased concern for human rights, for protecting the environment, and for promoting development programs that can be sustained.

Mr. Adler urged and applauded these developments and played a part in some of them, especially as a member of the prestigious Committee to Frame a World Constitution. He believed and believes that a world constitution, whether an amended U.N. Charter or an entirely new document, must be able to address economic, social, and human rights problems as well as security problems.

These developments meant that future proposals for a world federation would address a wider range of world problems than those addressed by most world federalists in the late 1940s. While many young world federalists were enthusiastic about a broader concept of world federalism, most adult world federalists tended to be more conservative. At its founding convention in 1947, UWF wanted a "security only" federation. But it soon moved to a position of neutrality on the question of whether the proposed world federation should have additional powers. Today UWF's successor, the World Federalist Association, calls for a much broader concept of world federalism than UWF ever did.

While the broadening of the concept of world federation was a very constructive development, it did not add much to UWF's membership. The Cold War was persuading many federalists to use less and less of their time discussing and working for world government and more and more of it working for "interim goals," e.g., arms control and disarmament, foreign aid, human rights, and the protection of the environment. However, the political and financial constraints of the Cold War severely limited the progress that could be made toward those interim goals. So did the Vietnam War. That tragic event turned the attention of many American activists away from world federalism, away from U.N. reform, and away from interim goals. They spent most of their time and energy protesting against that war and trying to end it.

Can the Post–Cold War U.N. Keep the Peace: Three Tests

When the Cold War finally ended in 1989, many U.N. supporters believed that the U.N. would now be able to do its job and that few, if any, changes would be needed in its structures and powers. While the permanent members' would keep their veto in the Security Council, a Gorbachev or a Yeltsin would be less likely to use it than a Stalin, a Khrushchev or a Brezhnev. A Communist China inside the U.N. would be more cooperative than the Communist China that the United States had kept outside for so many years.

The U.N. coalition's victory over Iraq in the 1990–91 Gulf War seemed to support the view that the U.N. did not need to be strengthened. The coalition had put down an aggressor, and it had not required a Charter change to do so. The post–Cold War U.N. had lived up to its responsibility under Article 1 of the Charter to take effective collective measures for the prevention and removal of threats to the peace, and for the suppression of acts of aggression. The coalition's victory seemed to confirm the view that the Charter did not need to be amended.

The Gulf War was hardly over when a savage war broke out in the Balkans. Within three years some 200,000 people had been killed. But this time the U.N. members chose not to honor their Article 1 obligations to stop the aggressor. Why not? Many people concluded that the U.N. coalition's war against Iraq had had much less to do with upholding the U.N. Charter than with seeing that the world's oil reserves did not get into the wrong hands. When Iraq conquered Kuwait in late 1990, it conquered the nation that has the world's third largest oil reserves and was a threat to nearby Saudi Arabia, the nation with, by far, the largest oil reserves. Had Iraq, with the second-largest oil reserves, conquered both those countries, it would have had control over almost half the world's oil reserves. With so much at stake, the U.N. coalition decided to go to war to free Kuwait and to protect Saudi Arabia.

The early 1990s saw a third major test of the post-Cold War U.N., i.e., the starvation and/or slaughter of half a million persons in Somalia, Sudan, and Rwanda. The U.N. and its member nations quickly brought in food and medicine. These were civil wars rather than inter-state conflicts, and for that reason the U.N.'s duty to intervene was somewhat less clear. But Article 1 of the Charter states that a major purpose of the U.N. is "to achieve international cooperation in . . . promoting and encouraging respect for human rights and for fundamental freedoms. . . ." The U.N. and U.N.–member nations quickly brought in food and medicine. But should the U.N. use force to stop the slaughter? In Somalia, the U.S. military used force against one of the warlords, and a number of American soldiers were killed. This generated strong congressional and public sentiment for removing U.S. troops. President Clinton announced he would remove them in the near future, and he did so. And though many U.N.–member nations gave humanitarian aid, most U.N. members felt that their peoples would not approve their using force to protect the citizens of those unfortunate African nations.

The end of the Cold War has made nations even less willing to live up to their Charter commitments. Many national political leaders have said that they and they alone will decide whether and, if so, how and when their governments will live up to their Article 1 obligations. Most nations conclude that they cannot count on the U.N. for their security. They must depend on their alliances, their diplomacy, their weaponry, and themselves. In some cases this will mean covert action or pre-emptive strikes against potential enemies.

Huge arms transfers to the Third World have added greatly to the problems of security and stability. But they are only part of the problem.

The weaponry of 1995 is far more lethal than that of 1945. Among the new or improved weapons are hydrogen bombs, new or improved atom bombs, nuclear submarines, the intercontinental ballistic missile (ICBM), anti-personnel mines, germ warfare, biological weapons, more effective poison gas, and 2,000–mile-an-hour jet planes. Because aircraft carriers are very expensive and may soon be very vulnerable, the U.S. Navy is designing arsenal ships which, it is reported, will cost about one-tenth as much as the carriers and require only 20 personnel rather than the 4,500 required by the largest aircraft carriers.

Today satellites circle the earth at tremendous speeds and can easily be converted into dangerous weapons. This has generated congressional support for expensive defense shields. Another danger is that the increasing power of explosives tempts fanatics to commit suicide if by so doing they can destroy thousands or millions of people. The World Trade Center was heavily damaged by one such attack. Another was planned for United Nations headquarters in New York.

The post–World War II arms race imitates the arms races that occurred in Europe after the defeat of Napoleon in 1815. Soon after Waterloo it became clear that neither the Holy Alliance nor the Quadruple Alliance could be counted on to keep the peace. Between 1815 and 1914 European generals, admirals, and inventors did not sit still. They invented or produced or bought improved rifles and artillery, machine guns, iron or steel battleships, submarines, tanks, combat airplanes, and poison gas. They developed steam engines and laid down railroad tracks. They built trucks and road networks. They also built much larger armies and much more efficient communication systems, and drew up much more sophisticated plans for the rapid mobilization of their troops. Their much-improved armament contributed greatly to the horrors of World War I.

Soon after the Versailles Conference it became clear that the League of Nations would not be able to keep the peace. The munitions makers went back to their drawing boards and developed fighter planes, bombers, and transport planes, aircraft carriers, tank and personnel landing craft, radar, and, of course, the atomic bomb.

But not at Vienna in 1815, not at Versailles in 1919, not at San Francisco in 1945 did the Great Powers try to build world institutions which could effectively keep the peace and accommodate change. At the U.N.'s fiftieth anniversary celebration in San Francisco, the most prestigious groups made relatively timid suggestions which, if adopted, would do little to cure the anarchy of the nation-state system.

If the existing United Nations–states cannot stop wars and if the world is becoming a much more dangerous place, we must ask why more people in more countries are not working harder to reform and restructure the U.N. and to give it the power to keep the peace, to protect the global environment, and to promote justice and human rights, i.e., to transform the U.N. into a world federation.

The Realists: A Major Obstacle to World Government

In my view the major obstacle to world government is not political, or financial, or ideological. The major obstacle is intellectual. Since World War II a school of thought known as "realism" has dominated the discussion of international politics and, to a considerable extent, the implementation of it. This is especially true in the United States. Most, if not all, of the realists have insisted that the national interest must be the determinant of national policy—not ethics, not international law, and certainly not the United Nations, whether in its present form or in any conceivable form. However, the brilliance and learning of the realists are no guarantee that their judgment is sound.*

Realists expect their own and every other nation to relentlessly pursue its national interest and, for no logical reason, hope or even expect that this will result in a happy convergence of those national interests. Shades of Adam Smith's "hidden hand"! Their theory assumes that many or even most statesmen will be wise enough to discover mutually

---

*I think I know the realist mind. I had the good fortune to be a student of three prominent realists: Nicholas Spykman and Arnold Wolfers at Yale and Hans Morgenthau at The University of Chicago. And Professor Morgenthau supervised my doctoral dissertation on a fourth realist, Edward Hallett Carr. Although I respected all those realists and others, such as George Kennan and Reinhold Niebuhr, I agree with Adler that their dismissal of world federalism has discouraged constructive thought about what institutions are essential to world peace and how to get them.

beneficial policies, and persuasive enough to get their own people and the leaders and people of other nations to support those policies. But the clear implication of the realists' thought is that persuasion, embargoes, and the threat of war can effectively keep the peace at the world level. Most realists seriously believe that well-managed anarchy can keep the peace at the world level. It is an absurd proposition but one they fiercely cling to. They also insist that world government, a system of law, order, justice, and enforcement is a utopian idea, an idea that could not work, or could not get adequate support, or, if established, would probably be a disaster. One suspects, one knows, that no realist would believe that anarchy can keep the peace at the local, state, or national level, that every realist would call that a utopian idea. Fortunately, a few realists have seriously pondered the case for world government, but many give little thought to it and, in some cases, belittle those who do.

In the United States and in many other countries, the beliefs of the realists have had a powerful—and, in important ways, a destructive—hold on policy elites, in academia, in the business community, and in the highest levels of government. Their hold is as powerful—and as destructive—as that of the Manchester School in the nineteenth century. Those ardent disciples of Adam Smith held that laissez-faire capitalism, i.e., anarchic capitalism, was a workable and desirable economic system. They believed that government should do little more than provide national defense, public order, a monetary mechanism, and the enforcement of contracts. They said that it would be counterproductive for government to concern itself with such problems as poverty or unemployment or health or social security.

The economic views of the Manchester School were strongly and sincerely believed by many political, economic, academic, and religious leaders. They were soon translated into public policy and, not surprisingly, had catastrophic effects on millions of wage earners and their families. The novels of Charles Dickens chronicled the degradation which they visited on the English poor. The views and policies of the Manchester School alienated working people and persuaded many intellectuals and some labor leaders that capitalism inevitably meant poverty and exploitation and that only communism or fascism or state socialism could answer the needs of wage earners and their families. Communist and fascist dictatorships took power in a number of countries. Their leaders, at least the early ones, wanted to help poor people but felt that that required not only firm control over the economic system but also firm control over the political system.

The ascendancy of the Manchester School was eventually undermined by intellectual critiques, by the growing power of labor unions, and by politicians who addressed the needs of working families with practical political and economic programs which would make capitalism socially responsible. Today there is a widespread belief that capitalism can survive and prosper if—and only if—it is supplemented by economic and social security. That conviction and the humane policies it fostered were the basic reason for the resurgence of capitalism and the collapse of communism and fascism.

Although the Manchester School's influence on economic and social policy has faded, the realist school's impact on foreign policy-making is still very strong. Its anarchic views continue to dominate discussion and decision-making in the realm of international politics. Those views encourage a Machiavellian approach to international politics. In situations where realists think it is vital to stop aggression, they invoke provisions of the U.N. Charter which require nations to help stop the aggressor. But if stopping a particular aggression is not vital and would be politically expensive, they ignore those Charter provisions. If action is vital but politically unpopular, they may arm and bankroll poor countries who are willing to fight and, if U.S. forces are essential, they may undertake covert operations, enabling them to deceive the public and most of the Congress.

Realists are aware of the problems that come with anarchy but believe they can be managed by classic diplomatic techniques such as consultation, alliances, bargaining, warnings, power-balancing, and spheres of influence. Henry Kissinger and other realist historians have romanticized the Concert of Europe and the Pax Britannica, i.e., the power-balancing policy of the British Empire. The Concert's get-togethers probably did stop or postpone a number of wars in the nineteenth century. So did Britain's shrewd diplomacy. But they did so at a great cost to the each of the Concert powers.

Soon, very soon, after Napoleon's defeat Britain had to choose whether to devote some of its energy and resources to building European institutions, as Foreign Minister Lord Castlereagh and Czar Alexander wanted, or put most of its energy into being the power-balancer in the European system. (Castlereagh remembered Britain's long—and sometimes lonely—struggle against Napoleon and feared that something like it would happen in the years ahead. The Czar remembered that Napoleon's troops had taken Moscow in 1812. The Czar and the British Foreign Minister were an odd couple.) Their hopes for powerful European institutions were strongly opposed by Parliament and by Castlereagh's successor, George Canning. In 1818, France joined Austria, Russia, and Prussia in the Quadruple Alliance, but Britain withdrew in the same year. As Canning withdrew, he said, "Each nation for itself and God for us all." Britain did not have to pay the price for her "loner" policy until 1914 and 1939, and then she paid a great price indeed.

Nineteenth-century Britain had many assets and, or so it would seem, used them shrewdly. Though part of Europe, Britain was an island nation. It had the world's most powerful navy, was a leading industrial power, and had a huge empire, with guaranteed access to large markets and major sources of raw materials. It had control of key ports and waterways in many parts of the world. British leaders used these assets and their own diplomatic skills to see that no nation got too powerful or was too isolated.

But an effective Pax Britannica seemed to require, probably did require, British domination of Ireland and India, Gibraltar and Malta, Egypt and South Africa, and many other places. For the first half of the century it was helped by the limited size of the British electorate and the Foreign Office's relative insulation from Parliament. But in the latter part of the century nationalism and democracy were sweeping Britain, Europe, and much of the rest of the world. They made British governments less and less able to withstand the growing power of "Little Englanders," who questioned the wisdom and the cost of the policies which Pax Britannica seemed to require, and to withstand independence movements in Ireland, India, and other parts of the Empire. In relative terms, Britain's power was waning while Germany's was waxing. The Pax Britannica was threatened by a very unified Germany and a unified Italy, by growing German military and industrial power, by German and Italian colonial ambitions, and especially by a growing German army and German aspirations for a large navy.

To play its role of power-balancer Britain had eschewed alliances. But power-balancing was and is a delicate and dangerous game. As the century neared its end, Germany abandoned the restraints of former Chancellor Bismarck, built up a mighty army, began to dabble in colonialism, threatened to build a large navy, and engaged in some very undiplomatic conduct. Early in the twentieth century the menace of a powerful Germany persuaded Britain to ally itself with France and with Russia. Meanwhile Germany allied itself with Austria-Hungary and with Bulgaria and Turkey. Now, there was no power-balancer, and in 1914 the international system broke down. It took four long years of death and destruction before the victors could begin to patch the system together. Many realists see a Pax Americana as the best—or the least bad—foreign policy the United States can have in the years ahead. It is certainly much more likely to win support than any proposal to empower either the one nation/one vote General Assembly or to empower the present or a somewhat larger Security Council. For many reasons the United States will not and should not turn its back on the world. It has the strongest economy and, by far, the strongest military machine. And there are many reasons for thinking that at the present time the world would welcome a Pax Americana and that Americans officials would be flattered to take on that job. But there are other reasons for thinking that neither Congress nor the American people would support such a policy for very long. And even if they did support it, there are reasons for thinking that presidents and their advisers would eventually back away from it.

The arms race continues. In the decades ahead it will be more and more difficult and dangerous to be the world's policeman. With missiles becoming more and more accurate, able to go farther and farther, and carry more and more dangerous explosives, the world policeman's lot will not be a happy one. The economies of a number of middle- or large-size countries are expanding rapidly, and the U.S. economy's lead will probably diminish. The world desperately needs order, especially to control and, it is hoped, stop the arms race. The American people have to decide whether they prefer isolation or participation. If they choose participation, they have to decide whether they want to invest the precious years just ahead in an ego-satisfying Pax Americana policy which cannot last for long or in a bold attempt to replace the anarchy of the nation-state system with a world commonwealth which has the power and the authority to make, interpret, and enforce world law, limited world law.

Some realists have seen the limitations of the realist approach to international politics and viewed world government as the necessary solution. But most of them feel that for the time being it is impossible to achieve. The late Hans Morgenthau, a very prominent realist, said this in the 1978 edition of his book *Politics Among Nations:*

> There is no shirking the conclusion that international peace cannot be permanent without a world state, and that a world state cannot be established under the present moral, social and political conditions of the world. . . . there is also no shirking the further conclusion that in no period of modern history was civilization more in need of permanent peace, and, hence, of a world state, and that in no period of history were the moral, social and political conditions of the world less favorable for the establishment of a world state.

Unfortunately Morgenthau did not draw the conclusion that Mortimer Adler draws in this book, that is, that because world government is necessary, "the moral, social, and political conditions of the world" which do not permit it to be realized must be changed—and soon. Professor Morgenthau died before the end of the Cold War, so we cannot know whether the dissolution of the Soviet Union and the Soviet Bloc would have convinced him that a world state is now a possibility.

Another realist, Robert Strausz-Hupe, founding director of the conservative Foreign Policy Research Institute, also sees the necessity for a world government. In 1992 he told the Philadelphia hearing of the U.S. Commission on Improving the Effectiveness of the United Nations:

> What is needed first and foremost in order to make the United Nations more effective and viable is candor. The peoples of the world need to be told that a more effec-

tive United Nations comes at a price and that this price is the delegation of national sovereignty; in the beginning, not all of it, but as the process continues, more and more of it.

Recently, George F. Kennan, one of the most prestigious of the realists, gave an eloquent—and probably unintentional—call for world government. In his 1994 book *Around the Cragged Hill*, the former Director of the State Department's Policy Planning Staff said:

> Government is a universal feature of civilized life. Whatever the form it takes, however liberal or oppressive it may be, however large or small the community to which it extends, government is an absolute necessity. The only conceivable alternative would be a state of anarchy which would constitute self-destruction for the community in question—which is, in effect, no choice at all.

Alexander Hamilton saw the suicidal implications of the nation-state system. In *Federalist* No. 6 he said:

> To look for a continuation of harmony between a number of independent, unconnected sovereignties, situated in the same neighborhood, would be to disregard the uniform course of human events and to set at defiance the accumulated experience of ages.

The Internationalists and the U.N.

Another school, the internationalists, has played an important part in foreign-policy–making. Unlike the realists, the internationalists are, or seem to be, very pro-United Nations. But, like the realists, they spend little, if any, time advocating comprehensive U.N. reform and empowerment. They assume that U.N. restructure and empowerment must and can come gradually, like the development of the European Union. Thus, most of the proposals made by prestigious internationalist groups at or before the U.N.'s fiftieth anniversary celebration in San Francisco are more remarkable for what they do not advocate than for what they do.

Good examples would be the recommendations of two U.S. groups, the United Nations Association-U.S.A. and the U.S. Commission on Improving the Effectiveness of the United Nations, and two international groups, the Commission on Global Governance and the Independent Working Group on the Future of the United Nations. Though each of these groups made interesting and useful proposals, none of their proposals called for changes in the one nation/one vote system of representation in the General Assembly. None called for a significant rise in the meager funding that the U.N. now has or for a method of ensuring that that funding is dependable. While the Global Governance Commission talked boldly about getting rid of the veto, its provisions for enforcement would continue to require economic sanctions or war, two very undependable systems. There is much talk of international criminal courts but no credible suggestions for extraditing indicted war criminals so that they can be tried.

Why don't most liberal internationalist groups call for a Charter amendment to change the one nation/one vote system of decision-making in the General Assembly? U.N. watchers know that Monaco, with some 30,000 people, has the same voting power as the United States or China. They also know that the U.N. is not going to be empowered until the one nation/one vote system is abandoned.

Can it be changed to a system which also gives some attention to population and, possibly, to economic power?

The conventional wisdom among U.N. watchers is that the many poor and/or sparsely populated Third World countries can and will round up enough votes, i.e., at least one-third plus one, to defeat any amendment providing for change in one nation/one vote. Certainly they would oppose—and probably defeat—a Charter amendment which dealt only with voting power. But suppose the amendment included an entire package of reforms, including provision for substantial and dependable funding for the U.N. and authorization of some of that funding for development, education, health, and other programs of great concern to many Third World nations? My guess is that many Third World countries would support that kind of amendment package.

There is an interesting analogy in American history. Soon after the signing of the U.S. Constitution, state conventions met to consider ratification of that document. One of its key features was a reduction in the voting power which small-in-population states had had under the one state/one vote Articles of Confederation regime. Nevertheless, three of the smallest-in-population states, Delaware, New Jersey, and Georgia, were among the first four states to ratify the Constitution. Each did so by a unanimous vote of 94–0. They preferred a strong constitution in which they would have less voting power to a very weak constitution in which they would retain their equal voting power.

Would the developed countries support an amendment package which abandons the one nation/one vote formula and restructures and empowers the United Nations? Would the permanent members of the Security Council support it? It is hard to say. One thing is certain. If they did not support it, the developed nations, rather than the Third World, would be blamed for the failure of U.N. reform and the retention of one nation/one vote.

I have suggested that a comprehensive or package approach is the easiest way to change the Charter. But most internationalists believe it is easier to get one or two of the necessary parts of an effective and desirable world federation than to get comprehensive change. That is a very dubious assumption. It is also a very destructive one, because it implies that if you cannot get a part or parts of a comprehensive package of reforms, you cannot get the whole. But the truth is just the opposite.

Most internationalists do not understand a paradox which the American Founding Fathers understood and which Mr. Adler understands, i.e., that it will be much easier to get comprehensive reform of the U.N. than to get gradual or partial reform of it. After trying hard to make partial changes in the Articles of Confederation, the Founding Fathers came to Philadelphia and tried the comprehensive approach. In four months they wrote a new and much stronger constitution, and in nine months they sold it to the American people.

The World Federalists

The world federalists say that their goal is a world federation that can make and interpret world law, limited world law, and enforce it on individuals, a world federation that has substantial and dependable funding, a world federation that is democratic. They want that federation to champion social and economic justice, human rights, and protection of the environment, not only in the world government that they want to see in the near future, but also in the existing nation-state system.

But while early world federalists were urging comprehensive reform of the United Nations, some recent and present leaders of the world federalists have become sincere champions of the gradual, partial approach, a strategy very similar to that of the liberal internationalists. The present leadership of the World Federalist Association, the largest U.S. world federalist group, frequently uses the vague term "global change" and the obscure term "global governance" rather

than the words "world government" or "world federation."
The distinguished international Commission on Global Governance insists that the term global governance does not
mean world government. This raises an important question:
Is vagueness in its most central terms an asset for the world
federalists or a liability? Is it an asset or a liability for the
Commission? It is of some interest that one of the most distinguished members of the Commission, Sir Brian Urquhart,
a former U.N. Under Secretary General, has said it is a meaningless word.

World federalist groups increasingly insist that all the
member nations in a world federation must be democratic,
a position that Mr. Adler has consistently taken. The case for
requiring member states to be democratic is a strong one.
But a doctrinaire definition of democracy could be counterproductive. If the definition rules out nations with established churches, then Britain will not be eligible for
membership. If each nation's electoral districts must be approximately equal in population, then the state of California
must have sixty times as many senators as Wyoming. Since
that is unlikely to happen, the United States will also be ineligible for membership in that kind of world federation. Many
nations, including the United States, will be ineligible if the
federation's constitution requires member nations to adhere
to the U.N.'s Declaration of Human Rights.

Should all nondemocratic states be kept out of the federation until they are full-fledged democracies? If no such provision is made, it may be very difficult to get many democratic
states to join a democratic world federation. For, as Mr. Adler
stresses, all the members of the world federation would have
to give up control of their foreign policy and most of their
military forces to a federation government. That federation
will be able to send their citizens into battle without asking
the permission of member governments. Students of world
federalist history will recall that the idea of a "democracies

only" federation was advocated with eloquence by Clarence Streit and his organization Union Now in the 1930s, during World War II, and in the decades after. However, in spite of dedication, hard work, and endorsements by many distinguished persons, it never really got off the ground.

Perhaps there can be a compromise which allows nondemocratic states to join the federation if they agree to disarmament, taxation, and other requirements when they join, and agree to have federally supervised elections within a stated number of years and reduced representation until that time. This would pose some danger to the federation but probably much less danger than having all nondemocratic states staying outside and increasing their armament.

I believe there is a real possibility that some dictators would be willing to lead their countries into a democratic federation and gradually devolve their power to their people. In the Soviet Union Mikhail Gorbachev welcomed *glasnost*. There is also reason to believe that Poland's dictator, General Jaruzelski, was happy to devolve some of his power if it would prevent the Soviet Union from intervening.

Let me add that while many people assume that the European Union will soon become a federation, I seriously doubt it. I do not believe that in the near future Britain or France or Germany will allow a European Assembly to decide whether, and with whom, the federation will go to war and which young people will be drafted to do the fighting.

Why are individuals who call themselves world federalists so taken by the idea that it can be or must be reached by a gradual-partial approach? I believe that a major reason is their admiration for the success of the European Union, a regional organization which has evolved slowly over the last forty years. They believe that that approach can be usefully applied to the problem of reforming and empowering the United Nations. I do not agree.

In my view the real reason for the success of the gradualist approach to building the European Union was that U.S. troops in Europe guaranteed the security of each of the Union's members, not only against the Soviet Union but also against the other members of the Union. After World War I a European prime minister would have risked political suicide if he urged generous and statesmanlike policies toward his country's recent enemies. But after World War II a European prime minister might gain rather than lose public support by calling for just such policies. If the U.N. or the U.S. (or Mars!) could guarantee the security of each nation during a slow evolution toward a U.N. world federation, a gradual approach to U.N. restructure and empowerment might be possible. But that is most unlikely to happen. In my view—and, I believe, Mr. Adler's—a world federation is much more likely to come through adoption of a comprehensive package of interdependent reforms involving, among other things, voting power, substantial and dependable funding, provision for the enforcement of U.N. law on individuals, and checks and balances to prevent usurpation of power by the U.N. executive.

Enforcement by Collective Security

The major reason why nations ignore their obligations to enforce the provisions of the U.N. Charter is that it establishes an unworkable system of enforcement. It is usually called "collective security." In the *Federalist Papers* Alexander Hamilton said that it is madness to make warfare the instrument for enforcing law. That is what the Articles of Confederation did, what the League of Nations Covenant did, and what the U.N. Charter does. As Walter Lippmann once said, collective security is an unworkable system which will work only if all the great powers feel threatened at the same time. The 1991 Gulf War was one of those rare occasions when the Big Five were in agreement, although two of them, Russia and China, made no military contribution to Operation Desert Storm.

However, if their own national interests are not involved, presidents and prime ministers will continue to be very reluctant to go to war. They may try economic and political pressure measures, but if the outlaw nation is powerful and persistent, they will probably not take up arms against it. Forced to choose between doing nothing, i.e., appeasement, and risking a quagmire like Korea or Vietnam, presidents and prime ministers usually decide that it will cost less politically to appease the outlaw nation than to go to war with it. That is what happened in Munich in 1938 when British Prime Minister Chamberlain and French Premier Daladier gave into Hitler's demands for the Sudeten region of Czechoslovakia and thereby made the rest of Czechoslovakia undefendable. That is what happened in Bosnia in 1992. But appeasement can be very costly. The Munich settlement was probably one of the major reasons why the Soviet Union signed a nonaggression treaty with Germany. That pact saved Hitler from a two-front war, allowing him to conquer Poland and then go westward to take on Denmark and Norway, then France and Britain.

The Virginia Analogy

In 1787 the Virginia delegation to the Constitutional Convention decided that the best way they could serve the interest of Virginia was to propose and promote a Virginia Plan to restructure and empower the weak and poor United States of the Articles of Confederation years. That plan, with important modifications, became the Constitution of the United States.

It is surprising that it does not occur to American realists that the best way they could serve the national interest of their country would be come up with an American Plan for a world federation and to sell that plan to the American people and to the people of the world and their national governments. America is one of the few powerful countries where realpolitik is still distrusted by a large part of the population. Typically, the substitutes that have been offered for it have been unrealistic, e.g., disarmament, international law, weak international organizations, good will, etc. The great advantage of world federation is that it is a realistic idea, infinitely more realistic than the fragile balance-of-power systems which the realists try to sell.

Americans know federalism. They know sharing of power. They know checks and balances. They know judicial review. They know grants-in-aid. They are wise enough to understand something that most realists deny: that the American experience and the American analogy do have great relevance to the urgent problems facing the world today. They can follow the example of Virginia, which urged the thirteen states to devise national institutions and powers and restraints not unlike those that Virginia and some of its neighbors were quite familiar with. Or they can follow the example of nineteenth-century Britain and try to balance the power for two or three decades until the American people—and the world's people—tire of that Pax Americana and the arms race gets totally out of hand.

I believe that Mortimer Adler's book shows us the way.

* * *

A Postscript: Needless to say, many people are curious as to the mechanics of bringing a democratic world federation into existence. The United Nations could become a world federation if an appropriate package of amendments to its

Charter is approved and ratified by two-thirds of the members of the United Nations, including all the permanent members of the Security Council. If that procedure seemed unlikely to succeed, a democratic world federation could also come into existence by having an appropriate body draft a new U.N. Charter, i.e., a replacement charter, with or without the name "United Nations," and getting that charter ratified by whatever process the charter provides for. The replacement Charter might or might not permit one nation to veto its adoption. A third possibility is that the federation of democracies would be formed within the existing United Nations. The U.N. would keep most of its present functions, including serving as a world forum and a meeting place for diplomats and for representatives of nongovernmental organizations. It is to be hoped that in a transition period the nondemocratic members of the U.N. would gradually decide to become democracies and apply to join the federation of democracies. At some point there might be a consensus to transfer the name United Nations to the federation of democracies.

A Plea to the Reader

BY CLIFTON FADIMAN

I CALL these words a plea because it is that and only that, and not a foreword, an introduction, or a preface. I make it because the author is by nature a limited man. He is incapable of making pleas, being capable only of making demonstrations.

Now, this plea of mine is unimportant, except insofar as it may move you to pay attention to the demonstration. That demonstration *is* important, being quite literally a matter of life or death. I do not mean that you cannot survive without reading it. I do mean that it deals with survival, perhaps yours or mine, but certainly the survival of civilized man.

I am pleading with you to do something difficult—to read a book that has to be hard in order to be good, and is both. These pages (and this is not praise) are swept bare of emotion. They are minus the seductions of a personal style. They do not glint with humor. The delightful pleasures of mental compromise may not be sought here. Yes, this is a hard book, hard not because it is involved or obscure, but because it gets down to bedrock, to hardpan. It is hard because it is basic; because it asks us to think things out to the end; because it asks us to grow greater than ourselves, to undergo a conversion of the passions and the intellect almost as awesome as that higher conversion that comes only by the grace of God.

The title of this book is *How to Think About War and Peace.* Not *How to Prevent War.* Not *How to Make Peace.* But how to *think* about war and peace. And right there is where the screams of anguish start. Very few of the rest of us who *say* we hate war and want peace are willing to do the hard and painful thinking that must precede the abolition of war and the creation of peace. For that kind of thinking leads to the conclusion most of us are willing to face only at the point of a gun: the conclusion that *we must change our minds.* But, when the gun is there, it is already too late.

Who is doing this kind of thinking today? Precious few men in high positions. Mainly plain citizens here and there, mothers and fathers and soldiers, businessmen and mechanics and farmers. These are not yet articulate, though their time is coming. In the meantime, this kind of thinking has come to my attention recently from two odd sources. One is the brain of a philosopher working at his desk in the city which many think of as the very center of American isolationism and nationalism. The end product of that thinking is the book you hold in your·hands.

Odder still is the second source. Now that I am no longer a member of the staff of that deeply and seriously civilized humorous magazine, I can say without embarrassment that in the editorial columns of *The New Yorker* during 1943 there appeared the clearest political thinking (presented in the most casual and even whimsical form) that American citizens have produced since the war began. You will find several quotations from *The New Yorker* in Mr. Adler's pages. Indeed, his whole book is but a systematic and logical extension of these quotations.

Because I would like you to know and trust him, may I say a word or two about the man who wrote it? He has been my friend for over twenty years, and I have been in hearty intellectual *dis*agreement with him for many of those years. But I am not engaged in puffing the work of a friend; I am engaged in pleading for the work of a wide-visioned fellow citizen.

Mortimer J. Adler, now forty-one, is Professor of the Philosophy of Law at the University of Chicago. A few hundred thousand Americans know him as the author of that surprising best seller, *How to Read a Book.* Thousands of teachers, here and abroad, know him (not always with unalloyed affection) as the gadfly of American education, a denying spirit who is dissatisfied with the quality of the production of our educational mill and with the quality of the minds of our teachers who turn its handles.* He is deeply learned in philosophy and cognate subjects, which is nothing to his credit, for the same is true of hundreds of his colleagues.

Amazingly fecund and at the same time intimidatingly non-superficial, he has written many books on problems of morals (including one on the morals of the movies) and metaphysics, books beyond my depth and read by but a small minority. He is to my mind a great, though not a popular, teacher.

An analyst in the field of democratic philosophy, he has grown out of many errors and false turnings into larger and larger truths. He possesses little of the charm, the passion, the artistic talents of those thinkers, like Pascal and Rousseau, who, though much greater men, nevertheless inhabit his universe of discourse. He is only clear, only logical, only uncompromising; and these, though they may be enduring qualities, are not endearing ones.

I referred above to "errors and false turnings." Mr. Adler himself, in an Augustinian confession in his Preface, cries out his own *mea culpa*. It is not important, however, that this book is Mr. Adler's attempt to set himself right; it is important that it is an attempt to set you and me right.

This attempt may not make Mr. Adler a highly beloved figure. We all love what is pleasant; and much of what Mr. Adler has to say is not pleasant. The Moscow Pact is a good thing; the ideas of Senator Ball are good; even the vague resolution of Representative Fulbright is good; but none of them can secure peace, any more than Locarno did. Those publicists who assure us to the contrary are doing us a disservice, because they are unwittingly leading us up to the brow of the cliff from which we shall some day fall in disillusionment.

I am myself less cautious than Mr. Adler and believe that there

---

* If any of my readers is similarly dissatisfied and would like to know why he is dissatisfied, I refer him to Mark Van Doren's *Liberal Education*. (Henry Holt, N. Y., 1943.)

is no theoretical obstacle to the creation of universal (though not necessarily internal) peace after this war. Yet I applaud his resolute determination to accept halfway measures only for what they are, and not as the panaceas our well-meaning optimists would make them out to be.

There have been a hundred books about peace and postwar planning; and, let us confess it, we are confused by most of them, and bored by the others. Here is still another. How does it differ from its competitors? It differs in that it is written from the point of view of a citizen of the world, not that of an American, a Frenchman, an Englishman, a European, a politician, an economist, a geographer, a Communist, a Fascist, or a moralist. "It differs," says the author, "from most of the current books about peace in that it is primarily concerned with the ideas that should be in every citizen's mind, not the plans or blueprints which deserve a place at the peace table." It is concerned only with *how to think* about peace—and war. "It is a book of ideas to think with."

What are some of these ideas? First, read the six questions that begin Chapter 1. Is there a thinking man or woman alive who is not interested in finding the answers to them? Are there any other questions, short of those that pertain to religion, that are more vital, more awesome, more overpoweringly necessary for us to answer? I can think of none. They are the questions, phrased simply and in their proper order, the answers to which will determine the major course of our lives and the lives of those to come after us. If you are not interested in them, then this book is not for you, and you are willing to let another man, who may turn out to be a Hitler, do your thinking for you.

First to grasp, then to answer these questions, we must consider what Mr. Adler calls the Four P's of Peace—the Problem, the Possibility, the Probability, the Practicality.

It is the second of these P's that, I conceive, stops many of us dead in our tracks.

Is perpetual peace at all possible? If we think it is not, we shall merely try to work out coalitions, balances of power, alliances, whose aim will be not *to make or preserve the peace,* but *to prolong the truce.* Then we shall call ourselves, with a certain satisfaction, "realists," as if there were some special virtue in the mere limiting of our objectives.

But what if it can be demonstrated, far more cogently than the "realists" demonstrate the opposite, that perpetual peace *is* possible, not tomorrow, not necessarily in our lifetime, but within the conceivable future? What if it can be shown, as I think the author does show in his third chapter, that war is *not,* like death, inevitable? How if it be more like chattel slavery which not so many years ago was considered the inevitable lot of some men—but which now we know to be a totally eradicable evil? What then? It is with this "What then?" that much of Mr. Adler's book deals.

If you are a Fascist, if you are a special kind of hard-boiled sentimentalist, you will asseverate that war is the normal condition of man. If you are a rational animal, as I conceive every reader of this book to be, you will come to Mr. Adler's conclusion, that *war is an abnormality,* that it is the *natural* condition of man to live in peace—and, furthermore, that history itself provides us with varied proofs that this is so. But what this peace *is* that man aspires to, it is necessary to define clearly; and one of his many brilliant insights lies in Mr. Adler's precise clarification of a word used far too loosely by too many respected thinkers and by many too respected thinkers. You will, among other things, learn that peace is not perfect concord or harmony, and has nothing to do with Utopia.

Something *causes* peace. It is government. Something will *cause* world peace. It is world government. Something *causes* war. It is anarchy. Something *causes* world wars. It is world anarchy. For the logical and reasonable demonstration of the truth of these simple affirmations, see the whole book, but more particularly Chapters 6 and 7.

Mr. Adler takes the bull by the horns. By this time we know

what the bull's name is. The bull is called Sovereignty. Sovereignty may be defined in many ways; it may be defined, for example, as an idea which certain Senators and Congressmen are unwilling to examine reasonably, preferring instead to orate about it emotionally. More useful definitions you will find in Chapter 8; there, too, you will find that, in Mr. Adler's opinion—which is open to argument—if we really wish for world peace, we must be prepared not merely to *limit*, but to *relinquish* entirely our *external* (as separate from our *internal*) sovereignty to a world government, as the thirteen colonies relinquished their *external*, not their *internal*, sovereignty to a federal union.

But this idea is a hard one to accept. It is hard for me to accept it, because I am so used to the idea of a sovereign nation, and so attached to my own sovereign nation. Most of my readers will feel the same way. The Pennsylvania farmer, the Virginia planter, the Massachusetts mechanic felt the same way in 1787. How do they feel today?

I am putting the problem far too simply. Mr. Adler devotes several chapters to a rational, even-tempered discussion of the idea of the relinquishment of sovereignty and the many objections that may be urged to it. I do not ask you to agree with him; I ask you to listen to him. His inquiry into the subject is *the* question of the next fifty years. No man alive, however unpolitical he thinks he is, will be free from the influence and effects of that inquiry; as no American alive in 1861 was free from the influence and effects of a somewhat similar inquiry that came to a head at Fort Sumter.

Mind you, Mr. Adler is not asking for the immediate relinquishment of sovereignty. He does not expect a world government tomorrow. He merely proves that the surest way of getting *peace* tomorrow—or, at any rate, a long and fruitful truce—is to work for a world government that may come at some remote but not unimaginably remote date. He is an idealist only in that he believes in the tendency of man toward peace. He is a practical idealist in his perception of the slow tempo at which that

tendency works. In my opinion, he is *too* practical, too conservative in his estimate of the length of time needed to establish
peace.

He is convinced that the existence of democracy and its gradual, though often interrupted, extension comprise true and valid
grounds for optimism. He is a rational optimist in that he insists
on examining carefully and without passion all the well-known
obstacles to world peace, and all the moral factors that make it
highly improbable in the immediate future. He cannot be accused of wishful thinking; he can only be excoriated, by the irra-
tional, for thinking at all.

Well, how do we go about it? What can education do, what
can the growing unity of the globe do, what can the abandon-
ment of race prejudice, imperialism, economic injustice do?
Much? Little? Nothing at all? Mr. Adler has pertinent and fresh
things to say on all these matters.

He reminds us that, though we in our generation cannot in
all probability *make* peace, we can *promote* it by action open to
all of us, action in thorough consonance with our pride in ourselves as citizens of a democracy. What action? See the chapter
called "Means." It is not exhaustive, it is open to argument; yet
it is a clear-visioned start.

But, even if we all work busily and with all our hearts toward
world peace, we must work toward it with the full and grave
consciousness—I would call it a religious, a truly Christian consciousness—that the work is being carried on by men who will
not live to see it finished. As Mr. Adler points out, the builders
of the Gothic cathedrals worked for hundreds of years, knowing
that only some future generation would enjoy the full glory of
these temples of God. Are we less men than they were?

No, it cannot be done tomorrow. But how many of our important actions are determined by the assurance that we will
enjoy their fruits tomorrow? Do we pay life-insurance premiums
for tomorrow? Make last wills and testaments for tomorrow?
Build up a happy family life only for tomorrow? Instruct our

children for tomorrow? Revere God for tomorrow? In sober truth, much of the life we live today is but posthumous, and the actions of our mortality are fit only for the creation of things immortal.

So, let us ask ourselves, is a remote objective to be cast aside merely because it is remote? Or has this terrible war matured us at last, filled us with the quiet determination that we must, sooner or later—and better sooner than later—escape from this devilish cycle of self-annihilation. Has it taught us that truces are not enough, treaties not enough, a narrow and self-glorifying patriotism not enough?

It is my firm conviction that here, in the most democratic of countries, a growing minority is ready to cry, "These are not enough!" To them, to their friends, and even to their enemies, this book, offering as its only charm the dry light of reason, humbly, modestly submits itself.

One last word before I turn you over to Mr. Adler. During a war, the dread pair of alternatives facing the soldier, and less directly, the civilian, is: *Fight or Die*. But below this set of alternatives lies a deeper and more persistent one, for it will confront us when the fighting is over. That set of alternatives is: *Think or Die*. Mr. Adler's book is highly undramatic in tone, yet underlying the quietest, the most abstract of his sentences is that dread, concrete imperative: *Think or Die*. We didn't *think* in 1919; and we are dying now.

If you say, "Thinking is not enough," who would disagree? But action without reflection, the jerry-built formulas that our legislators are presently emitting, this is still worse. We are not a lethargic people, and move fast enough once we understand something; but we hate (who does not?) to go to the painful *trouble* of understanding it. All Mr. Adler asks us to do is try to understand, for proper and orderly action will follow proper and orderly thought, if the thought is common to a sufficient number of people.

And when that thought at last is common, or at least prevalent, we will inevitably be set firmly on the one road this bleeding globe must traverse if ever its perennial wounds are to be stanched. For these wounds will be stanched only by a Veronica's veil woven of the intangible threads of thought and conscience, the thought and conscience of all men and women working together with the grave resolution that there shall some day be, not a society of nations, but, as great thinkers from Marcus Aurelius to William Penn and Tom Paine (with Jesus standing sorrowfully above them all) have imagined—A Society of Men.

November 1, 1943

Preface

THIS BOOK contains the facts and ideas I wish I had been taught in school and college. It contains the principles and conclusions which I should have been teaching students in every class these last twenty years. I was given no understanding of war and peace at any point in my own education. And I have failed as a teacher to give a later generation the fundamental insights which should be everyone's possession.

In the introduction to his recent book on American foreign policy, Mr. Walter Lippmann described himself as "one young man who was not mentally prepared for the age he was destined to live in." Neither Harvard nor travel abroad nor years of editorial work on *The New Republic* and the old New York *World* gave him the education he needed in American history or the understanding he now has of the problem his country faces in foreign affairs. "The conclusions set down in this book," he wrote, "represent what I now think I have learned, and not at all what I always knew."

Without having gone to Harvard, most of us are as vague about the significance of American history as Mr. Lippmann confesses himself to have been. Most of us, without having written editorials on the burning issues of the day, are as unaware of the principles which should determine a country's foreign policy and its thinking about war and peace. The fault is not that American history is slighted in school or college, but that American history—in fact, all history—is so poorly taught, so blindly written, and so blindly read.

There is a deeper failing which Mr. Lippmann's admirable candor inspires me to confess—for myself at least. Until very recently, I was ignorant of more important things than American history. I had no understanding of the basic simple truths which make peace on earth an intelligible ideal; I had no conception, which historical insight might have given me, of man's progress toward peace and the probability of its eventual accomplishment.

I must add, with immodesty, that my shame is greater than Mr. Lippmann's. I profess to teach the philosophy of law. I have taught political philosophy for many years. Now that I think of it, it seems to me that I should have known better. I should have known that the theory of law and government is, above all, concerned with war and peace. I should have known that any philosophy of history worthy of the name has a profound bearing on this problem.

I should have taught my students that war and peace are the central terms in political theory, and that the gradual development of peace is the deepest trend in the world's history, as well as the deepest aspiration behind man's struggle to civilize himself.

It took the present war to arouse me, as it has aroused others, from neglect of these matters. In the last five years I have discovered what every schoolboy should know about war and peace through a study of history and politics. The terrible magnitude of this war and its ominous foreshadowing of the future made it impossible to be satisfied any longer with hazy ideas about the conditions of peace, or vague presentiments about the wars to come in endless succession. Utter despair seemed too high a price to pay for disillusionment; and it seemed as if it should be possible to hope, and even to act, for a better world without complete self-deception.

I cannot give the war itself full credit for my enlightenment. Within the last few years, the war has produced a series of books about the peace which should follow it, written from many angles and with different purposes. I have read a great many of these, only to become, at first, confused and of many minds where before I was ignorant and of no mind at all. I say "at first" because discontent with this dubious frame of mind led me to look for the principles and notions which might clarify the problem and bring all its elements into perspective and good order.

I found, what I should have suspected, that the history of human thought contains all the ideas anyone needs with which to think clearly and with reasonable certitude about peace; and that the history of human action records all the developments needed to infer what can be done from what has been done, and to inspire faith that what can be done will be done.

As a result of such efforts at self-clarification, this book tries to expound the rudimentary notions which anyone must use to think clearly about war and peace. It tries to set forth the fundamental facts of history on which anyone must rely to make his thinking certain and definite rather than full of doubts and cross-purposes. I hope that reading it may prove as clarifying to others as writing it has been for me.

Because it is a reaction to other books on the subject, as well as a consideration of the subject itself, this book may serve to mediate between the facts all of us have to think about and the thinking many of us have already done for ourselves, or the thinking of others with which we are acquainted. *It differs from most of the current books about peace in that it is primarily concerned with the ideas which should be in every citizen's mind, not the plans or blueprints which deserve a place at the peace table.*

The title is accurate. It is not a book about *how to make* peace after this war is over or about what should be done at the peace conference. It is concerned with *how to think* about peace—and war—and how to do that from now until peace is finally made. But it is not a book of rules, as was *How to Read a Book. It is a book of ideas to think with.*

Finally, it is a book for Americans only by reason of the accident that it is written by an American and published in America. In writing it I have tried to keep in mind that what I had to say could have been written, as it can be read, by men of any nationality or culture. The problem of war and peace is a human problem, not a provincial one. The ideas which can solve it are universal, not American or European. The facts on which sound conclusions rest belong to world history, not to the history of this country or any other.

World peace, more than any other practical problem, requires men everywhere in the world to acknowledge the same facts and to be guided by the same ideas. The members of the human race must be able to think about war and peace in the same way—without the distortion of local prejudice or the blinders of partisan interest. Until they do, they do not belong, in thought or action, to the one world whose physical unity sets the stage for a peace that is likewise one and indivisible.

Mortimer J. Adler

August 31, 1943

Postscript:

This book was written in the summer of 1943. Since August, a number of significant events have taken place, and a number of significant statements have been issued by political leaders and influential public groups. To take account of these, I have made additions to the original manuscript and in the revision of printer's proofs.

The careful reader will find reference to the following items: the Mackinac Statement made by the Republican Post-War Policy Committee; Secretary Hull's radio address on foreign policy; Herbert Hoover's speech before the Kansas City Chamber of Commerce; the report of the Foreign Relations Committee of the American Legion; the Fulbright resolution adopted by the House of Representatives; the Connally resolution adopted by the Senate, including a clause from the Moscow Pact; Sumner Welles' address at the twenty-fifth anniversary of the Foreign Policy Association; the seven-point declaration on world peace issued by 144 representatives of the Protestant,

Catholic, and Jewish faiths; and the Pledge for Peace written by some members of the Writers' War Board.

Extensive comment on these current proposals and formulations is not necessary; for the principles and ideas with which this book deals enables the reader to form his own critical estimation of their significance. The reader can easily decide for himself whether, for example, the Senate resolution and the Moscow Pact envisage anything more in the way of international organization than was contained in the Wilsonian formulae for a League of Nations and, if so, what this portends for the future of war and peace.

Present issues should always be viewed in the largest possible perspective that history and philosophy can provide. In thinking about war and peace, as in thinking about any other basic practical problem, the man who brings general ideas and principles to bear upon particular problems and current formulations has a unique advantage. He can make effective contact with the concrete and the immediate without losing a dispassionate vision of the universal and the timeless. He can exercise that critical detachment necessary for a thoughtful, rather than an emotional, judgment upon the conflicting policies which solicit his adherence.

M. J. A.

December 15, 1943

PART ONE

THE PROBLEM
OF PEACE

CHAPTER 1

The Questions Men Must Face

THESE ARE the questions which every sober free man must face in the modern world.

1. Will there be a world war after this one?
2. If so, will it occur in my lifetime or in the lifetime of my children and grandchildren?
3. If there is to be another world war, what can we do to postpone it?
4. Will there ever be peace on earth—not just a breathing spell between wars, but lasting peace?
5. If so, will it come in my lifetime, in my grandchildren's, or centuries from now?
6. If there is any probability of perpetual peace, what can we do to hasten its coming?

Though the problem of war and peace is as old as human society, and though men have discussed it for many centuries, they have not always asked these questions. They have usually assumed that there would be another war, during their children's lifetime if not in their own. Believing future wars to be inevitable, rulers and representatives have been concerned only with the time, the place, and the alignment of forces.

For sixteen hundred years of Christendom nobody seriously thought it possible for men to perpetuate peace. It was not that antiquity and the Middle Ages neglected the problem. The problem has always been the occasion for laborious reflection; it has always excited hard debate. But the fundamental issue usually turned on a choice between the peace of Caesar and the peace of God—the pacification of the world by conquest and the soul's eternal rest in heaven.

On earth, the individual might achieve peace *with himself;* but political peace, the peace of an earthly community embrac ing all men, remained an ideal for men of good will, because good will never seemed adequate to the task of making it an enduring reality.

Only in the last four centuries have a few men proposed practical means for accomplishing by institutional changes what good intentions alone could never realize. Only in our own day has a substantial number of men begun to consider both the possibility and probability of lasting peace.

2

In our century, the problem of war and peace has changed in these significant respects.

Ordinary citizens now discuss issues which once engaged only statesmen and philosophers. We ask, not about local wars from which our nation may stand free, but about world wars into which all peoples will inevitably be drawn. And those who believe that the future threatens such wars naturally seek to postpone what they dare not hope to prevent.

Some men now have a higher aim because they have greater hope. They think that wars, especially world wars, can be prevented. They think that peace can be made world-wide and perpetual.

Though the notion of perpetual peace made its appearance before our time, the earlier projects for permanent peace seldom planned for more than the world of Europe, which is hardly the world. It was natural for a truly universal conception of peace to await the century when world wars first began. We are the first generation to possess a veridical image of the world and thereby to envisage peace as global in extent. But even that is not our most important distinction.

Today for the first time there are enough men who think that a durable peace is possible to make that the central issue. They form a minority, but a very articulate one. They insist that a lasting world peace is a genuinely practicable objective. From their point of view, the various plans for postponing the next world war fall short of the goal at which we should aim, not merely because real peace is better than a prolonged truce, but also because the better goal is now at last attainable.

There can be no doubt that this is the central issue raised by the six questions we are considering. If perpetual peace is impossible, then it makes no sense to ask whether it is probable now or later; we should not try to make plans or take action to bring it about. Our only *practical* problem is limited to keeping out of local wars and postponing the next world war.

But if perpetual peace is possible, then there are other problems which have practical significance.

We must try to estimate the probability that what *can* be done *will* be done by the men of our generation. With that probability in mind, we must determine what we *shall* do to expedite the most radical event in the world's history; supposing, of course, that we really want peace.

3

These questions require us to do three things:

First, to hazard a prediction about the future.

Second, to determine the objective or goal which merits our primary, if not our exclusive, attention and effort.

Third, to judge alternative plans or proposals, in order to choose the most efficient means for carrying out our aim.

All our discussions of war and peace would be greatly clarified and sharpened if we observed this order: *predictions, objectives, means.*

In practical affairs, we cannot choose means until we have settled on an end; and, except in dreams, we cannot pursue an end if it lies outside the bounds of possibility. Both possibility and probability limit the sphere of action, separating deed from wish.

Some conceivable events are merely possible—belonging to the future in that large sense which includes all time to eternity. Some are more than *merely* possible; they are not only conceivable, but predictable, having a definite probability within a certain time and under particular circumstances.

4

There is no way of avoiding the distinction between possibility and probability. These two terms have much more than an alliterative connection with the practicality of peace.

Only too frequently men say that a lasting peace is impossible, when all they mean is that it seems improbable after this war, or even in the next hundred years. And there are just as many who say that it is within our power to make this the last war, when they can only show reason for thinking that peace is possible— *eventually!*

The difference between possibility and probability is the difference between *can* and *may*, or between *any time* and *some definite time*.

There are many things we can do, which for one reason or another we may *never* do. Marriage is a possibility in *any* man's life; but whether it is probable for *this* man depends upon a wide variety of circumstances. The possibility never changes. It is never greater or less. But the probability varies with age and opportunity, inclination and impediment.

When we talk of probabilities, we are obligated to specify the time of the event predicted. Something which is only slightly probable in the near future may be much more probable in a longer time. But whether something can *ever* happen, without any determination of date, is a question of sheer possibility.

Any man knows with certitude that he will die; but when and under what circumstances he will die, and what can be done to prolong his life, are questions calling for prediction by the insurance expert and the medical scientist. Longevity is a matter of probability; mortality is certain.

When we argue about the possibility or impossibility of perpetual peace, we are dealing with certainties no matter how we answer the question. But we can predict the probability of future wars, or the probability of preventing them, with much greater modesty—admitting doubts and allowing for all sorts of unforeseen contingencies.

Life, or at least thinking, would be simpler if our actions did not require both a judgment of the possible and an estimate of the probable. The problem of war and peace has, unfortunately, tempted a great many persons to indulge in such simplified thinking. It is unfortunate because permitting our thinking to be simpler than the case demands merely puts off the complications until disaster uncovers the matters we have neglected.

CHAPTER 2

The Answers Men Have Given

CONTEMPORARY THINKING about war and peace seems to divide into two major patterns.

According to the predictions men make on this most predicted-about-of subjects, they can be classified as pessimists or optimists. According to their objectives, and the means they recommend, they are usually characterized as realists or idealists.

By seeing these two classifications in relation to one another, we can avoid the invidious tone which attaches to the words "realist" and "idealist." If his optimistic predictions are sound, the man who proposes the more desirable goal is thoroughly realistic. His ideal solution cannot be dismissed as utopian if the facts show it to be quite practicable. And the man who advocates the less perfect solution does not necessarily relish making this choice. He need not cynically reject all lofty aspirations in order to insist that we make facts rather than wishes the measure of the attainable.

Ideals are no more the exclusive possession of the idealist than reality is the private property of the realist. Nevertheless, it is difficult to overcome the associations which make "realist" and "idealist" name-calling words. I shall, therefore, use the more descriptive words "pessimist" and "optimist" in describing the two main positions taken on the question of peace in our—or in any—time.

2

The pessimistic position can be summarized as follows:

PREDICTIONS

Future wars, including world wars, are inevitable. The extreme pessimist will add: "until the end of time." The more moderate pessimist will be content to say: "for some time to come."

In terms of perpetual peace, the extreme prediction is that it is utterly impossible on earth. The more moderate prediction is that its realization is improbable for many centuries, that improbability being even greater if we consider our own lifetime.

OBJECTIVE

The only practicable goal for which we can work is the prolongation of peace in our time, or the postponement of the next world war. It would be too much to suppose that we can prevent all forms of war, but not too much to aim at preventing for several generations another world war.

MEANS

We must employ the familiar devices of power politics, whether or not we call them that: such things as treaties, alliances, or coalitions, aiming at a balance or a predominance of military power.

Agreements for collective security and an "international police force" to execute repressive or punitive measures must be regarded as implements of a coalition of great powers.

Such things as a league of nations, world courts for arbitration of international disputes, and other international agencies can be recommended as supplementing the nuclear alliances; but they cannot be advocated as adequate by themselves to postpone the next world war, and certainly not to prevent it.

If the pessimist is cynical, he does not add any qualifications concerning justice and liberty; he does not pretend that the game of power politics need be played more politely, or can be played more effectively, by a just administration of the world's affairs, and with some regard for the liberties of smaller or less powerful nations. But if he is a "liberal," he usually seeks to incorporate the ideals of justice and liberty into his plans for postponing war by coalitions of power, insisting that there is a greater chance of succeeding this way.

REMARKS ON THE OPPOSITION

The pessimist does not deny that world government or world federation could abolish international wars, local or general. He merely says that any scheme which goes beyond a confederacy or league of *independent* nations is at present out of the question, precisely because it requires the abrogation of national independence and all that that implies.

Only despair and disillusionment can result from trying to put such schemes into practice before the time is ripe. The optimist, he contends, fails to recognize the existing realities—the economic rivalries, the diversity of cultures, the bellicose nature of man, the inequalities in education, standard of living, and political maturity, and, above all, the ever-resurgent nationalistic spirit, whether it be condemned as pride or praised as patriotism.

3

The optimistic position can be summarized as follows:

PREDICTIONS

International wars, local or general, can be prevented.

It is highly probable that permanent peace can be made at the end of this war.

OBJECTIVE

Perpetual peace is not the only goal for which we *can* work, but since it is obviously so much more desirable than merely postponing the next world war, it is the only goal for which we *should* work.

MEANS

We must establish a world government, federal in structure, including all the peoples of the earth.

No form of power politics and no merely international organization are adequate either for initiating or preserving world peace.

Beneath the diversity of plans for the institution of world government, there is agreement that such government must be constitutional rather than despotic; that it must be built upon principles of political justice and liberty for all; and that it cannot be accomplished by conquest or imperialism, but only by voluntary acts of union on the part of all the states to be federated. If the optimist is clear, he recognizes that federated states retain *none* of their sovereignty in external affairs, and hence that world government requires the complete abolition of national independence. If he is confused, he tries to say that world government is incompatible *only* with "absolute" sovereignty, and that federation permits nations to retain a "limited" sovereignty, or some degree of independence in external affairs.

REMARKS ON THE OPPOSITION

The optimist calls attention to the fact that his opponent identifies peace with a mere absence of shooting. But the sheathed sword is still a sword; the bomber will not be beaten into a transport so long as nations remain potentially at war. The very phrase "peace treaty" is a contradiction in terms, for treaties make, not peace, but truces—temporary interludes between periods of shooting.

It is the pessimist, therefore, whose proposals are dangerously deceptive, likely to result in disillusionment and depair; for the pessimist promises peace when what he really means is the maintenance of large military establishments to safeguard a tenuous truce.

Furthermore, despite anyone's liberal pretensions, an alliance of the victors to preserve what they call "the peace" cannot help becoming, like all monopolistic enterprises, an effort in self-perpetuation and aggrandizement. A less polite, but more honest, name for this proposed nuclear alliance would be "world domination." Despite all the talk about liberty and justice, there is enough dynamite in the pessimist's plans to blow the world wide open again—and sooner than he thinks.

4

In summarizing these two positions I have omitted the variety of detail which occurs on the level of specific plans and blueprints. I have not tried to give a digest of the reasoning—the evidence and principles—in support of each point of view. In matters of argument, as in specific proposals, individuals in each group differ from one another.

The purpose of these summaries is to focus attention on the main points of opposition. That purpose has been served if the issues are now clear on a high level of generality.

The pessimistic position is best exemplified in the writings of Mr. Walter Lippmann. I refer particularly to *Some Notes on War and Peace* (1940), and to *U. S. Foreign Policy* (1943).

In the earlier book, Mr. Lippmann says:

Perpetual peace which eradicates all evils is not an attainable ideal at this stage in the slow process of civilizing mankind. . . . We must aim at the possible, or we shall accomplish nothing at all. We must aim at a peace which is good enough to endure without serious interruption in the world as it is and among men as they are—for perhaps fifty years. . . . I do not believe that anyone will ever possess enough force to impose a general peace, and I do not believe we shall live to see the miracle of universal consent.

Mr. Lippmann declares his objective to be a "good peace" in the relative sense of "durable for a time."

There is no warrant in human experience for a pessimism which insists that no war can ever end in a good peace. If this war, for example, could end in as long a peace as that which most of mankind enjoyed for the hundred years between the battle of Waterloo in 1815 and the invasion of Belgium in 1914, we should be entitled to say it was a good peace. To be sure, there were wars in the nineteenth century.

But the wars were local and limited; the injustice and oppression was remediable and diminishing.

In his later book, Mr. Lippmann proposes a nuclear alliance of three or four great powers—the United States, Great Britain, Russia, and China—as a coalition which will do for the world in the twentieth century what the Congress of Vienna and the subsequent concerts of European powers did for Europe in the nineteenth. A resurrected League of Nations unsupported by such a coalition would not work now, as it did not work before.

The will of the most powerful states to remain allied is the only possible creator of a general international order. . . . It is only around this strong nuclear alliance that a wider association of nations can constitute itself. If that condition is accepted, and once it is accepted, it will become evident that the combination of the great powers cannot, despite their common vital interests, be made to hold together except as they respect the liberties of the other peoples and promote them by the maintenance of law.

Mr. Lippmann is much clearer and more cogent than any other representative of this position; and more honestly liberal, despite his effort to be honestly realistic at the same time.

By comparison, the work of Mr. Herbert Hoover and Mr. Hugh Gibson (*The Problems of Lasting Peace*, 1942) resembles, as Miss Rebecca West suggested, "a Channel fog." These men talk in terms of "co-operation" and "joint action" by all nations; they use the phrase "lasting peace" when they can mean only a temporary truce; they go no further than some sort of retailored League of Nations. But through all the fog one thing is clear: they are against aiming *now* at the kind of peace which could be perpetuated by world government alone and nothing less.*

* Since the publication of his book, Mr. Hoover has made his real position only too painfully clear. In a recent speech, he said: "Lasting peace will not be built on the surrender of the independence of the sovereignty of nations, but it must be built upon the collaboration of free peoples . . . Therefore, I suggest that plan-

I cite other representatives of the pessimistic position, with the single comment that they come to the same general conclusions from quite different origins and by quite different routes: Sir Halford J. Mackinder ("The Round World and the Winning of the Peace," in *Foreign Affairs*, July, 1943); Lionel Gelber (*Peace by Power*, 1942); Edward Hallett Carr (*Conditions of Peace*, 1942); C. J. Hambro (*How to Win the Peace*, 1942); Arthur C. Millspaugh (*Peace Plans and American Choices*, 1942); Ross Hoffman (*The Great Republic*, 1942); and Nicholas J. Spykman (*America's Strategy in World Politics*, 1942).

5

The optimistic position is best exemplified in Mr. Michael Straight's *Make This the Last War* (1943). This war, says Mr. Straight, "is the crucial phase of a larger struggle to achieve world unity." It cannot be won "until the underlying conditions of world unity have been attained." There will be no end to wars, and world wars, until the world becomes a single economic and political community under federal government.

This is not a utopian objective. "The time is now," says Mr. Straight again and again. The United Nations already exist as a substructure on which to build. If space and time can be conquered to wage war without territorial limit, they can be transcended for the sake of terrestrial peace. If economic barriers can be torn down, and resources pooled, for the sake of efficiency in war, then certainly these economic factors can also be manipulated to support peace.

Nothing external prevents us from forming the political union which the physical and economic unity of the world calls for.

ners of peace incorporate into their thinking the idea that nations will maintain their full independence and their full sovereignty. And it is only on such a common ground that we must and can build a lasting peace." What Mr. Hoover has made clear is that he wants no "sacrifice of the independence or sovereignty of the United States." Wanting that, he should not deceive us or himself by talking about a *lasting peace*.

Nothing will keep us from making peace, instead of a truce, after this war, except our own lack of enterprise and courage.

The flood tide is upon us that leads to fortune; if we let it pass, it may never occur again. We need now to declare that in our acts of liberation we are opening the flood gates to a new course of history, a new direction of time. . . . We must now declare that the joint boards of the United Nations are the beginnings of the permanent structure of world government, that the combined Chiefs of Staff are the leaders of a world army that will be the only armed force in the future peace. We need to declare now that the Supreme Council of the United Nations which we form is the central executive of a provisional world government; that the full Council of all the United Nations will become the provisional assembly of a world legislature; that the twenty-eight states of the United Nations, like our own original thirteen, will grow until the United Nations becomes the United Nations of the World. *The time is now.*

Mr. Straight's book of over four hundred pages, with its admirable concreteness of detail, seems to be fully cognizant of all the economic and political realities on which the pessimists rest their case. He differs from them in his fundamental prediction because he does not regard nationalism in all its forms as an insuperable obstacle to the institution of world government. World federation is not merely possible; it is highly probable that we can attain this objective within the present century.

Mr. Straight recognizes—in fact, embraces—all the difficulties of the enterprise.

For at least a century after this war is over, our main objective will be to prevent civil war in our world society. We shall not prevent it by one armed force, or one assembly, or one judiciary with its carefully prepared body of law and its constitution, however fine and clear. . . . Our only assurance against a final world war will be to bring our social systems into harmony with each other. . . . Everywhere in

the world for the next century it must be the right and the
duty of all peoples to bring their social systems into the
essential pattern that is demanded by world unity. It will be
the constitutional right and the constitutional duty of those
who live under constitutions; it will be the revolutionary
right and the revolutionary duty of those to whom constitutions are denied.

Other writers, notably Mr. Emery Reves (*A Democratic Manifesto,* 1942) and Mr. Nathaniel Peffer ("America's Place in the
Post-War World," in *Political Science Quarterly* for March, 1942)
share Mr. Straight's objective and concur in the general principle that world peace can be instituted and perpetuated only by
world government; but few if any have his undaunted optimism
that these things can, or will, be done now. Of the others, the
most hopeful is Mr. Edward J. Byng (*A Five Year Peace Plan,*
1943).

There are other representatives of this position, but none is
as clear, as realistic, and yet as uncompromisingly idealistic, as
Mr. Straight. I must mention Mr. J. B. Condliffe (*Agenda for a
Post-War World,* 1942); Mr. Clarence Streit (*Union Now,* 1940);
John T. McNeill ("Preparing for a Durable Peace," in the collec-
tion *Religion and the Present Crisis,* 1942); and Mr. Robert Mac-
Iver (*Toward an Abiding Peace,* 1943).

I feel justified in excluding from this company such writers as
Sir Norman Angell (*Let the People Know,* 1942), and Mr. John
Foster Dulles ("Toward World Order" in the collection *A Basis
for the Peace to Come,* 1942), on the ground that they propose
means which are inadequate for consummating peace at the end
of this war. No fault can be found with their meliorist conception
of slow stages of progress toward peace, unless it be their failure
to acknowledge that if we cannot immediately achieve more than
a truce, we must face the probable consequences—war and more
war before peace is finally made.

For example, the "Six Pillars of Peace," formulated by the
Commission of the Federal Council of Churches, of which Mr.

Dulles is Chairman, includes the notion of world government, but that is regarded as a remote objective to be approached through stages of progressively mitigated nationalism. "Until we have world government," says Mr. Dulles, "ultimate power would rest with the nations, subject to arrangements for its concerted use." Mr. Dulles sees much farther than Mr. Lippmann, but he does not seem to see all the problems of the immediate future as clearly.

Not substantially different from the "Six Pillars" is the seven-point "Declaration on World Peace" recently issued by 144 prominent representatives of the Protestant, Catholic, and Jewish faiths. The fifth point calls for "the organization of international institutions, which will (a) develop a body of international law, (b) guarantee the faithful fulfillment of international obligations, and revise them when necessary, (c) assure collective security by drastic limitation and continuing control of armaments, compulsory arbitration and adjudication of controversies, and the use when necessary of adequate sanctions to enforce the law." Such phrases as "collective security" and "international law," "control of armaments" and "compulsory arbitration," symbolize a lack of hope for world peace *in our time.*

In this group also belong those who would revive the League of Nations, changing its buttons but leaving it, no less than before, a mere diplomatic conference of quite independent states. Their aim is peace, not a truce; but their means are poorly calculated for the end they espouse. Their proposals, like the peace plans of the recent Popes (*Principles for Peace,* 1943), are so inadequate that only self-deception can save them from regarding themselves as pessimists.

6

So far as popular opinion is concerned, the pessimistic position prevails in this country, and probably in all others.

A recent nation-wide survey undertaken by the University of Denver recorded that only twenty-six per cent of the people think it probable that "after this war a way will be worked out to prevent any more wars." Another fourteen per cent believe that "some day wars will be prevented, but this war will not be the last one." And fifty-five per cent take the pessimistic position that "no matter what is done to prevent them, there will always be wars" (36%) or that "it is possible to prevent all wars, but people will never do what is necessary to prevent them" (19%).

It is worth observing the distinction between those who think that perpetual peace is *impossible* and those who think it possible but highly improbable because men *will not do* what they *can do*.

Except for those who straddle the fence, the two positions seem to present an inescapable dilemma for thought and action. The straddlers do not really escape. Anyone who understands the minimum conditions of world peace, especially with regard to national independence, knows on which side of the fence they are doomed to fall. The advocates of merely international agencies (as opposed to truly *supra*national government) propose means for peace which cannot prevent war.

It matters little whether they include an international police force. They must face the question raised by a recent editorial in *The New Yorker* magazine:

> You people realize, of course, that a police force is no good if simply used as a threat to strengthen agreements between independent powers, that to have meaning it must be a certified agent of law, that to have law we must first have a constitutional world society, and that to achieve that each nation must say good-bye to its own freedom of action and to its long established custom of doing what it damn well pleases. *Now* how many of you want an international police force?

The implication of the question lies in the choice it offers between international anarchy and world government. That public-opinion polls have recorded a large majority favoring an international police force must remain a fact of ambiguous significance until such sentiment is clarified by reference to the real issue. The Editors of *Time,* in one of their "Background for Peace" series, shrewdly observed:

> A world cop attached to a world court, standing alone, could never serve to keep the peace of the world. To achieve this end, the world cop would have to be backed by a full-fledged world government—by a legislature to translate political decisions into written laws and an executive to give such laws substance in action. John Citizen may not have contemplated any such far-flung scheme when he upped with a Yes to the notion of an international police force . . . The whole idea of establishing such a force inexorably raises all the problems connected with the creation of a complete world government.

Those who talk about international police in the absence of world government, like those who try to smile away the contradiction of *united* but *independent* nations, must fall off the fence, and usually fall into pessimism and power politics, as soon as they abandon the weasel words which cannot bridge the unbridgeable chasm between *alliance* and *federation.* As Robert M. Hutchins, President of the University of Chicago, pointed out in a recent address: "In the absence of world law and world government . . . conquerors asserting a right based on power alone are no more entitled to the name of police than Himmler's men in Czechoslovakia."

7

The issues are clear, and the consequences of a clear choice are plain.

If any compromise is tenable it is not immediately apparent. Until we can see a way of finding *some* truth and practical wisdom on both sides, we must either suspend judgment entirely or take sides decisively. Suspended judgment can neither prevent wars nor postpone the next one.

We must take sides. But which? We must add up the facts and weigh the reasons to justify our pessimism or our optimism, to acknowledge whatever objective our basic attitude imposes on us, and to throw our individual strength behind policies or plans to which we are committed by our prediction and our aim.

There are many plans and policies under discussion, but each of us can, in ultimate judgment, adopt only one. And that one will be, in general principles and pattern of thought, one of two main views on the problem of war and peace.

Again I quote from an editorial in *The New Yorker,* whose facetious rigor is so much more serious and binding than the loose logic of more solemn utterances:

> Mr. Edwin L. James told some journalism students recently that what this country needs is *one* peace plan. He sort of hinted at which one, just in passing. That's the trouble with the one-plan idea; it may not be the one you like. Take us, for instance. Mr. James' pattern for peace fails to satisfy us. Ours, from what he says, would certainly fail to satisfy him. He wants strong treaties, a revived League, firm action against aggressors. We want international law, a United Nations of the World, and relaxation of nationalism. He says our kind of talk is dream stuff, impossible of fulfillment. We say his is hoop-skirt stuff, proved to be unreliable. How are we going to get one plan which truly represents Mr. James and us and a hundred and thirty million other planners? Well, we will get it in the usual manner—talk, talk, talk, everybody beating on the table and pacing up and down. It's going to be a colossal debate, but at least it's going to be a debate and not a monologue. As for us, we shall not back down merely because we've been assured that our head is in the clouds. Who's afraid of getting his hair wet in the cumulus? Besides, it's quite nice up here in the clouds. Surprising number of planes, too.

8

It is always pleasant to find some points on which opponents can agree. We feel reassured that they are moving in the same universe of discourse. Not only do their differences become more intelligible in the light of some common understanding, but in their agreements may be found the beginning of a resolution to their dispute.

The pessimist and the optimist do agree on certain fundamentals: not the extremist or the befuddled in either camp, but the *liberal* exponent of the position that the next war can be postponed and the *clearsighted* exponent of the position that all wars can be prevented.

The liberal pessimist tries to *combine* power politics with international morality. The clearsighted optimist denies that international morality *without* supranational government will work.

Neither is an isolationist, a militarist, or a pacifist.

Neither is an isolationist because neither thinks that the next world war can be effectively postponed or prevented by an effort on the part of his nation, or any single nation, to keep out of world affairs.

Neither is a militarist because neither admires war as a noble enterprise fulfilling the human spirit; both feel that the prevention of war to any degree, temporarily or permanently, is an unmitigated good.

Neither is a pacifist because neither is satisfied that a widespread desire to avoid war is sufficient to postpone it, much less to abolish it entirely. Both think traditional pacifism *impractical,* even as they regard unregenerate militarism as *immoral.*

Underlying these three points of meeting is their most fundamental agreement: *power is needed to prevent war or to maintain peace.* Either independent nations, separately or in coalition, must exercise the ultimate power in world affairs, or that power must be wielded by a single government to which all peoples are equally subject.

Both accept this dilemma, choosing opposite horns. Both agree that there is nothing in between these alternatives. Those who would insist that a league of nations is in between are saying that it is nothing—*powerless*. It may be something in the sense of a promise of better things to come, but the gap between promise and performance is infinite in the sphere of practice.

Powerless conventions or congresses or courts either provide the façade behind which real coalitions of power must operate or they dangle in mid-air, like good will without foundation in force. To whatever extent a league, or any other international agency, is a *powerless* institution, to that extent it provides no solution to the problem—neither the postponement of future wars nor their utter prevention.

Agreeing on this, the opponents may nevertheless take quite different attitudes toward a league of nations, old-style or new. Agreeing on the necessity for a leverage of real power, they disagree about where the fulcrum should be placed: either (1) in a system of alliances which can make the promises of a league negotiable instruments in international affairs; or (2) in a real grant of power to international councils and courts, which would necessarily transform a debating society into a government.

The first of these solutions would make a revived league no more vital than a diplomatic clearinghouse, a servant, not a master, of the great powers. The covenants of a league, the decisions of its councils or courts, and the conventions of international law cannot be any stronger than the obligations which nations are willing to fulfill or than the pledges which the might of a predominant alliance can force unwilling nations to respect. Nothing more can be expected than is obtainable from backing a real convergence of interests by a teaming of real power.

The second of these solutions would revive a league only to transmute it from a conference of self-governing nations into a government of federated states. The basic insight here is one of the great lessons of American history. A federal constitution must always supplant articles of confederation. As every schoolboy knows, the sole usefulness of the latter is "to demonstrate to the feeblest intelligence the necessity of a more perfect union."

A monopoly of power offers the only solid ground for any

practical solution of the problem of war and peace. But shall it be concentrated, by treaties and alliances, in the hands of those nations whose mutual self-interest dedicates them to the "pursuits of peace"? Or shall it be consolidated in the institutions of world government?

9

We have considered the questions which all men must face. We have examined the answers some men have given. The answers raise more questions, the ultimate issues on which practical policy depends.

The course of the present inquiry is determined by all these questions and issues. It aims to expand the agreement between the liberal pessimist and the clearsighted optimist. Accepting the principles in which they already concur, it seeks the reasons and evidences which can bring open minds into fuller agreement.

The reader who is still trying to make up his own mind must judge this undertaking on the following counts:

(1) Does it prove the possibility of a durable world peace? And in attempting this, does it demonstrate the minimum conditions, necessary if not sufficient, for so desirable a future?

(2) Does it properly assess the evidences *pro* and *con* which bear on the probability of peace– within our century or in a more remote period?

On these two considerations rests anyone's prediction of what men can do and when they will do it. On that prediction rests all further practical determinations. The reader must, therefore, judge this book on one further count:

(3) Does it establish the practicality of peace as an objective for which men can work now? Does this objective free us from the grave practical concerns involved in prolonging a truce at the end of this war, or does it require us to aim at postponing the next world war as well as at the prevention of all wars?

PART TWO

THE POSSIBILITY
OF PEACE

CHAPTER 3

The Inevitability of War

How can we *know* that world peace is possible, that war is wholly avoidable? There always have been wars. How can we know that wars are not inevitable?

It is certainly true that during the last twenty-five hundred years men have lived with the belief that war is inevitable, that another war will occur in a short time. On point of fact, this belief has been completely verified. No decade has passed without one or more wars somewhere in the world. In the more civilized parts of the world, the average family has not survived three generations without some of its members being directly engaged in war, or at least suffering from the social and economic convulsions which follow in its wake.

But do these facts justify the inference that war is inevitable? "What always has been always will be" is not always true. A valid inference here depends on a knowledge of causes. If the reason why something has always happened is a cause rooted in the very nature of things, then it will continue to happen as long as its cause remains operative, and that will be until the underlying nature is itself destroyed.

If the cause can be controlled or eradicated, the event which once *seemed* inevitable may be avoided. But even when something is avoidable in the very nature of the case, it still may not be avoided. That will depend on us—on our learning the causes to control, and on our making an adequate effort to control them.

The history of medicine records the shifting of many diseases from the incurable column to the list of the curable and the cured. With gains in knowledge and advances in therapy, we have learned, not only how to prevent and cure such ills as typhoid fever and diphtheria, but, what is more important, we have learned that they were never incurable in the first place. The discovery of our error in thinking the *merely uncured* to be *incurable* gives us confidence that other ailments still uncured will turn out to be curable as medical science progresses.

We have come to suspect that all diseases are curable, and that it is up to us to find out how to cure the ones which still prove fatal. But we also distinguish between the ills of human flesh and its mortality. We do not expect to cure death—by heart failure or other lethal degenerations of the vital organs. Heart failure is not a sickness; it is simply dying.

Is war like disease, or is it like death? Is it intrinsically curable, though still uncured? Are we in danger of making the same sort of error about it that men once made about typhoid and some still do about cancer?

2

A problem in the field of social phenomena provides us with a closer parallel to war and peace.

We now know that chattel slavery can be abolished. For the most part, it has been. But suppose we were living in the eighteenth century and had to judge whether chattel slavery would always exist. To say that it could be done away with would be to fly in the face of overwhelming evidence that slavery has always existed.

In China and India, Egypt and Persia, Greece and Rome, in the Middle Ages and even in modern times, human beings were bought and sold. The forms of slavery vary with the civilizations and the centuries. The condition of the slave becomes somewhat ameliorated by legal safeguards which limit the abuse he may suffer at the capricious will of his master. But throughout all these variations the bondsman remains a chattel. He does not own his own life or the fruits of his labor. He is not his own, but another man's. With few more rights than the domesticated animal, he lacks the rights proper to a human person.

In the eighteenth century, men could not help being impressed by the fact that slavery had always been a social institution. Reading history as if it revealed a necessity, they argued that so enduring an institution must have an ineradicable cause.

Even wise men, men who understood and practiced justice, argued that some men are by nature slaves and fit only to be used as instruments. The Roman jurists, the Christian theologians, and the American constitutionalists did not find the proposition "all men are born free and equal" incompatible with the existence of chattel slavery. To their minds, it was an institution inseparable from the fabric of human society.

As late as the middle of the eighteenth century, men who had struggled for their own liberties were not shocked by slavetrading. The New York *Gazette* for September 4, 1738, carried an advertisement offering for sale, "Englishmen, Cheshire cheese, Negro men, a Negro girl, and a few Welshmen." Its duplicate could be found in the colonial papers of Philadelphia or Boston, as well as in the South. Not until 1799 did the efforts of the Quaker Society for Promoting the Manumission of Slaves succeed in passing a bill which began the gradual emancipation of human chattels in New York.

At the end of the eighteenth century, and in the first half of the nineteenth, all the abolitionist movements flew in the face of history. Unable to deny that chattel slavery had always existed, they could only argue that its existence was never due to an ineradicable cause—a difference at birth and in nature between some men and others.

It was not easy for them to say what we proclaim with confidence: that no man is by nature a slave; that neither social organization nor economic welfare demands this unjust institution. Our ancestors who thought otherwise had cause to be deceived. It was difficult for them to see that the slavish appearance of some men resulted from the way in which they had been treated, not from the nature with which they were born.

3

Chattel slavery is, however, only one form of social inequality and economic exploitation. There is grim irony in the fact that the Common Council of New York in the 1730's "designated a popular meeting point, Wall Street, as the place where Negroes and Indians could be bought, sold or hired."

Waiving the question whether every sort of economic exploitation can be remedied, let us ask whether all social inequalities can be eliminated. The answer to that question is no.

That all men are born equal is only half the truth. The other half is that individuals, equal in the endowments *specific* to human nature, vary widely in the degree of their talents and virtues. The historic Declaration of the Rights of Man and of the Citizen acknowledged this inequality. While denying that such inequality could justify the deprivation of a single political right or exclusion from citizenship, it recognized that society and government require organization, and that organization requires a diversity of unequal functions.

All men should be called to citizenship, but not all should be regarded as equally competent for all political offices. In political life, as in the arts, men of superior skill should be chosen to perform the more difficult tasks, even though that may involve the direction of some by others for the sake of a good common to them both. But the architect who directs the artisan does not *enslave* him.

There is, in short, a form of social inequality which is functional. It occurs wherever the organization of men in any common work involves a division of labor, and where different tasks require different skills. Such social inequality is unavoidable *in the very nature of the case.*

4

Is war like chattel slavery, or is it like the functional inequality of superior and inferior engaged in a common work? Is it a curable social ill, or does it belong to human life because of what man is and what human society must be?

The answer to these questions depends on the view we take of the great injustices which have stained human history. Some of these have been rectified. There is good ground for the faith that all can be remedied—ameliorated, if not abolished. War belongs with these if it is essentially abnormal, a violation rather than a fulfillment of human nature.

We cannot rightly think that war is normal merely because it has always plagued the social life of man.

CHAPTER 4

The Abnormality of War

THE PERSON who thinks we cannot *know* whether war is avoidable may argue that before the end of the eighteenth century men did not *know* chattel slavery could be abolished. Before that time most men had not even dreamed of the possibility.

This mode of argument runs itself into the ground. It amounts to saying that, until a basic social reform is accomplished, it must appear to be impossible. It commits the error of confusing history with nature, and makes knowledge that something is *possible* entirely *ex post facto*.

If this were so, then the abolitionists of the nineteenth century were trying to do what they must have admitted was impossible. They were, however, eminently practical men aiming at an objective they conceived to be quite practicable, not only because it seemed to them intrinsically possible, but more than that—attainable in their own day.

According to the kind of argument which relies solely on history, no one will ever *know* that perpetual peace is possible until after it exists.

To consider the matter properly, we must go beyond history to the political nature of man. Does the political nature of man make peace the normal condition, war the abnormal? At once the man who relies on history will say that nothing can be regarded as abnormal which has everywhere and always prevailed.

Without appealing to the facts of human nature, his error cannot be shown. Yet even so far as history goes, he has looked at only half the picture.

2

There are two great historical facts, not one. The first is that there always have been wars. The second is that there always has been peace.

There always have been wars. Up to the present, men living in distinct social groups have always had to resort to fighting to settle their differences. There always have been wars *between* organized groups of men, whether the level of social organization is that of tribe or village, city-state, empire, or nation.

The word "war" should not be used to cover every sort of violent conflict between men. That would blur everything. Criminals, individually or in gangs, do resort to violence, but every sort of violence is not war. In its commonest usage, the word "war" refers to violent conflict between separate communities. The social organization which characterizes the communities reflects itself in the socially organized character of the violent conflict we call "war."

There always has been peace. Up to the present, men living within each socially organized group have been at peace with each other. That peace has not, of course, been perfect or uninterrupted. It has usually been attenuated by civil disorder; but so long as the political community itself endures, the *civil* peace it creates is not entirely destroyed.

Strictly, we should use the word "peace" in the plural, just as we speak of "wars." Disregarding euphony, we should say that there have always been as many "peaces" as there have been relatively stable social organizations. Each peace, existing among the members of a given community, has been local.

The fact that separate communities have been destroyed by conquest does not mean that the men who survived ceased to live at peace with one another. By force or consent, they became members of another community, and continued to enjoy the peace of community life to some degree, even though they may have been willing to sacrifice that peace to regain their former independence.

Neither the wars nor the peaces which the world has seen have been continuous. Wars between communities have been interrupted, for longer and shorter periods, by truces—by the cessation of hostilities which we sometimes call "international peace."

The civil peace of most historic communities has frequently been sundered by revolution or civil strife of some sort.

3

Despite these obvious facts, the man who thinks future wars are unavoidable may say that he sees no reason to alter his view. The only difference between the future and the past will be world-wide wars in place of local wars; but then the truces will also become world-wide in extent.

The man who still thinks that a lasting world-wide peace is impossible will say that the ambivalent facts of history do not prove him wrong. He is right in one sense. By themselves, the facts of history do not constitute the proof. They must be interpreted to discover the critical bearing they have on the issue. They must be made to show us something about man.

The cardinal fact that men can and do live at peace with one another signifies that wars do not flow from the very nature of man. If by his nature each man could live in no other way than at war with his fellows, then local peace would never have existed anywhere in the world.

The facts are otherwise. We find men living at peace everywhere in the world and at all times. Even in a world at war, men live in peace with the members of their own community. Paradoxical though it may seem at first, civil peace, like political unity, frequently is intensified within a community which is at war beyond its borders. The other face of the paradox is that the inhabitants of a country at war cannot enjoy the "pursuits of peace" which make peace more desirable than war.

War as we know it—war between communities—would not be possible without the existence of communities, and except in the context of the various local peaces which these communities establish.

The state of war which Thomas Hobbes describes as the "natural" condition of man has never existed on earth, *so far as individual men are concerned.* There has never been "the war of all against all" because men are not by nature solitary beasts. They have always lived together in societies. Hence the war of *each* against *every other* has never occurred among men, as it does occur in the jungle among the solitary beasts of prey. When Hobbes wrote of the natural state of man as a state of war, he knowingly invented *an hypothesis contrary to fact.*

4

The proof is not yet completed. The ambivalent facts of history, it can be argued, seem to show that war is a normal condition for men, as much as peace. Why are we not obligated to admit that both war and peace flow equally from human nature?

The answer is that men live at peace *only under certain conditions,* namely, the conditions provided by an organized society. Now, if it can be shown, as I think it can, that these social conditions respond to a natural human need, then it will be seen that peace is indispensable to the normal development of human life. If we see why a man cannot live humanly except he live at peace with his fellows, we shall understand why human nature requires peace. We must also see why the opposite is not true—why a man can live humanly without being in a state of war with some of his fellow men.*

Still the question arises: why, then, have there always been wars, if war is not required by the nature of man?

The answer is that men have so far failed to establish the social organization identical with total peace, as they have never yet failed to institute the social organizations identical with local peaces. That failure up to the present does not support the inference of perpetual failure. On the contrary, the fact that men

---

* The members of the American Psychological Association were recently polled on the question, "Do you as a psychologist hold that there are present in human nature ineradicable instinctive factors that make war between nations inevitable?" Seventy per cent of the members answered as follows: No, 346; Yes, 10; Unclassified, 32.

know how to make local peace shows that they know how to make total peace.

There is absolutely nothing in the nature of man repugnant to the existence of a world community, as there is something in the nature of man repugnant to the existence of no communities at all. The nature of man makes world peace possible, for the same reason that it makes the war of *each* man against *every other* impossible. The reason is man's need for society and, in order to preserve the society, for peace.

The fact that wars have always existed between communities signifies only man's past failure to eradicate the cause of war— a cause which lies outside his nature, a cause which must be found in the character of his social institutions. These are ultimately the work of his intelligence and will. They have been made by man. They can be changed by man.

Just as the existence of slavery implies the existence of free men, the existence of war implies the existence of peace. We cannot even conceive of a society in which *all* men are slaves. But, Hitler to the contrary, we know that it is in no way impossible for all men to be their own masters. Nothing in the nature of man prevents a social organization in which all men are free.

The historical fact which enabled some men to understand the possibility of abolishing chattel slavery was the fact that freedom had always coexisted with slavery, even as peace has always coexisted with war. That helped them to see that slavery resulted from alterable social institutions, not from the essence of human nature which man cannot change at will.

Freedom and peace correspond to the deepest aspirations of human nature. That man is by nature *rational* makes slavery repugnant, even as the fact that man is by nature *political* makes war abnormal.

5

Other animals are gregarious, but only man is by nature political. Some of the gregarious species live in relatively stable family groups; some move in herds; some, such as the social insects, belong to elaborate organizations involving a hierarchy of functions and division of labor. But in every case the form of social life is instinctively determined. Generation after generation, the social structure of the beehive or the ant mound remains the same. As long as a given species endures, its social pattern, like its modes of reproduction or nutrition, does not vary appreciably. And the social patterns of the gregarious animals vary from species to species, not within a single species.

Though man is naturally gregarious, instinct does not determine the human forms of social organization. They exhibit a tremendous range of variation. Wherever one finds a beehive, one expects to find the same social arrangements. Such uniformity cannot be found in human communities. Furthermore, even within the same community of men, the social structure undergoes transformation in the course of generations. Man is the only *historical* animal, as well as the only *political* animal.

Like some other gregarious animals, man needs the society of his kind, not merely for pleasure but for survival. This basic biological need can be regarded as an instinctive drive toward association. Because they are not self-sufficing, men are instinctively impelled to live together. But instinct goes no further than this fundamental impulse.

Human intelligence devises the forms of association and conceives the institutions through which the social impulse of man is realized in a wide variety of organizations. Hence to say that man is by nature a political animal means two things: first, that man cannot live except socially; second, that the forms of his social life result from the exercise of his intelligence and freedom. They are not predetermined to any particular form.

Even when, under primitive conditions, man lives in a large family or a small tribal organization, his political nature expresses itself in the fact that the social arrangements are conventional. Though the customs of the group may appear to run back to time immemorial, they reflect intelligent decisions to arrange affairs this way rather than that. Customs which have long persisted unchanged have had a history of development and an origin. They must have originated through the voluntary adoption of certain practices.

While the family and the tribe satisfy man's fundamental biological needs for society, affording him the bare conditions of subsistence and survival, they do not answer all the needs of human nature. Man's political character tends to express itself in the formation of larger communities which go beyond the bonds of consanguinity and which, being more populous, permit a more elaborate division of labor. Such communities afford more than the bare conditions of subsistence and survival—for some of their members, if not for all. In such communities, leisure and a degree of freedom from the daily ordeal of keeping alive enable the arts and sciences to flourish. The higher levels of civilization can now be reached.

Because the larger community had these advantages, the ancients regarded it as the *political* community par excellence. It was the highest expression of man's political nature. It not only satisfied the needs of his daily life, but also provided him with occasions and opportunities for developing his talents—the capacities of his intellectual endowment.

The human race would not survive at all if every individual man attempted to lead a solitary life. The smallest social group, the family, may be sufficient to solve the problem of survival. But the political community or the state—I shall use these words interchangeably—enables men to do more than barely live. It makes it possible for them to live well, to live humanly, to culti-

vate their talents, and so, through the growth of culture, to mag-
nify the characteristic features of human civilization.

The civil, as opposed to the domestic, society is the basis of
civilization. The tribal group represents an intermediate stage
of development between the family, or domestic society, and the
state—the civil society or political community.

6

There is no conflict between the modern theory of civil society as formed by a social contract and the ancient view that
man is by nature a political animal.

The great political thinkers of modern times did not suppose
that the human race could survive a single generation if all men
tried to lead solitary lives. When they talked about man living
in a "state of nature," which he abandoned to live with his fellows
in a "state of civil society," they had no historical event or process
in mind. They simply meant that man's natural need for social
life must be supplemented by the activity of his reason in devising, and the activity of his will in instituting, the political community.

The word "contract" signifies a voluntary or free engagement.
Men do not have to live in civil societies. They are not instinctively determined to do so. They do so only when their
reason tells them it is the best thing for them to do; and then they
do so freely—by conventions which they voluntarily institute
or accept.

In short, civil status, or membership in a political community,
is both natural and non-natural to man. It is non-natural only
in the sense that it is noninstinctive; or, to put it positively, in
the sense that it is conventional—like any human artifice, the
result of intelligence and volition. It is natural in the sense that
it is natural for man (who does not act according to definite instinctive patterns) to exercise his reason and will to devise those

institutions which most fully satisfy his human needs, the demands of his nature.

Both the ancients and the moderns saw that peace between men exists only within the bounds of a community and pre-eminently under the auspices of the civil or political community. Aristotle, for example, who first enunciated the truth that man is by nature political, made a point of adding that the man who finds himself an outcast from society for whatever reason is "forthwith a lover of war."

Hobbes and Locke and Rousseau all identified their hypothetical "state of nature" with a "state of war." Though the war of each against every other never existed as a condition prior to all forms of social life, a "state of war" has always existed historically among sovereign princes or independent communities.

To explain what they mean by a "state of nature" in contrast to a "state of civil society," these modern thinkers always point to the relation of sovereigns—independent princes or states—and contrast this with the relation of men living under the auspices of a single political community.

7

Men form political communities in order to have peace, in order to live without fighting and violence and to enjoy the positive benefits which peace confers. Peace, which is identical with the order of civil life, represents the normal condition toward which the nature of man aspires. War, identical with the absence of civil order, violates and frustrates human nature. *That is why war is abnormal.*

Rousseau recognized the paradox that the abnormal is as prevalent as the normal. Just as he said, "Man is born free; and everywhere he is in chains," so he might have said, "Man is born for peace, yet everywhere he is at war." What he did say amounts to this: "As individuals, we live in the civil state, under the control of law; as nations, each is in the state of nature. . . . Living as we do at once in the civil order and in the state of nature, we find ourselves exposed to the evils of both conditions, without winning the security we need in either." How can we account for the fact that most of the great political philosophers who understood the abnormality of war also accepted war as unavoidable? Plato and Aristotle, Saint Augustine and Saint Thomas, Grotius and Hobbes, Locke and Hegel, differing on many points, concurred in thinking that war could not be eliminated from human affairs. Even Kant and Veblen, who wrote tracts on peace and understood the conditions of its perpetuation, regarded a lasting and universal peace as an ideal, a goal toward which men *should* strive but which they can *never* reach.

The answer is simply that none of these men were in a position to imagine the development of a world political community as a real eventuality in the course of history. We might say that they should have been able to foresee the event in terms of their fundamental insights about war and peace. But that is asking too much. Historic limitations prevented most men, even the most enlightened men, from seeing that war could be eliminated, as it prevented most of them from seeing that chattel slavery could be totally abolished.

8

The abnormality of war is further evidenced by its effect on the highest forms of political life.

Men established themselves in a civil society in order to live well. The conditions of its origin thus show the state or political community to be a means, not an end. Its purpose is to serve the happiness of individual persons. When the state subordinates the good of individual lives to its own welfare, it violates its own reason for being.

Such violence is done by the totalitarian states, whose exponents declare the good of the state to be an ultimate end, and who practice this false religion of "statism" by sacrificing men to the idol. We know totalitarianism to be a monstrous perversion of the natural order. But we frequently forget or overlook the fact that during a war every society tends to adopt the disorder of totalitarianism to some degree. Every departure from the normal mode of the citizen's life signifies a degree of that disorder in which men serve the state rather than the state men.

In a world in which wars exist, and in which nations feel that they have to struggle for their honor or existence, all the impulses of patriotism are natural and justified. But this does not make it any the less unfortunate that patriotism should have to go to the excesses which war, and only war, demands.

The more justly constituted the society, the more admirable its political form, the more war threatens to weaken its institutions and to pervert them. And it is also true that the best form of government is that which is least adapted to the exigencies of war.

Not all political communities exist under constitutional government. Both historically and in the present, a large number have been and are under despotic regimes. Under despotic government, whether by absolute kings or by absolute parties, the governed do not enjoy the rights of citizenship.

Not all constitutional governments are democratic. Many historic and existing constitutions have been and are instruments of class privilege, embodying all sorts of unjust discriminations, including disfranchisement of large numbers in the population. The democratic constitution extends the franchise to every normal person, and repudiates wealth, birth, and other accidents as conditions of privilege. Only in a democracy are *all* men citizens, and are *all* equally entitled to hold public office at the pleasure and discretion of the electorate.

Democracy is the only completely just form of government, for it is the only form of government under which *all* men receive what is their due—the rights and privileges of equal political status. If the political community originates to help men *live well*, then the history of political life does not reach the natural term of its development until democracies come into being. Only then does a society exist in which *all* men, not just *some*, can live well.

In short, it is not civil society under any form of government, but only constitutional democracy, which adequately fulfills the needs of man's political nature. Anything less necessarily frustrates and degrades, even when it does not enslave, the many who, while members of the population, cannot call themselves and each other "citizen."

Now, it is a significant fact that the enterprise of war is more injurious to the political processes of a democracy than to the governmental procedures of the less advanced forms of civil society. Despotic government can undertake war without deviating from its ordinary pattern. But a constitutional democracy requires all sorts of emergency measures in order to engage efficiently in warmaking. The worst forms of government—the least just and the least mature—are those most inclined toward war and the best prepared for its trials.

This confirms the abnormality of war—or the normality of Fascism! The form of government which is best adapted to the nature of man is least adapted for the nature of war. War runs counter to man's nature, even threatening to destroy the very institutions which represent his achievement of political maturity.

The abnormality of war is in no way lessened by the distinction between good and bad wars, just and unjust wars. *All* wars violate the nature of man and defeat his normal aspiration for the goods of social life—the goods which reflect the beneficence of peace.

CHAPTER 5

What Peace Is

"WAR CONSISTETH not in battle only, or the act of fighting," wrote Hobbes, "but in the known disposition thereto, during all the time there is no assurance to the contrary. All other time is Peace."

The peace which Hobbes has in mind is *civil* peace, not peace between independent nations. It is "the king's peace," against which criminals offend when they commit "a breach of the peace." It is the sort of peace which civil war disturbs, but seldom destroys; the sort of peace which can exist *within* a country while it is waging war on foreign fields.

The conception of war as not limited to battle, and of peace as not being merely the *absence* of fighting, applies to the external relationships of a state, as well as to its internal condition. Rousseau generalized Hobbes's basic insight in the following manner:

> War between two Powers is the result of a settled intention, manifested on both sides, to destroy the enemy State, or at least to weaken it by all means at their disposal. The carrying of this intention into act is war, strictly so called; so long as it does not take shape in act, it is only a state of war. . . . The state of war is the natural relation of one Power to another.

The fact that we call states or nations "powers" confirms the truth that distinct political communities are always in a *state of war,* which becomes *actual warfare* when the shooting begins. Rousseau observed that we use the word "power" only when we wish to refer to the state in its foreign relations.

In diplomatic intercourse, adds J. A. Hobson, "states are represented in their capacity of 'Powers.' " And Thorstein Veblen completes the picture by pointing out "that 'power' here means eventual warlike force."

44

Each state is a power to the extent that it has capacity for war, the great powers having greater warlike capacity than their smaller neighbors. During the period of truce or no-shooting, the nations defend themselves and prepare for war, not only through military establishments, but also through treaties and alliances and all the machinery of diplomacy. Because of its military capacity, each is a power during the period of a truce, just as much as during actual fighting when it exercises this capacity. The weight of a nation's words in diplomatic parley is seldom greater than the weight of its armament in battle.

2

These considerations oblige us to define our words.

The king's peace is maintained by his sheriffs and bailiffs operating under the laws of the realm, not by his armies or diplomats fighting or conniving abroad. The king's soldiers engaged in foreign combat do not breach the king's peace. Nor is that done by foreigners who undertake aggressive attack upon the king's people. The peace of the realm is disturbed by the king's own subjects when they violate his ordinances.

There seem to be two quite distinct situations for which we use the one word "peace," and two for which we use the one word "war." The following definitions are, therefore, needed to clarify any discussion of the problem of war and peace.

1. INTERNAL PEACE
   This is the peace which obtains *within* any political community. It is sometimes called "civil peace." Whenever the word "peace" is used without qualification, the reference will be to peace in this sense.

2. EXTERNAL PEACE
   This is the peace which obtains *between* distinct political communities, nations, or states. It is sometimes called "international peace."

Hobbes and Rousseau seem right in regarding it as, not peace at all, but a "state of war." Between nations there is always *potential* war when there is not actual fighting, the potentiality of the war being indicated by the fact that nations, in their external relations, are *powers,* which means a capacity for actual war.

This situation will never be referred to as "peace" unless the word is put in quotation marks to indicate that it is really a *truce,* which is the same as *potential war.*

3. EXTERNAL WAR
This is the war *between* distinct political communities, which we now call "international war," but which could have been called "interstate war" when states were city-states instead of national states.

Since such war always exists between communities, it is sometimes necessary to use such words as "fighting" or "shooting," "battle" or "combat," to distinguish the *act* of war, or actual warfare, from the potential war which is identical with an armed truce.

4. INTERNAL WAR
This is the war *within* a single political community, which we usually call "civil war" or "rebellion," "revolution" or "civil strife."

Even when such internal disorders reach the stage of *actual* violence, civil peace remains *potentially* present in so far as the community endures these convulsions and survives to reinstate the peaceful order which was temporarily in abeyance.

In order to distinguish the strife which reduces civil peace to potentiality from the strife which actualizes the potentiality for international war, the words "war" and "truce" will always be used for the latter, and the words "peace" and "civil war" for the former.

3

Once these fundamental distinctions are understood, it is not necessary to memorize the vocabulary. The context will always furnish sufficient indication of the sense in which the crucial words are intended. What *is* necessary is a conscious effort on our part, especially during a period of actual warfare, to overcome our natural inclination to look forward to the day when the shooting stops as the day when peace begins or can be made. The inveterate habit, on the part of most historians and journalists, to use the word "peace" for what is only a truce will, if we adopt it, blind us to the nature of peace and its causes. As Mr. Emery Reves has so well said:

> All those brief respites from war which we called "peace" were nothing but diplomatic, economic, political, and financial wars between the various groups of men called "nations," with the only distinction that these conflicts, rivalries, and hostilities have been fought out with all the means except actual shooting.

The tyranny of words is nowhere more destructive of good sense and clear ideas than in the discussion of war and peace. I cannot resist quoting my favorite authority on semantics, *The New Yorker*, which observes editorially that "this cantankerous attitude which we seem to be striking, this harping on the meaning of words, comes from our belief that there is a sharp need for definition and that, in the words of Saroyan's barfly, there is 'no foundation all the way down the line.' "

The New Yorker was commenting on the mythical sense of the word "law" when we appeal to international law. The comment, in paraphrase, runs as follows:

> Nothing is more frightening than to hear what is not law called law, what is not peace called peace. . . . To speak

as though we had peace when what we've got is treaties and pacts, to use the word "peace" for non-peace, is to lessen our chance of ever getting world peace, since the first step toward getting it is to realize with dazzling clearness that we haven't got it and never have had it.

4

What peace is and how it is made are not the same question. The two questions are, however, closely related; for what a thing is determines how it can be made.

Mr. Walter Lippmann, quite clear in his mind about the foreign policy his country should adopt, confesses to being *not so clear* about what peace is. In *Some Notes on War and Peace,* he writes:

Peace is as desirable, and just about as indefinable and elusive as good health. And war is as undesirable as a bad disease, but there are many kinds of disease. We may enjoy peace as we enjoy good health without knowing why, which is largely the case of the United States; or we may have bad health, like the wars of Europe and Asia, without knowing which pill, if any, will cure it.

It should be obvious that Mr. Lippmann is using the word "peace" in its internal sense when he refers to the United States, and "war" in its external sense when he refers to Europe. His main comparison, therefore, becomes misleading.

The health of a living body is strictly an internal condition, a harmony of its functioning parts. Health does not *consist* in a body's relation to other bodies outside itself, even though it may *depend* on these. When what we are talking about is the internal condition of the body politic, peace, like good health, does not defy definition.

The comparison suffers from another fault. The diseases of the body politic are both internal and external disorders, whereas in the case of the living body, disease is purely an internal disorder, whatever its cause. We do know how to cure many diseases once we know their causes; and knowing the cause of the political pathology that is war, we shall know how to cure it, too. Nor is this too difficult to know. The cause of war— *its only cause*, for all practical purposes—will become apparent as soon as we understand the cause of peace.

To know the cause of peace, we must first know *what peace is*. Let me appeal to a writer who thought he could define peace. In *The City of God*, Saint Augustine said:

> The peace of the body is ordered temperature of parts. . . . The peace of body and soul is ordered life and health of animate being. . . . The peace of man is ordered concord. The peace of the household is the ordered concord of commanding and obeying among those living together. The peace of the city is the ordered concord of commanding and obeying among citizens. . . . The peace of all things is the tranquillity of order. Order is the disposition of equal and unequal things attributing to each its place.

In this statement, several points should be observed. In the first place, Saint Augustine is considering both the peace of an individual living thing and the peace of a community which includes a multitude of distinct individuals. The latter is peace in the social sense, whereas the former is peace in an individual sense—the inward peace of the heart, the peace between man and God. These two should never be confused. Social peace is primarily an affair of political institutions, justice, and law; individual peace, primarily a moral matter, an affair of virtue and charity.

In the second place, any condition of peace involves these elements: a multitude of things; their concord with one another; and an order among them which establishes this concord. In the social sphere, peace consists in a multitude of persons living together in concord and enjoying the tranquillity of order.

In the third place, *order* is the central term. On the one hand, it establishes concord in a multitude; on the other, it confers a tranquillity upon their living together. And when the multitude comprises human beings who can live together by rules of their own devising, rather than by instinct, order results from two factors: from "commanding and obeying" and from "the disposition of equal and unequal things attributing to each its place."

Order results from the reign of law or from the operations of government, according to which men are related as rulers and ruled. Order in a multitude also results from the organization of that multitude, in suchwise that each member occupies a place according to his equality or inequality with every other member.

A multitude of things is nothing but a heap without organization. A multitude of persons is a mob, not a society or community, unless it is arranged according to some principle of organization. And any principle of organization involves some discrimination of likeness and difference among the things or persons to be organized.

Whether the discriminations are just or unjust, social organization always involves the distribution of status to the members of a community; and through the status they are assigned, they are related as equal and unequal.

5

Saint Augustine has given us not only a definition of peace, but also some insight into its causes. Postponing a consideration of the causes, let us look more closely at the definition.

It would seem that peace consists in making a *one* out of a *many*. The maxim *e pluribus unum* defines peace. But the natural unity of an individual thing must be differentiated from the social unity of a multitude of separate individuals.

An individual living body has parts or members. These parts are organized by nature to form a single whole, which is the one living thing. The parts do not associate themselves to form the organism. But when men form a society, they do voluntarily associate with each other to form a community.

The very word "community," which has the word "unity" at its root, signifies that here is *a unity which has come together*. The significance of "community" also involves the notion of many persons having something *in common*. When men associate for a common purpose and share in common benefits derived from their association, they form a community—whether this be a social club or an industrial corporation, a university or a political party, a family or a state.

However a community is formed, whatever be its size, its purpose, or the special characteristics of its personnel, social peace will be found wherever we find men living or working together in a community. The most important thing for us to see is that the peace of a family does not differ essentially from the peace of a village, nor does the peace of a small country, restricted in area, sparse in population, differ essentially from the peace of the largest state which has ever existed.

The same thing is true for all the other varieties of community. The characteristics of peace are everywhere the same.

Anyone who has belonged to a large family living together under one roof will know the meaning of domestic peace—the peace of the family community. He will also know that peace does not consist in the total absence of fighting or quarreling, that it does not require all the members of the household to agree about everything.

So long as the family holds together, it is an order of equal and unequal persons, each having a place and role in the group. So long as husband and wife, parents and children, brothers and sisters—and even, perhaps, the cousins and the aunts—have a way of settling disagreements and a way of patching up quarrels, the members will continue to enjoy the benefits of peaceful association, even as they will continue to collaborate for the family's good.

The familiar facts of family life remind us that peace can

exist in many degrees. It is seldom if ever *perfect concord or harmony*. Such imperfect peace, which is probably the only kind that will ever exist on earth, may be more or less imperfect according as elements of strain and discord tax the unity of any group and threaten to break it into utterly discordant fragments.

Hence, peace must be realistically defined, not only by reference to the ideal perfection, but also, considering its degrees of imperfection, by reference to the vanishing point at the other extreme. The vanishing point is reached, and peace disappears, only when the community dissolves. When, for example, the family breaks up into feuding clans, each with its own common purpose, that purpose being founded on rivalry and antagonism to the other fragment of the family, then the peace of the family is totally destroyed.

6

For the time being, I shall not discuss the degrees of peace. That becomes an important consideration later. What does matter now is the distinction between political peace and all the other forms of social peace—that of the family or the university or the business corporation.

To distinguish political peace, we must separate the political community from all others. This is not an easy task, but it can be done with sufficient precision for our purposes.

A distinguishing mark of the political community, which enables us to locate it by reference to obvious realities, is the fact that *it includes other communities and is included by no other*. It includes families, universities, and churches, political parties and economic associations. All these and many others are societies which it subordinates. These subordinate associations are among its members, even as individual persons are. They are to some extent subject to its regulations.

Every individual belongs to some all-inclusive political community, as well as to many subordinate communities. The various communities to which he belongs serve different purposes, which help to distinguish them. Through belonging to each, he participates along with its other members in the common good which that association aims at, and for which its members work co-operatively.

We could define the political community by specifying the political common good. But it is easier to separate it from all the others by its inclusiveness. By its "inclusiveness" or "comprehensiveness" I do not mean to imply that the political community should arrogate to itself every social function. That is the horror of totalitarianism. A well-ordered political community not only permits but also encourages the existence of subordinate associations to perform a wide variety of functions—economic, educational, or recreational.

When we understand what is meant by "inclusiveness," we see that the political community is distinguished by the *extent* of the peace it provides. Under the auspices of the political community, the individual lives at peace with a larger number of persons than he does through any of the other subordinate associations of which he is a member.

In consequence, the peace of the political community underlies and supports all the other instances of peaceful unity. Political peace is the paramount form of peace which the individual enjoys, just as the political society is the paramount community to which he belongs.

7

Under primitive conditions, a large family group may be the most comprehensive community to which a given individual belongs. If that family group is autonomous, if it does not acknowledge its subordination to any other group, it is at once both a domestic and a political society. We do not call such a family a "state," but it has much in common with the more elaborate political communities we do call "states."

Under modern conditions, incorporated towns and villages, chartered cities, and even states having their own constitutions may be included in a more comprehensive political community. It would seem that these subordinate societies should be called "political communities" even if they are not the most inclusive society to which their members belong. That cannot be denied. But its significance is controlled by the fact that these subordinate societies derive their political character from being the local or decentralized instruments of the one over-all political community to which their own members always also belong.

For our purposes, it makes no difference whether we consider the peace which belongs to the United States as a political community, or the peace of any of the forty-eight states, or the peace of their cities, towns, and villages. In each case we shall be dealing with a political community and, hence, with political peace. What is characteristic of political peace in the smallest of these communities will obtain equally in the largest.

CHAPTER 6

How Peace Is Made

THE CAUSE of peace is government. The effective operations of government make *peace,* and *keep* it.

Without government no community could long endure, if it could ever exist at all. Since peace is equivalent to the life of a community, since peace obtains only among the members of a community, whatever is needed to establish and sustain a community is needed for the establishment and preservation of peace.

The reader knows these things to be true of his local community—village, town, or city. He knows that such local peace flourishes only through the institutions of government and only to the extent that its instrumentalities function effectively. He knows in general what these institutions and functions are. He does not suppose that any of the basic elements of government can be dispensed with—that the community can get along without civic organization and some form of administration, without ordinances, without courts, without police.

The reader may remember what happened in Boston during the police strike, how even in the few hours before the governor of Massachusetts summoned the militia, the peace of a great city could be mocked by thugs and bandits. The laws of Boston, like international treaties, could be torn to shreds. He knows from this one historic example how truly Thomas Hobbes spoke when he said: "Covenants without the sword are but words, and of no strength to secure a man at all."

2

If the reader knows these things, as he does, can he claim that he does not know how world peace can be made and how it must be kept? Can he suppose that these fundamental truths he would never think of denying when he thinks of his immediat~

55

locality suddenly turn false, lose their significance, or become inapplicable when the size of a community increases?

The reader also lives in a larger community—in a state or province, in a nation. He knows that national peace requires national government no less than village peace requires village government, that state peace depends upon state government as city peace depends upon city government.

If anyone wishes to test his grasp of these truths, let him abstract his thinking from all the imagery of the actual communities in which he has lived or which he knows. Let him imagine instead any limited area of the earth's surface, vast or small, but less than the whole. Let him populate this area with human beings, sparsely or thickly. Add one further condition and only one: that no part of this population be completely isolated from any other, that no part be entirely self-sufficient, that contact and communication, commerce and culture, interlock their lives. Let him then proceed to solve the problem of peace versus war for this area of the earth's surface.

Can he, in the first place, imagine peace being *made* without the formation of a single political community? Can he, in the second place, imagine this community without political organization and government? Can he, in the third place, imagine the political peace of this area, once made, being kept for this population without the continued and effective operation of governmental machinery and some sort of legal system, formulating, applying, enforcing rules?

Though performed in the imagination, this is a crucial experiment in thought. Like any good experiment, it supports an induction of unlimited generality.

When Newton broke the sun's rays into the spectrum by means of a prism in his Cambridge room, he did not conclude that sunlight was complex in a certain room in a certain part of England in a certain century. A single well-conducted experiment told him the truth about the spectral variety in sunlight everywhere and at all times. Other scientists may repeat the experiment, altering the conditions to remove all accidental factors, but they will merely confirm the crucial character of the first experiment.

The political experiment we can perform in our imaginations is confirmed for us by all our local experience in civil communities and by all our historical knowledge. We see that quantitative variations in the extent of the area or the numbers of population are entirely accidental factors which do not affect the truth of our induction.

We see how Hamilton, Madison, and Jay, in the first nine of the *Federalist Papers,* could argue inductively from their own colonial experience and from the history of European affairs, to the conclusion that in the area between the Atlantic and the Appalachians and for the three million inhabitants of that long and narrow strip of land, peace could be *made* and *kept* in *only one way.* The Federalists could feel perfectly assured of the soundness of their conclusion, even though they were solving a political, not a mathematical, problem. They did not have to wait until the experiment was tried again in this new area to know how it would turn out.*

Let the reader then take the last step in this line of thinking. Let him extend the area he is imagining from any limited part of the earth's surface to the whole globe. Let him enlarge the population from some men to all. Let him retain the one essential condition that no part of this population live in isolation or self-sufficiency, without communication or intercourse.

Can anyone deny that *e pluribus unum* is the maxim of world peace—and for the same reasons that it is the principle of local peace? Can anyone think how to put this maxim into practice universally without satisfying the same conditions on which its practical realization depends locally? Does it make any difference that the *pluribus* now signifies the multitude of *all* men, not

* "To look for a continuation of harmony," wrote Hamilton, "between a number of independent, unconnected sovereignties in the same neighborhood, would be to disregard the uniform course of human events, and to set at defiance the accumulated experience of ages."

some; and that the *unum* now signifies the whole world, not a city, state, or nation?

If the reader has the faintest trace of doubt or reservation in answering these questions, it must be because he has somehow come to regard the "international scene" as utterly freakish—as a mysterious domain where none of the familiar principles of politics apply, or where they can be brushed aside with impunity. As if two plus two could make four here and there, but not everywhere!

3

There are as many types of governments as there are types of communities. There is familial government and business government. Within the sphere of civil government, there are many forms of political organization. None of these variations in type or form alters the principle that every sort of community requires government.

Under the term *government* I mean to include every aspect of a community's structure and organization. I mean not only the acts of commanding and obeying by which government most obviously manifests itself. I mean as well the disposition of status and function to every member of the community, the arrangement of public offices, and the distribution of rights and privileges.

Ordinarily when we speak of "*the* government" we mean the group of officials who occupy public office by election or appointment. Sometimes, we have an even more restricted meaning, referring to the executive branch of the government, in contrast to the legislature and the judiciary. But obviously the citizens who vote, who elect officials and can effect the amendment of the constitution, take part in the government of the country to which they belong.

Differences in form of civil government do not affect what we mean by the words "state" or "political community." Persia under an absolute despot and Athens under a constitution were both political communities, though they differed radically in form of government. And a political community remains the *same* state even when its form of government varies from time to time; as, for example, Rome under the Tarquins, under the Republic, and under the Caesars.

4

The chief function of government is to settle differences among men who engage to live together. That is the reason why government is needed to keep the peace.

Children playing sand-lot baseball soon discover this. They know that they have to have rules. They know that if a dispute arises about the rules, they must appeal to some ultimate principle of government, such as a majority vote, in order to get on with the game. They know that teamwork requires organization, that organization requires a division of responsibility, and that someone must usually be given the responsibility of making whatever decisions are not submitted to a majority vote.

The two ultimate principles of government are the principle of decision by a majority and the principle of decision by a leader. Both are methods of reaching a decision which will be acceptable to the group, despite the individual differences of opinion about what should be done.

It would be utter folly to trust to the possibility that a number of individuals will always agree about what is to be done. The fact is that they will very frequently disagree. Therefore, there must be some way to get men who may disagree to concur in a common action. When men form a community, they not only live together, but also work for a common good in which they all share. Just as all hope to share in, so all must co-operate for, the common good. They must have a way of deciding what should be done by all for the good of each, and by each for the good of all.

Each man cannot decide for himself what he should do or what the others should do; for if individuals disagree in their separate judgments—*as they will*—no common action can be taken. Nor can the principle of decision be the requirement of unanimity. That is equivalent to each man deciding for himself. Unlike the principle of a majority, a unanimous vote cannot be relied upon to settle differences *without fail*. One stubborn man who insists upon his own opinion is enough to hang up a jury.

5

In the administration of the common affairs of an isolated frontier settlement, all sorts of practical questions will arise, both questions of general policy and questions about what is to be done on particular occasions. Agreement on such matters cannot be expected. But neither can fundamental disagreements about urgent practical matters be permitted to go unsettled for long. Factions will form, and when argument is worn thin and patience frayed, the quarrel in words will become a quarrel in deeds. The community will be destroyed by violence.

Fundamental disagreements cannot be avoided, but recourse to violence can be. About difficult practical matters, even the most rational men, prudent men and men with the common interest at heart, are as likely to disagree as to agree. This unalterable fact requires any community, small or large, to adopt some rules of procedure for reaching a decision in which the dissident parties will concur.

Either the rule that all will abide by a majority vote or the rule that all will accept the judgment of some one given the authority to decide can effectively settle disputes when they arise.

Neither rule determines which side of a practical dispute is in truth the *right* side. In fact, the minority may be right, or a majority of the group, dissenting from their leader's judgment, may hold the sounder opinion. The rule of procedure is not a way of always finding the *right* answer to the question; it is only a way of always finding *some answer without recourse to violence.* That is the essential minimum condition which a principle of government must satisfy. In addition, one hopes that a rule of procedure will more frequently tend to produce a sound decision. Under different circumstances one may place one's faith in the wisdom of the majority, or in the prudence of those to whom authority has been given.

Recourse to violence will not be avoided unless rules of procedure can be enforced against those who may refuse to comply with the decisions reached. The force to be employed must obviously be the force of the group, supporting the authority of the rule which they themselves have voluntarily adopted.

If in a small frontier community, the dissenters on any occasion are numerous, the opposition of forces will tend to approach a balance of power. The exercise of force by one side will be resisted by force on the other. Unless those who would support the authority of the rule have a predominance of power against one or a few individuals, no rule of procedure will prevent violence or, ultimately, the dissolution of the community.

6

These simple facts help us to understand the distinction between authority and force, or power; and also to see that any principle of government must involve *both* in order to operate effectively for the end it was intended to serve.

The authority of a rule, or of any person upon whom a rule confers authority, consists in its voluntary acceptance by those who will be subject to decisions rendered according to the rule. They accept the rule voluntarily because they recognize its operation to be for their good.

In matters which are strictly private, every man can decide what is for his own good; but in matters which affect the individual's well-being *because* they affect the welfare of the community, or the common good, the individual cannot wisely insist upon his own decision. If he is wise enough to recognize that some principle of government, some rule of procedure, must be adopted to reach decisions for the common good, then he will acknowledge the authority of the decisions thus reached.

A rule, and everything which follows from it, has authority, in short, if it elicits an individual's obedience because his own reason tells him that the rule obligates him for the good of the community and ultimately for his own good. Wherever we find a man obeying a command even though no force existed which could compel him to obey, we perceive the operation of *naked* authority. The man who willingly submits to naked authority does so because he finds himself bound in conscience to obey, and for no other reason.

But naked authority and obligation in conscience cannot be depended on in all cases.

In any community we are always likely to find some men who will tend to disobey whenever their private judgment differs from the decision reached by a public rule. Even a man who recognizes the authority of the rule in most cases may be tempted to flout it on some particular occasion. Hence, authority must be clothed with power or force sufficient to compel obedience on the part of whoever does not obey through moral obligation.

The mere threat of coercive force may often suffice, but unless the sanction be forcefully applied when the threat fails, the threat will soon become empty. For coercive sanctions to be effective, the force on the side of authority must predominate by a large margin over the force that any individual or group of individuals can muster.

The authority with which any principle of government is invested is the authority of the community over its members. If individuals did not recognize the dependence of their own well-being on the existence of the community, neither the community nor the institutions of government indispensable to it would exercise any authority over them.

The authorized force which government applies should also be the force of the community, however it is recruited and wielded. But here there is always likely to be an opposition of forces, since public force need only be exerted against those who use private force when they seek to resist authority. We must, therefore, distinguish between *authorized* (public) and *unauthorized* (private) force, according as the force defends or opposes the community's rules of procedure.

Unless a monopoly of authorized force exists on the side of government, and unless the officers of government, exercising the *only* authorized force in the community, also exert a substantial predominance of real power, government will fail in its work. The peace of the community will be torn by factions in civil strife. The community may be destroyed. This group of men may no longer be able to live together peacefully.

7

Effective government must combine authority with force. Naked authority will not keep the peace because men are men, not angels. When Alexander Hamilton wisely said that "if men were angels, no Government would be necessary," he had in mind the need for coercive force to support the authority of rules "It is essential to the idea of a law," he wrote, "that it be attended with a sanction; or, in other words, a penalty or punishment for disobedience."

But why will not naked force do the work of government? Why must government have authority as well as power? If one man or a few have enough power to compel all the rest to obey their commands, will not the community be maintained and the peace be kept?

History gives us the answer. The tyrant maintains the community only for the sake of exploiting it. Tyranny always consists in the exercise of power for the private gain of the man possessing it, rather than in the interests of the community.

Whoever feels the oppression of the tyrant, whoever recognizes the injustice of the exploitation he suffers, will obey only under the threat of force. The tyrant's commands will have no authority, and his unauthorized use of force can have only one result, in the long run or less. When the people are finally driven to prefer the risk of death to further oppression, they will employ the only expedient available to them—the use of naked force against naked force.

Tyranny breeds civil strife, just as powerless justice permits it. From the point of view of peace, it makes no difference whether men must resort to violence in order to obtain justice or are able to employ violence in order to do injustice. Neither force without authority nor authority without force can protect the community from civil strife. Neither can perpetuate peace.

8

We have seen what must be done about disagreements on public policies or about actions for the collective good.

Another and equally important trouble zone includes all those disputes between individuals concerning the rights or privileges to which they think themselves entitled and which, in their opinion, others have violated; or concerning the injuries which they allege other men have done them and which these other men deny having committed.

A third sphere of controversy includes differences of opinion between private citizens and officials of the government concerning charges of misconduct brought by either against the other.

These three areas of practical dispute are fundamentally alike. They involve issues which *cannot* be settled in the way scientific controversies are usually resolved—by appeals to reason and evidence.

A scientific controversy can always wait until enough evidence accumulates or until the reasons become clear enough to warrant a unanimous verdict from all those competent to judge. It does not matter if such judgment must be suspended for a century or two. But serious practical issues have an urgency which requires decisions to be more speedily reached.

Moreover, the very nature of practical problems, concerning contingent matters, makes it doubtful that waiting, even if we could, would help. Evidence and reasons can never solve such problems with demonstrative certainty. The parties to the dispute are always likely to feel justified in persisting in their opposite opinions about what is right or wrong, just or unjust.

Since evidence and reason cannot be relied upon to settle such disputes, only two other remedies remain. One is resort to *private* force. The other consists in the operation of government, and includes the threat of *public* force.

Of these, the first, if it is the only expedient available, will tend to disrupt the community. Only the second can keep men living and working together peacefully despite the fact that the very business of living and working together necessarily involves them in all sorts of disagreements and disputes.

Quarreling cannot be prevented from occurring; but, having occurred, it can be prevented from turning into disruptive violence. To do this, three things are indispensable. (1) No *private* person can be permitted to determine which particular laws he will accept as binding on himself. (2) No individual can be trusted to act as judge in his own case when he becomes involved in dispute with another. (3) No party to a dispute can be relied on to comply with a decision which affects him adversely; nor can the other party be allowed to use his own private force to compel performance.

9

Government must, therefore, provide three institutions for the peaceful settlement of quarrels between members of a community.

   1. There must be *laws* of two sorts:
      a. General rules which determine the procedure to be followed in the adjudication of disputes; and

b. General rules which determine the standards of right and wrong according to which specific instances of conduct can be judged faultless or blameworthy.

It makes no difference whether these general rules express the long-prevalent customs of the community or whether they are expressly formulated and enacted by one or more persons who are given legislative authority by the community.

2. There must be *courts* which are designed to render an impartial verdict on the disputed issues and which, according to the laws of the realm, give judgment, commanding certain penalties to be imposed or certain compensations to be made.

3. There must be *sheriffs* or *police* with authorized force and sufficient power to execute the judgment against the party adversely affected by the court's decision.

These are minimum, not maximum, requirements.

In addition to these three elements, there is obvious need for police power competent to bring offenders to trial or to compel disputants, under certain circumstances, to submit their differences to a court. One might also add the deterrent and preventive efficacy of an adequately constituted and efficiently operated police power. But the main point for us to consider here is that *nothing less* than these three governmental institutions can discharge the task of keeping peace.

Unless there are laws—though these be rudimentary and incomplete—courts cannot even begin to operate. Once they begin to operate, a body of laws will grow through the accretion of judicial decisions.

Unless courts are adequately supported by police power, their judgments remain impotent, as impotent as any form of naked authority. And if courts devoid of a powerful executive arm cannot effectively prevent quarrels from turning into violence, how much less effective will be any set of rules, customary or enacted, which elicits no obligation except from those whom it binds in conscience.

Herein lies the whole difference between moral precepts and civil laws. The former bind only in conscience. The latter also impose a moral obligation in so far as just men recognize the rules to be just, but they do not stop there. In addition, they wield the big stick of coercive sanctions against any member of the community who does not acknowledge the authority of the community's customs or its enacted legislation.

Finally, if laws and courts lacking police power represent the impotence of naked authority, police power which operates independently of laws and courts is a violent imposition of unauthorized force—an instrument of tyranny.

10

The institutions of government can be regarded, in large part, as machinery for keeping quarrels on the level of conversation, and for sustaining conversation until disputes are resolved. When resolutions are reached, the machinery of government monopolizes the force required to translate words into action.

The use of language, as well as brawn, differentiates man from all the other animals. Men can settle things by words as well as by fists and stones or guns. Cicero wisely observed that

> There are two ways of settling disputed questions; one by discussion, the other by force. The first being characteristic of man, the second of brutes, we should have recourse to the latter only if the former fails.

There can be no peace among the predatory beasts of the jungle. There can only be a temporary truce when the brutes are well fed or exhausted, or their prey is in hiding.

There can be no war or strife among the members of a single beehive or ant mound, for they are instinctively determined to perform the acts which sustain their community.

But between men there can be either peace or war. They cannot live in interaction without quarreling, but they have two ways, not one, of settling their differences. Since they are both *rational* and *animal*, they can make peace or war—the one by discussion, the other by force.

Yet this is not the whole truth, for we must add that men can have peace only through the institutions of government. Without government, the conversation too frequently fails. Without government, discussion cannot be assured that its conclusions will prevail.

War can be made by force alone. When they make war, men can act like brutes, and worse than brutes because reason makes them craftier. But peace cannot be made unless force implements discussion. When they make peace, men behave reasonably, but never without a reasonable respect for *brute force*.

Human government, composite of law and force, reflects man's composite nature—his rational animality. Precisely because it corresponds to human nature, government and nothing but government makes the human community and keeps its peace.

CHAPTER 7

The *Only* Cause of War

THE ONLY cause of war is anarchy. Anarchy occurs wherever men or nations try to live together without each surrendering their sovereignty.

If a man or a nation could live entirely by itself, exercising no influence upon another nor suffering external influences, the word "sovereign" would not apply. Nor would "anarchy." Anarchy is the condition of those who try to live together *without government*. Only those who do not recognize any government over them regard themselves as sovereign.

Anarchy and sovereignty are inseparable. As we have seen, they both involve a social relationship, a relationship of reciprocal influence among free agents. But we should observe at once that the notions of anarchy and sovereignty are incompatible with the notions of society. A society or community cannot normally exist without government.

The words "an anarchic community" or "a society of sovereigns" may not be as self-contradictory as "round square," but certainly the word "society" or "community" changes its meaning radically when it occurs in these phrases. Unless we detect this shift in meaning, we will be deceived by a dangerous and insidious counterfeit. We will talk about a "society of nations" as if it were a political community in the *same sense* as a community of men.

One other point should be noted. Nowhere in the civilized world can we find an anarchic community of *men*, a society of sovereign *men*. A few experiments in anarchy have been tried, but their utter and speedy failure has verified the truth the experimenters should have known—that individual human beings cannot form a society without government, or live together without submitting themselves to the authority and power of the community.

This does not mean that the notions of anarchy and sovereignty lack practical significance or have no application to reality. On the contrary, throughout the whole of history and everywhere in the world today, the "social" relationship of states or nations exhibits the twin features of anarchy and sovereignty.

The astounding fact is that states or nations seem able to endure a condition under which individual men cannot survive. But the fact becomes less astounding when we remember the price the world has paid—war, continuous war, war without interruption, without any change except for the alterations between war by the diplomats and war by the generals. The price of sovereignty is war.

Individual men cannot live without living together, and they cannot live together in a state of war, actual or potential. States or nations, because each is much more self-sufficing than any individual man, can manage to live—even for fairly long periods—without living together *in peace*. But they are never so self-sufficient that they can manage to live without living together *at war*.

"Living together at war!" That strange and wonderful phrase tells the whole story of the tensions and frustrations which anarchy and sovereignty have bestowed upon man's corporate life. It also reveals anarchy—and with it sovereignty—to be the only cause of war among those who must try to live together.

2

The literature of the subject abounds with a large assortment of factors and forces called "the causes of war." Classifying the causes of war has been a favorite field for the professors of "international relations." Determining which were the predisposing and which the exciting causes of a particular war has occupied the attention of historians, and also the students of "international law," who, in addition, try to allocate guilt and innocence by applying the criteria of just war and unjust war.

Many books devoted to these problems were written about the

war which began in 1914. Many books of the same sort will undoubtedly be written about the war which began in 1939. Some have already begun to appear.

But one fact, which the professors themselves readily admit, changes the significance of everything they say. They admit that the war which began in 1939 represents a continuation of the war which ended in 1918. They sometimes even explicitly call the intervening period a "truce," during which the war was being carried on by other means.

This should lead them to see that the causes they talk about are *always* operative—just as much during the period of truce as during the years when the hostility and conflict between nations expresses itself on the battlefield rather than in the chancellories and foreign offices, through force of arms rather than through the guile of disarmament conferences. They should have learned from Machiavelli that the same end can be achieved by the cunning of the fox as by the lion's might.

The obvious point becomes obscured by the deceptive use of the word "peace" instead of "truce" to designate the period when the generals are waiting for the diplomats to fail. That makes it *seem* as if the so-called "causes of war" were inoperative or held in abeyance. But when we understand the truth that all the machinations of diplomacy, all the trickery of international relations, signify the operation of the identical causes, we see that the only difference between a shooting war and a "war of nerves" lies in the channels through which these causes operate.

3

A deeper truth remains to be seen. None of the factors cited produces war, either actual warfare or the potential state of war which always exists among sovereign states. A true analogue of every one of these factors will be found at work in the affairs of individual men living together in a single community. Yet, despite this fact, the members of a political community live at peace with one another.

Each of the following elements is *supposed* to operate as a cause of war between nations, yet each occurs in the life of a single society.

1. ECONOMIC RIVALRY
   Competition, even cutthroat competition, exists among the corporations and the individuals of most modern societies.

2. CULTURAL ANTIPATHIES
   These create friction among the members of a community. The clash of nationalities or races is present in the communities which have assimilated men from different historic backgrounds and of different biological stocks.
   Such conflict may be aggravated by the arrogance of majority groups and by the aggressiveness of the numerically inferior minorities.

3. RELIGIOUS DIFFERENCES
   The rift of deep religious differences has been present in historic communities. In modern times, a single society has embraced infidels and believers, atheists and God-fearing men, every mode of life which men of other persuasions call "paganism" or "heresy."

4. INDIVIDUAL ACTS OF INJUSTICE
   No society is ever free from the injuries which men do to men. When men live together, some will always injure others or take advantage of others, just as there will always be fundamental disagreements and disputes.
   Individual differences in talent and power always tend toward inequitable distributions of privilege, and privileged classes always tend to perpetuate themselves. Even in a community having the most just political constitution, there will be class distinctions.
   The so-called "class war"—the conflict between the *haves* and the *have-nots*—has always been present regardless of the particular form it takes, whether the *haves* have blue

blood or tainted gold or unmerited gifts of mind and energy.

5. HATE AND FEAR

   All the emotions supposed to underlie the antagonism of nations will be found motivating the actions of individuals in a single community. Men hate and fear *some* of their neighbors, distrust them, wish them ill, for a wide variety of reasons or rationalizations.

6. FACTIONS AND IDEOLOGIES

   Within any political society, and due to some combination of the causes already mentioned, men ally themselves into opposing groups, form political parties, foment factionalism of all sorts, and adopt the slogans and shibboleths of conflicting ideologies.

   If the unity which is the heart of a community had to be dead uniformity or complete unanimity, no political society would or could ever exist.

Everyone knows these facts about the society in which he lives. He does not have to be a psychologist or a social scientist, an economist or a political philosopher, to know that all these factors and forces activate the daily life of any community. He need only be wise enough to acknowledge that men are not angels and that no earthly society ever has been or ever will be like the community of saints in heaven—or, for that matter, like the association of the damned in hell.

On earth saints and sinners must live together, and there is a little of both in every man. How this can be managed successfully is *the* political problem. It is the problem of war and peace.

The foregoing enumeration is neither an exhaustive nor a subtle classification of the factors usually called "causes of war." But it is sufficient to make the point that everything which has ever been regarded as a cause of war operates within a single community *without causing war*.

None of these things is by itself or in itself a cause of war. Nor is war caused by a combination of all of them. Singly or together these factors and forces cause war *only when* their action is not restrained by the institutions and machinery of government. The *presence* of governmental controls prevents these factors from causing war within a single community. Hence we see that it is the *absence* of governmental controls which permits these things to cause war between communities.

To say that anarchy is the *only* cause of war is, therefore, to say that it is the *sine qua non* condition, the one indispensable factor without which every other we can think of would be an insufficient cause.

4

Anarchy—the *absence* of government—is a negative factor. The various forces or tendencies which lead to war, *unless restrained by government,* are positive factors.

How, then, can it be said that anarchy is the *only* cause of war? Must we not admit that the negative factor would not cause war between nations *unless* some or all of the positive causes of dissension and conflict also operated?

The question is fair. It can be answered by distinguishing between causes we can control and those we cannot. Only the former are significant for practical purposes.

There are some disease processes which result from a combination of positive and negative factors. The positive factor is the presence of certain bacterial agents. The negative factor is malnutrition, that is, a lack of certain vitamins in the diet. Neither the germ nor the vitamin deficiency is by itself sufficient to produce the disease. Only their concomitance will produce it.

If the bacterial agents are always present, and if there is absolutely no way of freeing the organism from such parasites, then the only controllable element in the situation becomes the negative factor—the vitamin deficiency.

When we have enough knowledge about vitamins to know which ones counteract the parasites in question, and when we know how to regulate the diet to ensure the presence of these vitamins, we can prevent the disease.

From the therapeutic point of view, there is much point in saying that a certain vitamin deficiency is the only cause of the disease. *It is the only cause we can control.* For all practical purposes, we can neglect the causes beyond our control.

We shall never be able to eradicate all the positive causes of war. From experience in our own community, we also know that these positive causes can be effectively counteracted by government. Total lack of government, or grave deficiency in its operation, then becomes, not only the negative cause of war, but also the only cause we can control. For all practical purposes, it is the only cause worth bothering about.

Our present situation is like the medical situation in which physicians know the precise vitamins that must be added to the diet, but do not yet know how to introduce these vitamins into the normal diet in sufficient quantity to prevent the disease.

We know *now* that only world government can *prevent* international wars. We know *now* the minimum *amount* of government which is needed, less than which could not effectively check the ever-present causes of war. But we do not *now* know how to inject the requisite quantity of government into world affairs or how to overcome the existing obstacles to such therapeutic procedure.

In so far as our concern with causes is practical, not academic or theoretical, there are only two things worth bothering about. *One is the single negative factor which permits the positive causes to operate. We know that we can prevent war by abolishing international anarchy. The other consists in all the obstacles which at present stand in the way of our abolishing anarchy.*

When enough people come to understand that anarchy is the *only controllable cause* of war, when they are no longer misled or deceived by irrelevant discussion about all the uncontrollable causes, then the chances increase of our being able to cause world peace by world government. Much else will remain to be done. But an understanding of causes which directs practical men to the only real remedy must be the first step in successful therapy. Everything men have done about war for centuries has been on the level of administering aspirin. Even if no aspirin had been given, the fever would probably have fluctuated up and down periodically in the intermittent phases of fighting and truce.

We have played around with all the superficial aspects of the human environment, neglecting the political neurosis which, from time to time, turns into the raving insanity of actual warfare. During the comparatively lucid intervals of potential war, we neglect the neurosis—the schizoid tendency in a world of sovereign states.

The psychologist will tell us that the only cure for the split personality involved in all neuroses is to get the parts of the soul to act together under some rule of order. The cure for international anarchy is the same.

5

In saying that anarchy is the only cause of war, I mean to imply that it causes the condition I have called "potential war," as much as the actual war all of us recognize when shooting begins.

Failure to understand that the absence of shooting is not the absence of war has blinded many persons to the realities of the international scene. They fail to see that no essential change has occurred in the transition from the diplomatic to the military means of carrying on the war between states.

Those who think that Prussian militarism is the cause of war often quote von Clausewitz, with the implication that if men did not think this way there would be no wars. Von Clausewitz said:

War is not merely a political act, but a true political instrument, a continuation of political intercourse, an execution of the same purpose with other means.

What he meant, of course, was that actual war or physical fighting merely continues the potential war or the economic, social, and psychological fighting that goes on during a truce. Overt war is merely the fulfillment of everything that is latent in international politics.

The cost of armaments is great, the risk in using them tremendous. Preference for gaining an objective by diplomatic means is not peculiar to modern civilized nations. Darius and Xerxes, Philip of Macedon and Alexander, Julius Caesar and other Roman conquerors, usually sent ultimatums before they undertook campaigns.

Under the word "diplomacy" I include every act, short of shooting, which one nation undertakes against another to better its position in the competition for power.

The power which a nation will have available when shooting begins depends, in large part, on the power it has accumulated by diplomatic means. The distinction between the great powers and the second- or third-rate powers holds just as much for their bargaining power in the council chamber as for their military power on the battlefield. Each in fact tends to vary with the other.

The diplomat or any other representative of a country on foreign soil works solely, or at least primarily, for his country's interests. In this he does not differ one bit from the general or the admiral. Sir Henry Wotton's definition of a diplomat as a man who lies abroad for his country distinguishes him from the soldier in one respect only. The soldier may have to continue lying there when the combat is over.

The saying that all is fair in love and war should be amended to include diplomacy and international negotiations of every sort. Diplomacy is, after all, nothing but war masquerading under the aspect of love. A former president of the League of Nations Assembly reports that in the Near East the letters "D.C." on the license plates of autos belonging to the diplomatic corps are rendered by the words "Distinguished Crook."

With malice to no individual, this epitomizes an obvious truth. In the anarchic world of sovereign nations, foreign policies and foreign transactions can be aimed *straight* only when they are aimed at the goal of self-interest. From any goal such as the *common* good of *all* peoples, they necessarily skew aside in all sorts of devious and crooked ways.

Von Clausewitz speaks the truth, but not the whole truth. Interested primarily in the military, he looks only at one side of the matter—the way in which actual war continues and fulfills a nation's trucetime maneuvers and deployments. But it is just as true to say that when the shooting ceases, diplomacy and international business take up where the soldiers leave off.

The victors try to consolidate and augment the advantages won by the sword. The vanquished try to undermine, or compensate for, those advantages. And in both directions, the pen is often mightier.

The diplomats work hard to give the generals an advantageous position in the next war, just as the generals work hard to give the diplomats an advantageous position during the next truce. Diplomacy may be a sublimation of the political neurosis underlying war. Actual fighting is needed periodically to relieve the impulses which diplomacy represses.

I do not say any of these things with a concealed moral judgment. So long as there are sovereign nations and international anarchy, war—actual or potential—is the order of the day. The morality which governs the conduct of individual men living together in a community and under law cannot govern the conduct of nations living together, but in no community and under no enforceable law. So long as national self-preservation remains the dominant end for which prudence must choose means, the principles of morality cannot be reconciled with the counsels of prudence.

Von Clausewitz may also have been a militarist in the worst sense of the word, a man who could think, as von Treitschke did after him, that military exploits alone bring out the highest virtues of a people. But that does not detract in the least from his realistic insight that, under existing circumstances, only the self-deceived can suppose that there is any moral difference between international activities in potential and in actual war.

In both cases, the lapses from morality have the same cause, for both are war. Militarism and armaments are no more the cause of war than pacifism and disarmament conferences are means to peace. Were universal disarmament to occur after this war, it would not signify the advent of world peace. The era of peace will not begin with a superficial Armageddon, but with the demise of diplomacy and with the end of all need for foreign policy.

Mr. Walter Lippmann has pointed out that failure to understand these things has misled people

. . . to entrust the conduct of war to soldiers who do not understand politics, and to leave the arrangements of peace [he means "truce"] to politicians who do not understand war. They have failed to understand the profound truth of von Clausewitz's doctrine that "war is nothing but a continuation of political intercourse." This failure has produced the militarist who supports wars but cannot conclude them, and it has produced the pacifist who declaims against wars but does not prevent them.

6

Though the positive and negative factors which produce potential or actual war are the same, the transition from the one to the other is usually brought about by special causes.

These causes are the occasions thought to justify military expedients—the so-called "last resort" when the penultimate pressures of diplomacy have proved too weak. They are the dramatic occasions and incidents which, in the judgment of a people or their officials, demand or warrant the substitution of overt war for covert war.

It makes no difference whether these *exciting* causes consist of acts of aggression which must be met by self-defense or acts which require a nation to be aggressive in order to defend what it *thinks* its interests to be. The traditional distinction between just and unjust war (meaning, of course, actual warfare) never goes deeper than the exciting causes of military action.

It overlooks the fact that no occasion or incident could excite actual warfare unless the nations were already potentially at war. The activating cause of military operations may be some real or fancied injustice suffered by one or both sides. But this by itself could not cause fighting. If law and government operated, the injustice could be rectified by peaceful means.

When we pay attention to the underlying causes of war, not to the last-minute incidents before military movements begin, we cannot find a single criterion for distinguishing between just and unjust war. Each sovereign nation participates in the international anarchy as much as every other.

In the eyes of God, justice may be more on the side of one nation than another at the moment when hostilities become overt. In declaring or undertaking overt warfare, nations usually appeal to God for victory, claiming He knows that justice is on their side. But only God knows. Nations are quite right in addressing their appeal to Him. They can appeal to no one else. They would do well to avoid couching their appeal in defiant language, and to speak, as Lincoln suggested, with the prayerful hope that "we are on God's side, not that God is on ours."

But, as a matter of fact, such humility seldom prevails. Mr. Emery Reves rightly points out that

> All wars in history were so prepared that the soldiers and nations who fought them were convinced that they were fighting a *Bellum Justum*. Every war of every nation was fought for a "righteous cause," for "justified national interests" and "in self-defense."

The theory of *Bellum Justum* can be used, he adds, "to justify *all wars* and, therefore, is merely a sophistic argument."

During all the ages when men have talked about just cause

in waging war, there has been no way of making the discussion of justice lead to a settlement of rights and wrongs in dispute without recourse to fighting. Men will continue to talk about just cause as long as there are wars.

Not until international anarchy is replaced by world government will it be possible to substitute effective courts and public power for self-judgment and self-help. But then there will no longer be any need to talk about "just war." War itself will be abolished by the very conditions which can make a determination of justice practically effective.

7

When we speak of "the occurrence of war," we mean nothing more than the transition from a potential to an actual state of war. But that is a great deal, indeed. It is the brutality and bloodshed of actual war we all abominate.

Whether men would perceive the evils of international anarchy *if nations always remained in a state of potential war* is an interesting, but academic, question. An extremely sensitive and refined conscience might deplore the discrepancy between the ideal of human brotherhood and the realities of national self-interest. But, with the facts as they are, anyone should be able to see that the state of potential war must be abolished in order to prevent the occurrence of actual war. Anyone who thinks the world should be rid of the horrors of martial combat must seek to abolish the state of potential war. Though its own horrors are more polite and less obvious, it cannot be absolved from the bloody violence in which it issues.

Nations *cannot* remain in a state of potential war. The truce always terminates in warfare, even as fighting always terminates in a truce. Anarchy is not merely responsible for the potential war between the nations. It also fails to prevent the transition to actual combat.

In the days just before "war" breaks out, diplomatic activity reaches feverish intensity. In the last hours of the truce, which journalists and most other men call "peace," the correspondents report, in the language of the foreign offices, that "conversations are rapidly deteriorating." At the end of one day we learn that "conversations have completely broken down." At the dawn of the next, the armies march, the navies sail.

Conversations are rapidly deteriorating. Conversations have ceased. Potential war has become actual. Whatever causes the breakdown of conversation causes the breakdown of "peace"— the onset of "war."

How could the conversations have been sustained? How could they have been made to produce reasonable decisions, instead of giving way before brute force?

We know the answer. Only the institutions and machinery of government can sustain the conversations. Only government can make reasonable the force needed to support reasonable decisions.

The language used by the foreign correspondents attending the birth of "war" epitomizes a truth every man should be able to see. But this truth is not new, nor is the language which so strikingly reveals it a modern turn of phrase.

In the fifth century B.C., Thucydides reported the opening of the Peloponnesian War—the war between the Athenian axis and the allies of Sparta. In the first book of his *History,* he recounts the events, the incidents and occasions, leading up to the outbreak of hostilities.

The dispute between Athens and Sparta and Corinth had been debated at some length by the envoys and diplomats of the several cities. But after many brilliant speeches on both sides, Thucydides tells us that "the envoys departed home, and did not return again." They were doomed to fail by the very conditions under which the conversations took place.

Then, at the beginning of Book II, Thucydides writes:

The war between the Athenians and Peloponnesians and the allies on both sides now *really* begins. For now *all communication* except through the medium of heralds ceased, and *hostilities* were commenced and prosecuted without intermission.

I have italicized the words which tell the story. That story is not simply the account of how the Peloponnesian War began. *It is the whole history of war and peace.*

CHAPTER 8

The Right and Wrong of Sovereignty

To THE proposition that war results from anarchy and anarchy from the sovereignty of nations, the most serious reaction is the one which affirms the truth, and accepts the consequences.

Holding sovereignty to be a natural and inalienable right of nations, some men take the position of the German philosopher Hegel: that peace is impossible, war unavoidable. World government cannot be instituted because that would destroy the sovereignty of independent nations. Sovereignty being indestructible, we can never eliminate the potential war or actual conflict between states.

I think this view is partly right and partly wrong.

It is right in regarding national sovereignty as incompatible with world government. On this matter, many persons take the flimsy position that only *absolute* national sovereignty rejects a supranational government. They think there is some way both to keep a multiplicity of sovereign states and also to have the people of the world live in a single political community under one government.

It is wrong in regarding a multiplicity of independent states to be the natural and necessary order of man's political life. Yet, on this point there are others who go to the opposite extreme of supposing that sovereignty is nothing but a misleading fiction, and that the theory of government would do well to get rid of this notion entirely.

2

Again we face a problem that is unduly complicated by the ambiguity of the principal word. We are helped here by our previous experience with "peace" and "war." For each of these words we found two chief meanings, one concerned with the internal condition of a community, the other concerned with its external relationship to other communities.

It is no accident that the two chief meanings of "sovereignty" should fall into the same pattern.

In one of these meanings, "sovereignty" signifies an attribute of civil government in relation to the individual men who are subject to its laws and administration. *This is the internal aspect of sovereignty.*

In its other meaning, "sovereignty" signifies an attribute of the political community as a whole, including its government, but now in relation to other, distinct, and independent societies. *This is the external aspect of sovereignty.*

In both aspects, the fact of sovereignty is as old as the historic institution of civil governments and political communities. I say this because the word "sovereignty" gained wide currency only in modern times, in the language of statecraft and in the writings of political theorists. In consequence, many historians falsely suppose that sovereignty is itself a modern phenomenon. They have allowed a word to deceive them about the facts.

It is important to get the history of these matters straight. Confusion on this subject has led many persons to identify sovereignty with the modern nation-state, in contrast to the Greek city-states, or the Roman Republic and Empire. This in turn leads them to think of national or dynastic aggrandizement as a peculiarly modern phenomenon, given impetus by pretensions to absolute sovereignty on the part of states or kings.

Finally, by a series of obvious steps, they come to think that there is a peculiarly modern problem of war and peace, which did not exist in the medieval or ancient world. Only in modern times is nationalism a cause of wars. Only in modern times is peace blocked by the sovereignty of states.

Against these views, I should like to insist that the problem of war and peace has always been essentially the same and always will be. Sovereignty has always been at the heart of the problem and always will be.

3

Two maxims formulated by the Roman jurist Ulpian help us to unravel the confusions about sovereignty. The first was: *whatever pleases the prince has the force of law*. The second was: *the prince is above the law and cannot be subjected to its coercive force*.

In these pronouncements, Ulpian did not invent a theory of what should obtain. He merely described the absolutism of the Caesars during the worst period of the Empire.

When the word "sovereign" is applied to an individual person —not to a state or an impersonal government—its meaning includes one or both of the elements formulated in Ulpian's two maxims.

Certain medieval rulers were sovereign *men* only in one respect, namely, that they were above the coercive force of the laws of their own realm. Since the king was himself the repository of public force and administered the law through officials responsible to him alone, there was no way of enforcing the law against him when he violated it. When his subjects were sufficiently outraged by his lawlessness, they could unite against him, using their own private force in armed rebellion.

Though the medieval ruler was above the coercive force of law, he seldom if ever regarded himself as the source of law. The law which he pledged himself to administer when he took his coronation oath did not consist of rules either adopted at his pleasure or ratified by his will. They were customary rules— the immemorial customs of the realm.

In the sixteenth and seventeenth centuries, kings tried to extend their personal sovereignty. They tried to make it complete by adding the other element involved in the absolutism of the late Caesars. Not only would they be above the coercive force of laws, but their will, and nothing but their will or pleasure, would give a rule the authority of law. In addition to being the repository of public force, they would become the sole arbiter of the law.

This effort on their part, which led to all the great modern revolutions, represents a departure only from medieval precedents. Far from being a startling novelty, it represents a return to the absolute sovereignty of the Roman emperors, of Philip of Macedon, of the Persian kings and the Egyptian pharaohs. We must also remember that the modern revolutions which set up constitutional governments had ancient models in the Roman Republic and in many of the Greek city-states.

With the revival of republics and constitutional government in modern times, there arose the theory of popular sovereignty. This denied both of Ulpian's maxims.

Sovereignty belongs to no individual man. No man shall be above the positive law or exempt from its coercive force—not even the chief magistrate of the land, certainly not its legislators, judges, or minor officials. The personal will of no man shall enact or set aside a law. The constitution itself, and all the laws which are made by due process under it, are formulated and instituted by the whole community, or by their chosen representatives.

Under republican or constitutional government, there are only citizens in private life and citizens who occupy public office for a time. No men are sovereigns; none are subjects. The citizen in office has no legitimate power or authority except that which is vested in the office he holds. No legitimate power or authority can be vested in a person, as opposed to an office.

According to the theory of popular sovereignty, the sovereignty which resides in the offices of constitutional government is derived from the authority and force of the community itself. A sovereign people confers sovereignty upon the government it constitutes. Being the source of all other sovereignties, popular sovereignty is unalterable. If the people of a particular community decide to federate with the people of another community, neither group relinquishes one iota of its popular sovereignty;

but, as I shall show presently, in setting up a federation, the sovereign people of the several communities confer some authority and force upon the newly constituted agencies of government, and so necessarily withdraw some authority and force from the governments of their several localities.

Because both local and federal governments must draw their sovereignty from the same ultimate source, each necessarily limits the scope of the other. The people who have joined to form a larger political community remain as sovereign as before, but the formation of the larger political unit *limits* the sovereignty of the governments of the previously independent communities, at the same time that it *annihilates* their independence. The fact that popular sovereignty does not suffer gain or loss must not mislead us into thinking that federation as an act of popular sovereignty does not involve a radical transformation on the institutional level.

4

It is fallacious to suppose that, with this shift from absolute monarchies to republican constitutions, sovereignty has disappeared from the political scene. It has merely changed its locus. The word "sovereign" can no longer be used to designate a man. It now designates the government of a community which has framed and adopted its own constitution.

Nor does the fundamental character of sovereignty change when it ceases to reside in persons and belongs to an impersonal institution, such as a constitution and the government it sets up. From the point of view of those who live under a constitutional regime, as well as from the point of view of those who live under absolute monarchy, the sovereignty of government consists in the same central fact: a union of authority and force.

In both communities, government has sovereignty because it has the authority which makes force legitimate, and the power which gives authority coercive force. The status of individual men differs radically according as sovereignty is personal or impersonal, but the sovereignty of government in relation to the community which lives under it remains the same. In order to understand this point, it is only necessary to separate authority and force. A friend who gives us good advice which we follow *only* because it is good exercises some degree of moral authority over us, but no sovereignty. A conqueror to whom we submit *only* at the point of a gun rules us by might, but not by sovereignty.

Without might, men are not governed. They are merely admonished.

Without right, men are not governed. They are merely overpowered.

Government combines might and right, and in consequence has sovereignty over those who acknowledge the right and recognize the might.

5

If and when world government exists, it will have to possess sovereignty in this sense. Lacking it, it would not be government. Anyone who conceives world government as exercising only moral authority uses the word "government" but does not understand the fact. Many who do understand the fact are opposed to world government exactly because it would have to possess internal sovereignty. It could not have such sovereignty and permit the existing nations to retain their external sovereignty.

What are the attributes of sovereignty in its external aspect? Again we shall find the answer by reference to law, to authority and force.

Let us suppose that a group of men tried to live together under the following conditions: (*a*) that each would recognize no law as binding him *unless* he agreed to it; (*b*) that each would regard any threat or use of force by one or more of the others as illegitimate; (*c*) that each would feel entitled to use force, or threaten its use, whenever that served his own interests, whether defensively or aggressively.

The situation we have just supposed is not a preposterous fiction. Preposterous or not, it is a fact exemplified throughout all history and in the world today—not by sovereign *men*, of course, but by sovereign *states*.

It makes no difference whether, in its internal aspect, sovereignty resides in an absolute monarch or in a constitutional regime. In either case, an independent political community regards itself as sovereign in its external relations. *Here it is the community as a whole, not its government, which has sovereignty.*

The absolute monarch recognizes this fact when he says, *"L'état, c'est moi!"* In relation to his own subjects, the absolute monarch identifies the government with his person. In relation to other despots and their subjects, the absolute monarch identifies himself with the whole community, signing himself "France" or "England" or "Spain."

It makes no difference to the facts of the situation whether one accepts this notion of the corporate or moral personality of the state, or rejects it as a myth, a fiction. In describing the interaction of independent communities, there is no way of avoiding language which personifies the corporate agents. In all its foreign relations, the political community acts *as if* it were an individual agent, making judgments, exercising free will.

Finally, it makes no difference whether a despot deals with a despot, a republic with a republic, or a republic with an absolute monarch. Regardless of their internal character, states act externally precisely as a group of individual men would act if, in their dealings with one another, each regarded himself and all others as having sovereignty.

Each tries to get along with the others only on terms entirely agreeable to itself, and submits to disagreeable terms only when compelled by naked might—power divorced from authority.

The plainest sign of external sovereignty in the affairs of independent states is, therefore, their insistence upon the principle of unanimity whenever they try by conference to decide anything affecting them all.

The embodiment of this principle in the Covenant of the League of Nations prevented the League from being anything more than a diplomatic conference. To be more, it had to be a sovereign government. But it could not be a sovereign government without abolishing the external sovereignty of each of the member states.

6

Failure to distinguish between the internal and external aspects of sovereignty leads to the most dangerous confusion of all.

Many persons today talk about "limited sovereignty" or about restrictions of sovereignty which would permit nations to remain sovereign to some extent and yet become members of a larger political community under a superior government. They frequently employ the federal structure of the United States or of Switzerland to illustrate what they mean by limited sovereignty. They point to the federal government of the American union as having one sort of limited sovereignty, and the governments of each of the federated states as having another sort of limited sovereignty.

Why, then, would it not be possible to form a world government by federation, in which the existing nations of the world could each retain some degree of the sovereignty they now possess?

Once we separate internal from external sovereignty, the answer becomes clear and indisputable.

Only in the internal aspect do the state governments of the forty-eight states have *some* of the sovereignty which they possessed when they were independent communities. They have *none* of the external sovereignty they once possessed.

The federal government, the state governments, and even the governments of chartered cities and incorporated towns have internal sovereignty to whatever degree *each regulates matters not regulated by all the others.* We do not ordinarily speak of the sovereignty of municipal governments because we regard sovereignty as inalienable. Theirs is revocable.

The Constitution of the United States defines the spheres of federal and state governments and, in doing so, apportions to each some measure of internal sovereignty. Each of the state constitutions proceeds similarly with respect to the subordinate local governments within its domain.

But no town, city, or state has any external sovereignty whatsoever. None has any foreign policy or foreign commitments. None has diplomats or armaments for dealing with other communities. None is an independent state in relation to other independent states.* In contrast, the self-governing dominions of the British Empire, such as Canada or the Union of South Africa, have *as much* external sovereignty as Great Britain. The dominions can make war independently of one another, conclude treaties, and enter into all sorts of foreign engagements.

We see, therefore, that there is no meaning to the phrase "limited sovereignty" in the sphere of foreign affairs. The external sovereignty of a political community is either complete or nonexistent. It is complete as long as the community remains an independent state. It is nonexistent when the state ceases to be independent and becomes part of a larger political unit.

There is absolutely no middle ground here—nothing between the independence of a single political community, which may be a whole of parts, and the nonindependence of its parts, regardless of what portion or kind of internal sovereignty they retain.

Those who persist in speaking of "limited sovereignty" *in the*

---

* The Constitution of the United States declares that "no state shall enter into any treaty, alliance, or confederation . . . [that] no state shall, without the consent of Congress . . . keep troops or ships of war in time of peace, or enter into any agreement or compact with another state. . . ." These provisions should not be referred to as limiting the sovereignty of the several states in the American union, or as merely taking away some sovereign rights. Sovereignty may be a bundle of rights, but the rights of internal and external sovereignty do not belong to the same bundle. The Constitution removes every vestige of external sovereignty from the states.

sphere of external or foreign affairs play fast and loose with the word. If in their dealings with one another, two states are exempt from the coercive force of law, they are absolutely sovereign. If the contracts or treaties they make with one another are reviewable by a higher juridical authority and if they are enforceable by law rather than by war, then they have no external sovereignty whatsoever.

When one independent nation makes a treaty with another, that act does not limit its sovereignty (Mr. Sumner Welles and the Editors of the *New York Times* to the contrary notwithstanding); for a contract voluntarily made by sovereign nations is binding *only at the pleasure of the parties.* Since self-coercion is impossible, and since the only limitation which can affect sovereignty must be coercive, treaties between independent nations do not represent limitations of sovereignty.

Nor can a state be conceived as retaining a limited sovereignty because it is permitted by a federal authority to negotiate or enter into contractual relations with other states which belong to the same federation. Unless such negotiations or contracts are subject to review and approval or disapproval by the federal authority, unless they are legally binding and enforceable by reference to the constitution and laws of a government superior to both of the contracting states, the contracting states cannot be conceived as belonging to a federal structure. They can be conceived only as absolutely sovereign. But if they do, by these criteria, belong to a federal structure, the contracting states cannot be conceived as having a limited external sovereignty simply because they are permitted to negotiate. The juridical conditions under which they exercise freedom of contract indicates that they have no external sovereignty whatsoever.

It is, therefore, an equivocation on the word "sovereignty" to regard freedom of contract as the mark of a so-called "limited sovereignty" which states can retain even though they have surrendered their absolute sovereignty by becoming subordinate members of a federation. This equivocation leads, in turn, to the more serious error of supposing that world government is incompatible *only* with absolute sovereignty on the part of the world's nations, but not with this fictitious "limited sovereignty."

The truth is that world government cannot co-exist with the sovereignty of independent nations, and such sovereignty either exists absolutely or it vanishes totally according as the nations of the world are independent states or subordinate members of a federation. It should be self-evident that a state must either be a part of some larger political whole or be a whole which is not part of any other. There can be no middle ground between subordination and independence.

7

The Editors of *Time* have performed a great public service by their effort to make Americans realize the difference in *kind,* not *degree,* between confederation (any sort of international organization, such as a League) and world government through federation. In a recent "Background for Peace," they wrote:

Experts in the field use two confusingly like-sounding names to describe the two very different kinds of organization that can be established by a group of states or nations. One is a "federation"—a real union like the United States today. The other and far looser kind of group government is called a "confederation." In a confederation, states are represented as states, rather than citizens as citizens. So in a confederation the real sovereignty, the ultimate power, remains in the national governments, which give up little or none of their sovereignty in the process of uniting. . . . This country was a confederation—and as such was fast falling apart—during the few years that intervened between the Revolution and the adoption of the Constitution. The League of Nations was a confederation. And despite the name, Culbertson's World Federation Plan is another. [Elsewhere they say of the Culbertson Plan that "for all its fine phrasing, it boils down to domination of the globe by the four victorious major pow-crs."] . . . A confederation is forever the creature, never the master of its members. It amounts to little more than an intricately formulated war-&-peace alliance.

If and when world government exists, both external sovereignty and political independence will become meaningless. Suppose that world government is federal in structure. Then neither the world community as a whole nor any of its parts under local government will stand as a sovereign in external relation to other communities.

Within the world community there will, of course, be divisions between federal and local authority. Accordingly there will be limitations upon the internal sovereignty of world government, as well as upon the internal sovereignty of the various local governments—the governments of the member communities. But such words as "foreign affairs," "foreign policy," "diplomacy" will become as meaningless as "independence." What they refer to will become as nonexistent as the armaments needed by a sovereign state to protect its independence.

Let no one who does not wish to fool himself think that his nation can remain an independent state or a sovereign community, in any external significance of these words, *without leaving the world completely anarchic.*

This is not a more or less proposition. There are no degrees of anarchy, as there are no degrees of external sovereignty. Any league of *independent* nations would leave the anarchy intact. Nothing less than world government would reduce the anarchy, and world government would reduce it to the vanishing point.

8

All this being understood, does Hegel's objection still hold? We must admit that states cling to their sovereignty, as individuals to their lives. But is it their natural right, as it is the natural right of individuals to preserve themselves?

The great political thinkers of modern times are in complete agreement on the relation of anarchy and sovereignty to war and peace. Yet except for Rousseau, they did not draw the implication that wars can be avoided. The issue raised by Hegel in criticism of Kant has had to wait for our own day to be resolved in favor of the possibility of peace.

It is worth while to examine the steps by which the issue of war versus peace reached its sharpest formulation.

In his *Leviathan* (1651), Thomas Hobbes pointed out that a state or condition of war is like the nature of weather. Foul weather consists

> . . . not in a shower or two of rain, but in an inclination thereto of many days together. . . . Though there has never been a time wherein particular men were in a condition of war against one another; yet in all times Kings and Persons of Sovereign authority, because of their Independence, are in continual jealousy, and in the state and posture of Gladiators . . . which is a posture of War.

John Locke, in his second essay *Of Civil Government* (1690), defined the state of war as the use of "force between persons who have no known superior on earth." Since this is contrary to the condition of men living together in civil society, Locke identified the state of war with the state of nature, which is anarchy. It is often asked,

> Where are, or ever were, there any men in such a state of Nature? To which it may suffice as an answer at present that . . . all princes and rulers of "independent" governments all through the world are in a state of Nature.

Anarchy, according to Locke, can be viewed in two ways. On the one hand, it results from the sovereignty of independent princes or states. On the other, it occurs wherever sovereign government is lacking for a group of men whose lives interact. In any community where law and force are shorn of one another, government ceases and anarchy begins.

If the laws already made can no longer be put in execution, this [reduces] all to anarchy.

Whosoever uses force without right—as everyone does in society who does it without law—puts himself in a state of war with those against whom he so uses it.

Writing about Saint-Pierre's scheme in his essay on *A Lasting Peace Through the Federation of Europe* (1761), Rousseau argued for federation as the only way to procure such peace on the continent. We must admit, he declared,

> that the powers of Europe stand to each other strictly in a state of war, and that all the separate treaties between them are in the nature of a temporary truce rather than a real peace.

This is due to the fact that the only

> recognized method of settling disputes between one prince and another [is] the appeal to the sword; a method inseparable from the state of anarchy and war, which necessarily springs from the absolute independence conceded to all sovereigns under the imperfect conditions now prevailing in Europe.

Immanuel Kant followed Rousseau, and less directly Locke and Hobbes, in stating the thesis basic to his essay on *Perpetual Peace* (1795):

> With men the state of nature is not a state of peace, but of war; though not of open war, at least of war ever ready to break out. . . . Nations, like individuals, if they live in a state of nature and without laws, by their vicinity alone commit an act of lesion. . . . Though a treaty of peace [between them] puts an end to the present war, it does not abolish a state of war, a state where continually new pretenses for war are found; which one cannot affirm to be unjust, since being their own judges, they have no other means of terminating their differences.

What is needed, Kant tells us, is

> something which might be called a pacific alliance, different
> from a treaty of peace inasmuch as it would for ever termi-
> nate all wars, whereas the latter only finishes one. . . .
> At the tribunal of reason, there is but one way of extricat-
> ing states from this turbulent situation, in which they are
> constantly menaced by war, namely, to renounce, like indi-
> viduals, the anarchic liberty of savages, in order to submit
> themselves to coercive laws, and thus form a society of peo-
> ples which would gradually embrace all the peoples of the
> earth.

At this point Kant exhibits a turn of thought which will be
found prevalent today. His own premises lead to the conclusion
that a lasting and universal peace requires the renunciation of international anarchy and, with it, the external sovereignty of independent states. But, says Kant, men are unwilling to go that far.

This prevents the realization of the plan and makes "them
reject in practice what is true in theory." For "the positive idea
of a universal republic" which would ensure world peace, we
must substitute the negative alternative of "a permanent alliance" which, since it cannot be stronger than the best treaty, will
merely prevent some wars and postpone others.

It is not entirely clear whether Kant thought the abolition of
external sovereignty utterly impossible or just highly improbable. Most interpreters of Kant hold that, for him, perpetual
peace was an ideal, a goal the world might approach, but never
reach. Against this we should note that Kant fails to give a satisfactory reason for thinking sovereignty cannot be abolished.

He says only that most men have "ideas of public right" which
make them hold on to the independence of their respective
states. He does not say that external sovereignty is inseparable
from the very nature of a political community. The reason Kant
gives makes perpetual peace seem highly improbable. It does not
make it impossible.

Other and later German philosophers argued differently.

Hegel agreed that states are in a condition of nature or of war "because their relation to one another has sovereignty as its principle." This principle of (external) sovereignty cannot be altered. It belongs to the very nature of states as political entities. Hegel pointed out that Kant's proposed alliance would not settle disputes. It does not and cannot provide a judge over states. "Therefore, when the wills of particular states come to no agreement, the controversy can be settled only by war."

Using Kant's premises, but adding the qualification that sovereignty must remain, Hegel concluded that international wars are unavoidable in perpetuity. International law cannot exert force. It can be no more binding than good intentions. The relation of states to one another cannot be restricted by the notions of morality or of private right. "As against the state there is no power to decide what is intrinsically right or to realize such a decision. . . . States in their relations to one another are independent and can, therefore, look upon the stipulations they make with one another as provisional."

9

The dilemma with which Hegel confronts us offers no loopholes.

Either the multiplicity of sovereign and independent states can be done away with *or* sovereign states, remaining above all positive law, remain judges of their own rights, and agents of force, responsive only to superior force.

It does no good to express abhorrence at Fichte's statement that "between states there is neither law nor right unless it be the right of the stronger." Anyone who thinks that the sovereignty of independent nations cannot be totally abolished must agree with Hegel, Fichte, and also von Clausewitz, even though he does so with a heavy heart.

Calling their points of view "Prussian" becomes an *ad hominem* which returns like a boomerang if we have nothing but fine sentiments to prevent us from agreeing with them *openly*. We should remember that the Englishman and liberal, John Locke, also thought that there would always be a multiplicity of independent states. Conceding thereby that anarchy and war must always prevail among nations, Locke would not disallow the further implications which Hegel and Fichte draw concerning international conduct.

There is only one way to disagree with Hegel—using his name to represent the position most men accept in heart and mind, though not in word.

Hegel's doctrine accurately describes the existing state of world affairs. It describes the whole of human history up to the present. About these things there can be no question.

But is Hegel right in assuming, or can he prove, that sovereignty is inseparable from the nature of a political community? I think the answer is doubly no.

Internal sovereignty is inseparable from effective and legitimate government, whether that be world government or the government of one among many independent states. But external sovereignty need remain the attribute of a political community only so long as it is one among many. The community founded by world government would have no external sovereignty.

The sharp separation of these two aspects of sovereignty uncovers the specious step in Hegel's reasoning. Because one aspect of sovereignty is inseparable from government, he allows himself to conclude, without cogency, that the other aspect must also be inseparable from the nature of a political community.

There are no grounds whatsoever for arguing that world government or a world political community is *impossible*. Certainly nothing in the facts or in the theory of sovereignty renders it impossible. But the question of its probable occurrence still remains.

CHAPTER 9

The Peace of Angels

ANOTHER REACTION to the truth that sovereignty causes war comes from the opposite direction. Whereas Hegel acknowledged the truth, but insisted that it meant the inevitability of international wars, this objection denies that the possibility of world peace depends on the abolition of external sovereignty. It really amounts to a defense of anarchy, for it consists in saying that nations can live at peace with one another despite the fact that they do not live together under government.

Surprising though it may seem at first, this is the position taken by the Papacy in the official pronouncements of the last five Popes. The paradox is hardly relieved by the fact that this view is shared by the Communist party when it adheres to the tenets of Marxism. This point of view even enlists those who oppose Marxism on grounds of economic individualism. But then, perhaps, we should expect strange bedfellows to be thrown together by anarchy.

2

The papal documents have recently been assembled in a single volume of 800 pages, *The Principles of Peace*. Throughout the encyclicals, allocutions, and letters runs one dominant theme: that peace is the work of justice and charity, both within the civil order of each state and in the international order. But equally conspicuous by its complete absence is the theme that world peace depends upon world government.

According to the Popes, international peace can be made and kept without the loss of national independence, without sacrifice of sovereignty, without eliminating anarchy.

In his Encyclical *Pacem Dei*, issued in 1920, Benedict XV

advocated that "all states, putting aside mutual suspicion, should unite in one league, or rather a sort of family of peoples, calculated to maintain their own independence as well as to safeguard the order of human society."

As recently as 1939, Pius XII declared himself in favor of an international organization "which, respecting the rights of God, will be able to assure the reciprocal independence of nations big and small." Later in the same year, the reigning Pontiff expressed this view even more emphatically:

> A fundamental postulate of any just and honorable peace is an assurance for all nations, great or small, powerful or weak, of their right to life and independence.

And in his Christmas broadcast to the whole world on December 24, 1942, the Pope said:

> International relations and internal order are intimately related. International equilibrium and harmony depend on the internal equilibrium and development of the individual States in the material, social and intellectual spheres. A firm and steady peace policy toward other nations is, in fact, impossible without a spirit of peace within the nation which inspires trust. . . . Every society, worthy of the name, has originated in a desire for peace, and hence aims at attaining peace, that "tranquil living together in order" in which St. Thomas finds the essence of peace.

But Saint Thomas also held that the existence of social peace, like the existence of a political society, depends upon government. It cannot be a matter of philosophic principle that the Five-Point Program of the Christmas Allocution in 1941 should have omitted the very *first* condition of world peace.* A similar omission from the Atlantic Charter puts both documents in the same category: high moral rhetoric, which inevitably misleads when taken as an adequate statement of practical policy.

---

* The Editors of *The Commonweal* interpret the present Pope's declarations as favorable to federation. Though *The Commonweal* is right in thinking that only

There are those who would try to tell us that the Popes favor world government (and recognize its indispensability for world peace), even though they continue to talk about the independence and sovereignty of nations. The Popes, they claim, recognize the necessity for abolishing *absolute* sovereignty as incompatible with world government and world peace, but see no reason for abolishing national sovereignty entirely—on the ground that world government and world peace are attainable with the retention of a limited sovereignty on the part of independent states.

But what is meant by "limited sovereignty"? Freedom of contract and capacity for negotiation, such as the formation of a concordat between a state and the Vatican? As we have seen, other questions must be asked. Will such contracts be reviewed by a higher or federal authority? Will they be tenable and binding only if they conform to the constitution of world government, and not simply at the discretion and will of the particular state? According to the way these questions are answered, we shall find either that world government exists and that the nations of the world are not independent and have no external sovereignty whatsoever, *or* that they are independent, have sovereignty (absolute, not limited in any way), and that world government does not exist.

The facts being what they are, the Popes must recommend either the full retention or the complete relinquishment of national sovereignty; they must wish either the continued existence of independent nations or their transformation into subordinate

federation, and no sort of alliances or leagues of independent nations, can maintain world peace, it seems questionable whether the words of Pius XII, in his Christmas allocution of 1939, can be so interpreted. The Pope said: "In order that peace may be honorably accepted and in order to avoid arbitrary breaches and unilateral interpretations of treaties, it is of the first importance to erect some juridical institution which shall guarantee the loyal and faithful fulfillment of the conditions agreed upon, and which shall, in case of recognized need, revise and correct them." The only sort of juridical institution which is compatible with the fulfillment or revision of *treaties* entered into by *independent* nations is an old-fashioned world court, not the judiciary of a world federation.

units of a world federation. When these inescapable alternatives are squarely put, without any fudging on the name or notion of sovereignty, the Papal documents seem capable of only one interpretation.

It is no criticism of the Papal pronouncements to say that they do not recommend so radical a step at the present juncture. The Popes would not be alone in their judgment that the time is not ripe for world peace by world government. But this should be frankly acknowledged in word, as well as in thought, to prevent deception.

It is quite possible to believe that peace cannot be made in our time and to propose immediate steps which may only promote a gradual advance toward peace in a more remote future, *without at the same time seeming to recommend half-way measures for more than they are worth.* If the Popes think that for the time being nations must remain sovereign, then they should also plainly admit that all of the measures they propose can do no more than prolong a truce. They should not talk as if their proposals were directed toward the institution of world peace *now*, or its perpetuation.

We may also be told that the Popes are concerned with alleviating the immediate sufferings of a war-torn world and hence that the Papal statements must be read as bearing on currently available remedies, one of which might be a revived League of Nations. But that does not alter the truth of the matter, nor can it evade the fundamental distinction between prolonging a truce and making peace.

Furthermore, it may be asked in rejoinder whether the Popes are justified in concentrating on problems of the immediate future, to the neglect of more ultimate issues. Of all the leaders to whom mankind can look for practical wisdom about ultimate ends, the Popes should be the pre-eminent spokesmen for peace, even if that is not immediately attainable. Their proper and practical interest in the reconstruction of the post-war world should not prevent them from accurately defining the minimum conditions of a universal and perpetual peace, that ultimate objective about which all men should begin to think now.

The failure to say plainly that peace is impossible so long as nations remain sovereign and independent will certainly not help men to think clearly about peace. There can be no reason of policy or prudence for obscuring this fundamental truth, even in the process of dealing with immediate rather than ultimate issues. *The Papal position is exempt from serious criticism only if peace—real peace, not a mere truce—is genuinely possible in a world of sovereign and independent nations.*

3

I turn to the earnest *obiter dicta* of a well-known literary critic who has read almost all the current books about war and peace. That may be his trouble, plus the fact that he may also have forgotten what he once read in the great books of political theory. In any case, John Chamberlain writes as follows, in a *New York Times* book review:

> Most people erroneously think of "total" war as a failure of international organization. A mere handful of intelligent souls—Guglielmo Ferrero, Peter Drucker, Mrs. Isabel Paterson—see it quite correctly as a disease which originates in wrong relationships in the civil order within a powerful nation. If such wrong relationships persist, if they cause the people of a great nation to fear their government and government to fear its citizens, the result will most certainly be violence against neighboring countries.

Plato had observed, many centuries before Ferrero, that the tyrant "is always stirring up some war or other." Ferrero, like Plato, rightly perceived that a tyrannical (or what Ferrero calls an "illegitimate") government inclines toward belligerency in foreign affairs in order to maintain its oppressive regime at home. The soundness of this point can be admitted without drawing the invalid inference which Mr. Chamberlain seems to accept. Alexander Hamilton recognized the point and rejected the inference. He wrote:

> Notwithstanding the concurring testimony of experience in this particular, there are still to be found visionary, or designing, men, who stand ready to advocate the paradox of perpetual peace between the States, though dismembered and alienated from each other. The genius of republics (say they) is pacific. . . . If this be their true interest, have they in fact pursued it? . . . Have republics in practise been less addicted to wars than monarchies? Are not the former administered by *men* as well as the latter? . . . Let experience, the least fallible guide of human opinions, be appealed to for an answer to these inquiries. Sparta, Athens, Rome, and Carthage, were all Republics . . . yet were they as often engaged in wars, offensive and defensive, as the neighboring Monarchies of the same time . . . The Provinces of Holland, till they were overwhelmed in debts and taxes, took a leading and conspicuous part in the wars of Europe. . . . In the Government of Britain the representatives of the people compose one branch of the national legislature . . . Few nations, nevertheless, have been more frequently engaged in war; and the wars in which that kingdom has been engaged have, in numerous instances, proceeded from the people. There have been, if I may so express it, almost as many popular as royal wars.

One need not deny the modicum of truth in Ferrero's insight to see that it is woefully inadequate as an account of the origin of international wars. Let me make the inadequacy plain.

Mr. Chamberlain seems to think that if nations, especially great nations, were internally well ordered, there would be no need for what he calls "international organization." His reason for thinking so must be that happy nations, like happy men, would have no grounds for quarreling or fighting with one another. Only when a nation, like a man, suffers internal disorder, does it become belligerent in dealing with its neighbors.

But, forgetting nations for the moment, is this true of men?

If Mr. Chamberlain could be assured that, in a group of human beings, all were well integrated, as the psychologist says, or all were men of virtue and good will, as the moralist says, would he recommend that they try living together without government? Would he suppose that such men could live together without any difference of opinion about practical matters affecting their separate interests as well as the common good, and could settle these differences without government?

If he would, then he does not understand why John Locke says over and over again that "government is hardly to be avoided amongst men that live together"; nor does he understand why Alexander Hamilton says, "If men were angels, no government would be necessary." Perhaps I can make the point clearer by reference to the position taken by Saint Thomas Aquinas against those earlier Christian thinkers who supposed that men must live under the dominion of government *only because* they have fallen from grace and are sinful.

Saint Thomas considers whether there would have had to be government in Eden if Adam had not sinned and the children of Adam had been permitted to dwell forever in the earthly paradise. Here would have been a community of morally and intellectually perfect men, more nearly perfect than any who have lived in the world. Yet, Saint Thomas thought, these men could not have formed a community, could not have lived together peacefully, without the institutions of government. Men remain men at their best, and at their best they have deficiencies of judgment which require some principle of government to bring them into concert for a common good.

I am not suggesting that government in Eden would have been like earthly government in every respect. My point is simply that what Saint Thomas says on this score becomes much truer in the case of men as they are.

Only angels can live together at peace without living under the coercive force of government. The peace of angels can be entirely spiritual because that is what angels are supposed to be. If men are not angels, nations certainly are not.

4

Mr. Chamberlain's position bears a striking resemblance to the Marxist view that when the injustice of capitalism is abolished, government will quietly wither away. There will be no need for government when no exploiters are left. And when the class war is over within states, there will no longer be wars between states.

To think this is to forget that though exploiters try to use government for their purposes, nothing but government can protect a just economy, once established, from the rise of a new exploiting class. It is to forget that capitalism and imperialism are not only interlinked, but that both thrive on the international anarchy.

Above all, it is to forget that, with men or nations, internal order and external relations affect one another at every point. *The influence works in both directions, not one.*

Such goodness as most individual men achieve is, in large part, due to their living under government, domestic and civil. International anarchy, permitting the growth and operation of cartels, making war the instrument of national survival or aggrandizement, requiring armaments and the deceptions of diplomacy, dividing policy into the watertight compartments of domestic and foreign affairs—international anarchy works against the existence of a healthy civil order within each community, be it large or small.

I repeat: no one who knows the facts of life and history can defend anarchy—either for men or for nations. No difference between individual men and groups of men allows us to suppose that individual men require government when their lives interact, but that groups of men, similarly interactive, do not.

Actual or threatening disorder within a powerful nation may certainly lead that country into war. Modern, not to mention recent, history offers numerous examples. But it would be just as true to say that nations with large standing armies are more inclined to begin fighting; and just as erroneous to infer that if all nations had small military establishments, or even total disarmament, the potential war between states could never turn into actual violence.

The error arises from neglecting the underlying cause of war—the cause of the potential state of war between nations, as well as of military action. The internal condition of independent nations is relevant to the immediate factors which lead one state to precipitate the conflict at a moment and in a manner favorable to itself. It may also be relevant to peace in so far as internal disorder or defect, moral, economic, or political, may lead a nation to reject the conditions of peace, the conditions entailed by world government. *Even though such obstacles to making peace must be removed before we can establish its minimum conditions, we must never identify overcoming the obstacles with enacting the positive institutions.*

CHAPTER 10

Civil War

STILL ANOTHER reaction to the insight that international wars result from international anarchy consists in making light of this truth by calling it a "tautology." This verbal subterfuge, the objection continues, conceals the fact that it will not profit men to have world government, if they lose their lives and property as frequently in world-wide civil wars.

The word "tautology" is merely an invidious way of referring to a self-evident truth. The American revolutionists could have said: "We hold these truths to be tautological: that all men are created equal . . ."

When anyone understands that all men have the same specific nature, he knows at once that all men are equal. When anyone understands the nature of man to be that of a rational animal, he knows at once that men are born or created for freedom. These truths are as self-evident—or as tautological—as the truth that a physical whole is greater than any of its physical parts. A self-evident truth is nothing but a proposition we know to be true as soon as we understand its terms.

2

In his preface to an English translation of Kant's essay on *Perpetual Peace,* Professor Latta of Glasgow quotes a line from Professor Ritchie to the effect that

There is only one way in which war between independent nations can be prevented; and that is by the nations ceasing to be independent.

The statement contains a tautology, barely concealed. If by "war" we understand military combat between *independent* nations, then of course it necessarily follows that when nations cease to be independent, wars can no longer occur.

I shall not attempt to deny the *similarly* tautological character of my statement that "war results from anarchy and anarchy from the sovereignty of nations." I shall, however, try to meet the challenge that a truth of this sort has no practical significance, because all the evils of war will remain even if you call them by another name.

Suppose you do eliminate wars between independent nations by abolishing their independence. Then there will be other forms of violent conflict between organized groups of men. If you refuse to call these conflicts "war" because they do not correspond to your definition of war as *international,* then you are hiding behind a verbal subterfuge, and letting wordplay blind you to the facts.

There are two answers to this charge of verbalism.

3

In the first place, let us agree to use the word "war" in two senses: (*a*) for violence between nations, and (*b*) for the violence of civil strife—revolutionary uprisings and what is called "civil war." In the history of the world up to the present, there have always been wars *in both senses of the word.*

Who would say that the total elimination of inter*national* war has no practical significance? Would that not be one of the most radical events in the whole course of human history? Yet it is a tautology which teaches us what we must do if we are ever to abolish war *in this first sense of the word.*

The tautology not only has practical significance in that it makes a *real* difference whether international wars are eliminated, and only civil strife remains. It also has practical significance in that it directs our attention to the one cause we can control if we wish to rid ourselves of this form of violence by eradicating its cause—by substituting world government for anarchy.

4

In the second place, when we use the word "war" in the other sense—for civil strife—the truth about government as keeper of the peace becomes applicable.

Anyone must admit that *nothing would be gained by eliminating international wars if, despite that fact, the total amount of violence in the world remains unchanged.* But can it be predicted that the amount and frequency of rebellions and "civil wars" in the world community will so increase as to make up for the elimination of international wars?

I think the answer is no, and for a reason not unconnected with the tautology under consideration. Anarchy would not be the cause of international wars, if government were not the cause of peace within a single political community. Though all forms of government are not equally effective in maintaining peace, some degree of peace obtains wherever the machinery of government works. The degrees of peace vary directly with the degrees of justice and efficiency in the institutions of government.

Call this a "tautology," too, but observe that it directs practical men in the course to follow if they wish to reduce the occasions and the opportunities for civil strife. A proper understanding of the functions of government tells us not only how to eliminate international wars, but also how to obtain, within the world community, the highest degree of peace that is possible in any society of men.

CHAPTER 11

The Degrees of Peace

PEACE ON EARTH is not paradise. No human community will ever be free from crime and violence, the injustice of man to man, deceit and treachery. No amount of social progress will ever provide man with a life unburdened by pain and sorrow, devoid of moral struggle, or unrivened by spiritual discords. Peace in the world will never, to the end of time, relieve man of the search for peace in his own heart.

The conditions of human life can be improved, but at their best they will reflect all the imperfections of man's imperfect nature.

Utopian fantasies set a false standard of perfection, one which does not fit human nature. They bring discredit upon the word "ideal." Rightly impatient with utopian thinking, the practical man tends to dismiss any discussion of ideal conditions as irrelevant to the real course of affairs. The false and extravagant idealism which sets standards of unattainable perfection is irrelevant, but a sober idealism should not be made to suffer for such utopian folly.

Universal and perpetual peace represents an ideal in the sense that it is a *better* condition than the world has yet experienced. It may even be the *best* condition of social life that men can hope to know on earth. But it is not utopian.

Universal and perpetual peace is a practicable ideal because it is possible for men as they are. Men do not have to become angels, or even saints, to achieve a better world than the one in which we live.

2

The most brilliant discussion of the problem of war and peace, written in our time, will be found in a book by the exiled German jurist, Hans Kelsen. In *Law and Peace*, Professor Kelsen defines peace as "a condition in which there is no use of force." This excludes even the exercise of police power to enforce the law and to repress crime. It obviously contemplates a community in which force will not be used in disobedience of the law—a community without criminals as well as without police.

Professor Kelsen knows that this does not define the peace of any possible human society. He writes:

> In this sense of the word, the law provides only relative peace, in that it deprives the individual of the right to employ force, but reserves it to the community. The peace of the law is not a state of absolute absence of force . . . but rather is a state of monopoly of force, a monopoly of force by the community.

In calling such peace "relative," we do not mean more than that it is relative to human nature. We do not imply that relative peace, in this sense, is imperfect, as if to say that only a peace which men cannot attain would be perfect peace. By "perfect peace" we always mean the best relative to human nature.

A practicable ideal must be approachable by a continuous series of approximations. Human institutions are not black or white. They are not wholly good or wholly bad, but better and worse. A reasonable standard of perfection should, therefore, enable us to define a scale of degrees, ranging from the barest minimum to the fullest maximum.

In setting up such a scale, the two most important problems concern the limiting points, the lower and upper extremes in the scale. The definition of peace solves both problems.

What is the lowest degree of peace, below which we may have something which resembles peace, but which cannot be called "peace" without equivocation? Here the definition sets the minimum requirements for any situation which deserves to be called "peaceful."

What is the highest degree of peace, above which men cannot go without leaving the earth and ceasing to be men? Here the definition determines what additions can be made to the minimum conditions, enabling us to see how the peacefulness of any situation can be improved to the utmost.

Let us begin at the lower end of the scale and work upward until we come to the perfection of perpetual peace, remembering that we are looking only for a realizable perfection consistent with the limitations of human nature.

3

We have called the international community "anarchic." But how can we use the word "community" at all, if we have to qualify it by the word "anarchic"? If there is any sense to the word "community" so qualified, must we not also find some degree of peace present *even in the anarchic community?* The importance of these questions should be evident to anyone who speaks of "a society of nations," of "the Atlantic community" or "the European community."

Since each of the members of an anarchic community is a sovereign state, recognizing no government above its own, the society of nations cannot be regarded as a political society in the same sense in which each nation is itself a political society—a community of individuals living under government. Hence we are certainly justified in calling the international situation "anarchic." But are we justified in calling it "a community"?

Here, as always, words are stumbling blocks. The word "community" can have one or two elements in its meaning.

The two elements are: (1) the fact that many live together and interact in some way; (2) the fact that they live together under government which regulates their interaction. When we speak of a community of sovereign nations, we are obviously using the word "community" to signify only the first of these two facts. When we speak of each of the nations as a community, we imply the additional presence of the second fact. One way of indicating which way we are using the word "community" is by prefixing to it the qualifying words "anarchic" and "political," according as the community exists without government or under it.

The difficult problem remains. We must have some reason for saying that there is no degree of peace in the anarchic community, that the difference between the least degree of peace and the most enduring truce is a difference in kind, not in degree. Difference in kind is the sort of difference between a straight and a curved line; difference in degree, the sort of difference between a longer and a shorter straight line. More or less of the *same* makes a difference in degree. When something *new* has been *added,* we get a difference in kind.

4

Professor Kelsen's discussion of law and peace is extremely helpful here. He calls our attention to the distinction between primitive legal systems and the mature development of law.

In some primitive tribes, all the rules of conduct belong to a tradition of customs. They have not been explicitly formulated or enacted by the tribal chieftain or a council of elders. This, however, is not the distinguishing mark of primitive law. Even in fairly advanced political societies, such as those of medieval Europe, a large part of the positive law has the status of abiding custom—"whereof the memory of man runneth not to the contrary."

The distinguishing mark of the primitive legal system is the way in which legal rules are administered and enforced, not the way in which they get formulated or adopted. In the tribes to which Professor Kelsen refers, each man decides for himself whether another man has committed an injury against him. He may appeal to the standards of conduct established by custom to make this judgment, but he, the party claiming injury, makes the judgment in his own case.

He may then proceed to exercise his own power to redress the injury, to obtain compensation or to punish the offender and get the satisfaction of revenge. The rest of the tribe may remain neutral during this process, or they may take sides, each exerting his own force to help the injured party if they think right is on his side, or to protect the accused person against the other's wrath if they think it unjustified.

In this situation, each man acts as judge in his own case in applying the law. Each man uses his own might, with or without the help of others, to enforce the law according to his judgment, or to resist what he considers an unjust use of force. These two elements—self-judgment and self-help—distinguish primitive law.

In more mature legal systems, the application of the rule of law, whether it be customary or enacted, is performed by a court. The society takes this function of judgment or law application away from its individual members, and concentrates it in certain persons whose authority to perform this function is acknowledged. This is the first stage of development above the level of primitive law.

In the second stage of development, not only the application of the law to particular cases, but also the enforcement of a court's judgment, becomes concentrated in the hands of officials appointed for the performance of this function. Neither self-help nor self-judgment is permitted. If in emergencies, men must still employ self-help to defend their lives or protect their property, they must also subsequently stand trial for their acts. A man is entitled to use his own might in resisting assault or ejecting a burglar, but not without having later to submit to a court's judgment, should the occasion demand an accounting for his acts.

The third stage of legal development consists in the transition from customary law to explicit legislation by persons or assemblies granted the authority to make, adopt, and change the laws of the community. At this point, we reach the full maturation of a legal system.

It should be noted that there is no legal system at all unless some community exists whose traditions of common life include customary standards of conduct, however few or ill-defined these be. From this primitive beginning, the steps of development consist in abolishing self-judgment and self-help, substituting in their place a *centralized* and *official* as opposed to a *decentralized* and *personal* performance of these functions—law application and law enforcement. The final stage of maturity is reached when the task of lawmaking is also discharged by officials or by some centralized body rather than in the diffuse and unofficial manner of custom formation.

5

These steps of development represent historic stages in the evolution of positive law, analogous to the gradual evolution of higher from lower forms of life. In biological evolution the continuous variation of living forms is interrupted by a distinction of species. So here in social evolution, we must observe a significant difference between primitive societies in which there is no centralization of the legal functions and all other societies in which one or more of these functions is centralized.

Professor Kelsen thinks that what we call "the political community" or "the state" comes into being only when the legal system involves courts and judges, police and other officers of law enforcement. So long as either self-judgment or self-help characterizes the legal order, the governmental institutions which give a society political structure and organization do not exist.

The society which lives under a primitive legal system is devoid of government in the strict sense of the word. It has one of the traits of a community: men live together, their lives interact. But lacking the other trait, government, it deserves to be classified as an *anarchic* community.

The sharp line we have been able to draw between the primitive legal system and all later stages of development, and, in consequence, the line separating the anarchic from the political community, enable us to distinguish the least degree of peace from no peace at all.

The least degree of peace requires some degree of government. In the anarchic community, devoid of government in the sense defined, there is only the counterfeit of peace which consists of interludes between unregulated violence. This counterfeit deserves to be called by another name.

When we call it a "truce," we recognize that the absence of violent combat is not due to any positive causes preventing men from taking the law into their own hands and using force to gain their ends. The interludes or lulls are due only to the absence of occasions or incidents to provoke quarrels. These, uninhibited by the legal devices of government, will usually turn to the wager of battle as a last resort.

That a primitive or anarchic community can long endure under these circumstances must be due to the fact that a sufficient number of its members do not get drawn into the struggle on any occasion. Should the members ever divide into approximately equal factions, the society would certainly be in danger of a permanent rupture.

Professor Kelsen makes one other point of far-reaching significance. He calls our attention to the striking resemblance between the anarchic tribal community and the society of nations—between the primitive legal system and the primitive character of international law.

There is only one difference. The men in the tribe do not regard themselves as sovereigns. They know that they are not self-sufficient, and so each is strongly motivated to keep the tribe together, to prevent violence from destroying the community entirely. In the historic past, when states were economically more self-sufficient than they are now, such motivation scarcely operated at all in international affairs. Even now, it is frequently overcome by other considerations.

Apart from this difference, all the elements of the primitive legal system will be found in the international situation. Each sovereign state is its own judge as to whether it has suffered an injury, by reference to the customary standards of international conduct which are called "general international law." And, having judged itself offended against, it exerts what power it can in self-help to punish the offender or remedy the injury, soliciting additional force from whatever nations it can inveigle into the struggle.

In the light of these facts, it is certain that there can be no degree of international peace so long as the international community remains anarchic. But when the international community ceases to be anarchic, it will also cease to be international in the sense of being a community of independent sovereign states. When the condition of world peace supplants the present situation, men will no longer speak either of international law or of international society.

A community of the world's peoples, living together under government, will not be a society of nations, but a society of men, divided into subgroups only according to the divisions of local government.

6

We have found the minimum conditions for *some degree* of peace, in either the limited communities which have so far existed or in the future community of the world's peoples. They are, briefly: impartial law, impartial judgment, impartial execution, as opposed to making the law to suit one's self, being judge in one's own case, and resorting to private might for self-help. These are the minimum conditions of government.

We have also found in certain primitive tribal groups and in the society of civilized nations the conditions which prevent *any degree* of peace from being present.

We must now try to ascertain the gradations of peace, and discover what additional factors are requisite for each degree in the ascending scale. To do this let us begin by considering a limited community, a single sovereign state. After we have found the conditions responsible for the perfection of peace within such communities, we can apply the same principles to the world situation.

Two things should be obvious at once:

(1) The peace of a political community is impaired by civil strife of all sorts. Whether or not we choose to call such civil violence "war," the fact remains that civil peace cannot be regarded as perfect until governmental machinery is able to cope with every form of dissension or dispute.

The perfection of peace does not depend on the removal of all causes for dispute or strife; nor even on the avoidance of force in the settlement of differences. It depends on ways of keeping quarrels on the conversational level, and on a monopoly of the legitimate force needed to execute decisions.

(2) Since peace, in any degree, depends upon government, the several degrees of peace will be correlated with the various forms of government. Forms of government vary in two ways. Some are intrinsically more just than others. Among governments which are equal in justice, one may be more efficient than another, that is, better able to do the work for which government is intended.

It would be reasonable to expect that the most just government and the most efficient will maintain the highest degree of peace. Neither justice without efficiency nor efficiency without justice can keep the peace perfectly. Defects in justice will occasion civil strife. Defects in efficiency will fail to provide pacific means for remedying injustice, or will fail to support them by public force.

7

What are the different sorts of civil strife?

We can eliminate at once the quarrels which occur between private individuals concerning injuries which one alleges another to have committed, and which the other denies. Such disputes fall within the domain of private, as opposed to public or constitutional, law. If the legal system of a government functions normally, it will settle such controversies and enforce the settlement.

Nor need we consider individual acts of crime, which disturb the public peace as well as affect the property, health, or life of law-abiding citizens. Crimes inflict injuries, but they may also result from injustice, from poverty or violence.

No degree of civil peace is so perfect as to be exempt from disturbance by crime. While it is true that an inefficient or corrupt officialdom will permit and sometimes encourage the ravages of crime, we cannot bother here with that quality of peace which varies with the quality of the personnel in the offices of government. Individual criminal acts, even those which are treasonous, breach the peace or disturb it in isolated spots; they do not, taken singly or collectively, disrupt it by dividing the members of a community into factions exerting brute force against one another.

We are left, then, with three major types of civil strife. Each of these is variously called "rebellion," "sedition," "revolution," or "civil war," but these names have no standardized meanings, and are usually interchangeable. Let us consider historic examples of each of these three types of organized violence within the political community.

I. **The revolt of the Helots in Sparta; the struggle between the plebes and patricians in the days of the Roman Republic; the fight of the English barons for Magna Charta; the peasants' revolt in Germany in the sixteenth century; the French revolution in 1789; and the Russian revolution in 1917. These exemplify the first type of civil strife.**

In each of these, and in all similar cases, some group in the population uses force to try to remedy the injustice it has suffered. The end in view may be only an alteration in the status, the rights and privileges, of the injured class; or it may include some radical change in the form of government as a condition prerequisite to preventing the further abuses of despotism or the recurrence of tyranny. The specific injustices suffered may involve the hardships resulting from an inequitable economy, or consist of crippling political discriminations.

I have failed to mention the kind of struggle which occurred between Caesar and Pompey in Rome, between the houses of York and Lancaster in England, between the Bourbons and the Guises in France, or between any set of rival claimants to a throne. Though on a more elevated social plane, these conflicts for power between individuals, and their retinues, are like the gang wars in Chicago. They seldom, if ever, turn on questions of justice. Furthermore, they seldom divide the whole civil population into warring factions, even though noncombatants may be unable to stay on the side lines without peril. The party purges which we have witnessed recently in Germany and Russia fall into this category.

II. The revolt of the Britons against their Roman conquerors; the rebellion of the thirteen colonies in North America against British rule; the wars for independence waged by the South American peoples against Portuguese and Spanish dominion; the revolt of the Swiss or of the Italian city-states against Austria. These exemplify the second type of civil strife.

Here, as in the first type, the cause of the armed uprising will usually be oppression, whether in the form of economic exploitation of colonies by the mother country or in the form of political subjection by the conqueror. But the difference here is that the rebellious group is not a class within the civil population. It is an alien population under the imperial dominion of a conquering state, or the inhabitants of a colonial dependency.

In consequence, the aim of the rebellion is to gain or regain political independence. If the rebellion succeeds, it does not affect the form of government of the defeated overlords. It merely detaches a colonial or imperial possession from their control. The other result, of course, is the setting up of a new political unit which now has sovereignty; or, in the case of conquered provinces and domains, the resurrection of the sovereignty which conquest had submerged.

The injustice of imperialism in the treatment of conquered peoples or colonial dependencies profoundly affects the peace of the imperial community—the political whole which must be viewed as including the annexed provinces or colonial possessions.

This has an obvious bearing on the sort of world peace which might result from world conquest. Ignoring for the moment whether conquest is itself unjust, we can admit the possibility of a conqueror who does not deal unjustly with the conquered. It is conceivable that the conquering nation might aim to set up a federal union of equal states.

It is conceivable, but history has no record of conquest issuing in this result. Napoleon may once have dreamed of a United States of Europe, but with the iron any conqueror must use, only an empire, not a federation, can be forged.

III. The American Civil War, or what is sometimes more properly called "the war of secession," is the outstanding, if not the only, example of the third kind of civil strife.

This type differs from the rebellion of dependencies in that it occurs between the members of a federal union. States which once had external, as well as internal, sovereignty seek to regain their original status, if only to form another federal union on new lines. Such civil strife must result either in the preservation of the union, or in its dissolution into two or more independent states.

Questions of justice may underlie a war of secession. If some of the states in a federal union *misconceive* their sovereignty as including the *right* of secession, the defenders of the union will appear to them to be unjustly infringing that right by using coercive measures to keep them in the union. That is one side of the picture.

The other side may involve an attempt on the part of the federal government to enforce the justice of the constitution within the domains of certain of the states, thus arousing armed resistance to armed intervention in the internal affairs of sovereign states. Or the desire to secede may be caused by impending changes in the federal constitution, aiming to increase its justice, supported by a majority of the states, and inimical to the unjust practices that a minority of the states regard as the prerogative of their sovereignty.

8

All three types of civil strife can be called "wars"—wars of rebellion or civil wars—but they differ from international wars in several significant respects.

In the first place, civil conflicts usually involve profound issues of justice, frequently lacking entirely or seldom plain in the struggles between independent nations. In historical retrospect, it is much easier to determine which party had just cause for armed uprising or armed resistance.

In the second place, during the intervals between civil strife within a single political community, an actual state of peace exists, not a state of potential war carried on by the intrigues of diplomacy. Even while the insurgents are fomenting a rebellion, a weak degree of peace obtains.

Civil war is truly a *breach* of the peace, however tenuous that peace may be. War between nations does not breach a peace, because none exists; international combats, along with armed truces, are merely the expression of an absence of peace. Precisely because civil war disturbs civil peace, it may be the inevitable expedient by which a community improves its political condition, perfects its government, and so achieves a more nearly perfect peace. But when fighting occurs between nations, no peace is broken, and so no peace is restored or perfected.

In the third place, civil wars seldom, if ever, end in truces or treaties between the contending parties. The conflict usually results in the reconstruction of the peace which was temporarily interrupted—either by a reformation of the government or by the creation of an independent community, for whose people peace is re-established under a new sovereignty.

The most significant fact about the American Civil War is that it did not terminate with a treaty, but with a declaration of amnesty. Lincoln's policy was that the South had never seceded, and so the rebel states could be reabsorbed into the peace of the Union, a peace not only restored but perfected. So long as the Southern states exaggerated "state's rights" into false claims to unabridged sovereignty, peace precarious, not peace perpetual, obtained within the territorial limits of the United States. It took a great and bloody war to achieve a more nearly perfect peace as well as a more nearly perfect union.

Finally, even if civil strife ends with injustice unrectified, the peace of the community can continue. The necessary reforms may yet occur peacefully before violent measures must again be taken.

With these things in mind, let us see what conditions can strengthen the peace of a community so that it is entirely free from the threat or outbreak of civil violence. Thus we shall be able to define perfect peace, and note the several approximations to it.

9

The most fundamental distinction among the forms of government is that between constitutional government and despotism, the absolute rule by one man who regards himself as a personal sovereign. Since the sovereign man is above the law, those subject to his rule can take no lawful stand against him. They lack juridical rights. They have no legal power to protect themselves against oppression, no legal means by which to seek remedies for injustice.

The despot may not always be a tyrant. Some despots have been benevolent, considering the welfare of their subjects as a father cares for children. But to treat adult human beings like children is itself a rank injustice, of which the people may not be aware as long as they are unjustly kept in an unnatural condition of political immaturity.

When the people can no longer stand the tyranny of the despot, or will no longer suffer the indignity of benevolent paternalism, they have only one recourse—violent rebellion. Despotic government provides them with no peaceful or legal means for obtaining reforms.

Constitutional government is intrinsically more just than the most benevolent despotism. It abolishes personal sovereignty. The basic political status under constitutional government is that of citizenship. The rights and privileges of citizenship can be legally safeguarded against the encroachments of public officials. Those who are admitted to the status of citizenship have the political equality and the political freedom which is the just due of every man.

But constitutional government can be defective in two fundamental ways—in justice and in efficiency.

If the constitution does not admit all the members of a population to the rights of citizenship, it is unjust. If the franchise is narrowly restricted, if some men remain in chattel slavery, if others are kept politically immature as wards of the community, political freedom and equality have been unjustly distributed.

The marks of the just constitution are universal suffrage and the abolition of all politically privileged classes. By these marks political democracy is defined, and so far as political justice is concerned, it is clearly the best form of government.

But political justice can be combined with economic injustice. Politically free men can be economically exploited, which means that they are enslaved, for slavery consists in being used by another as an instrument of that other's private profit. The perfectly just constitution must, therefore, remove all obstacles to economic reforms which progressively ameliorate the conditions of labor and which progressively approach an equitable distribution of economic opportunities and rewards.

Economic freedom is indispensable to the unfettered exercise of political freedom. Like political liberty, economic freedom is established by justice and by government, not in spite of justice and apart from government. Economic freedom cannot be defined in terms of free enterprise, ownership of private property, or being in business for one's self, though it is true that free enterprise and private property are essential safeguards against the sort of collectivism which substitutes one economic master, the state, for many. John Adams was right in thinking that no man who is dependent for his subsistence upon the will of another can fully exercise political freedom; but Adams, like most of the Founding Fathers, was an oligarch who advocated a suffrage limited to those fortunate enough to be born to, or to have achieved, economic freedom.

Economic democracy involves economic *justice* for all men, as well as economic *freedom* for all. The theory of free enterprise fails to solve the problem precisely because it insists only on the necessary autonomy of the economic life, and neglects the just regulation of the economic order to prevent exploitation. The ultimate natural right to be protected is not the right of private property, but rather freedom from exploitation, based on the equal right of every man to work for his own happiness and the common good.

Whenever a man works for the *private good or profit* of another man, he is that other's economic slave, even when not his chattel. In an industrialized economy and under the conditions of efficient mass production, it is impossible for every man to be in business for himself, as the isolated farmer or the lone shoemaker once was. Hence either some men must work for others or all men must work together *in such a way that none works for another*. The theory of free enterprise does not tell us how to avoid the first of these alternatives, or how to achieve the justice and freedom of the second.

10

So long as the constitution itself remains politically unjust or so long as it protects economically privileged classes, the community lives under the threat of civil strife. Men will not forever suffer constitutional injustice any more than they will endure despotism. They will not forever submit to economic disadvantages any more than they will accept political disqualifications.

At this point, the efficiency of constitutional government becomes a factor in preventing civil violence. By "efficiency" I do not mean the use of police power by the vested interests to put down militant reform movements, labor strikes, or other popular uprisings. The efficiency I have had in mind varies with the degree to which governmental machinery provides legal means for settling every sort of civil dispute, whether it be about political rights or economic privileges.

If political and economic reforms cannot be accomplished by *due process of law,* they will have to be accomplished some other way, and the only other way is violence. Hence, a constitution which does not provide legal means for its own amendment, or which provides no legal means for the impeachment of persons who have abused their public office, or which fails to provide sanctions to protect the rights of citizenship, will fail to make the principle of constitutionality work in practice.

The constitutions of the Greek city-states and of republican Rome were defective in these respects, as well as in justice. Hence, the working classes in Athens had to throw the oligarchs out by violence in order to set up a more democratic constitution. The plebs in Rome had to engage in civil war to get constitutional reforms. But in modern England and in the United States, at least some basic constitutional reforms have been accomplished by due process of law. The justice of the constitution has been improved, and glaring injustices rectified, without recourse to civil strife.

The measure of efficiency in the practice of constitutional government is the extent to which due process of law, supported by legitimate public force, can settle every controversy involving real grievances. But the forces of political or economic reaction must always be dealt with. To whatever extent a constitution is just, its justice must be protected against the return of the oligarchs or the rise of despots, be they persons or parties.

In listing the varieties of civil strife, I did not mention the rebellion of the fascists against constitutional government. Such civil violence can be prevented, not by the justice of government, but by the efficiency of government in using legitimate force to protect whatever justice it provides.

The rights of free speech and public assembly belong to all who would use these rights to procure constitutional changes or legal reforms. They do not belong to individuals or groups who seek to abolish the constitutional rights of free speech and public assembly. That amounts to overthrowing constitutional government, not reforming it.

The reason why we can usually tell on which side justice lies in civil strife is that the natural law provides us with standards for recognizing tyranny and despotism, and the constitution or its positive laws provide us with standards for recognizing reactionary efforts to do away with what justice has been achieved.

If, however, the constitution is unjust, if it deprives some men of political status or economic rights, and if it offers them no legal means to remedy their situation, then justice lies on the side of the revolutionary movements. They are justified in attempting to overthrow a constitution which does not permit free speech and public assembly to effect constitutional reforms or the gradual rectification of abuses by legal means.

11

We have now seen the steps by which the institutions of government can be perfected in justice and efficiency. By improvements in justice, the occasions for civil strife can be removed or reduced. By improvements in efficiency, the occasions which remain to generate grave dissensions can be prevented from issuing in violence as a last resort.

There are two other causes of civil strife which require different remedies. Let us briefly consider these.

The justice and efficiency of government—even of constitutional and democratic government—so far as one part of the population is concerned, may be combined with the injustice of imperialism. It makes no difference whether the subjugated portions of an empire have been acquired by military conquest or by colonization. The civil peace of an empire is as imperfect as the civil peace of a despotism.

The subject peoples in the conquered domains or the colonial dependencies are, in fact, living under despotic government, for they are deprived of the rights and devoid of the liberties which belong to them as well as to their conquerors or masters. In addition to such political indignities, they may suffer from the hardships of economic exploitation.

Let us have no illusions about the *Pax Romana*. Just as democratic Athens subjugated the cities under its imperial sway and exploited its far-flung colonies, so republican Rome brought peace with its rule of law but it did not always give the subject peoples the rights and liberties of Roman citizenship.

Julius Caesar repeatedly refers to his conquests of Gaul and Britain as a process of *pacification*. From the Roman point of view, there is an apparent truth in this interpretation of conquest as pacification. The gifts of Roman law and Roman rule were being bestowed upon barbarian communities.

According to Virgil this was Rome's great destiny. The mission of Rome was to *impose* a peace upon the world. The very word "pax" meant to the Roman a pact imposed upon the vanquished —a pact by which they exchanged their independence for the advantages of Roman government, even if that did not include equality with Romans.

But the Roman point of view on these matters must not obscure the other point of view. These things looked different to the conquered peoples. The ungrateful Britons preferred their independence to Roman dominion, and they were willing to break the imperial peace to get it. Tacitus reports the British chieftain Calgacus as thundering this retort, right but discourteous, to the Caesars: "Those deadly Romans, who plunder, butcher, steal, and misname these things 'empire,' who make a desolation and call it peace."

This cause of civil strife can be completely extirpated, but only by a complete renunciation of imperialism.

The one remaining cause is the factor operative in the American Civil War.

The sovereignty of states belonging to a federation is entirely the internal sovereignty of local government dealing with local affairs. By the very nature of federation, federated states cease to be sovereign in any external sense. Their sovereignty does not include any right of secession. A federal government is therefore justified in using force to preserve the union.

But the questions of justice go deeper than that. The constitution of the federal government must provide standards for measuring the justice of the constitutions of the federal states. That is why, for example, the federal Constitution of the United States guarantees to the peoples of the several states a republican form of government. That is why the basic political principles upon which a federation is founded must be uniformly adopted by all the member communities. The latter can vary only in matters of detail, not with respect to anything fundamental in the institutions of government.

In consequence, a federal government can and must use legitimate force to intervene in the internal affairs of its subordinate communities whenever basic constitutional rights are violated or privileges denied. Not only do the subordinate communities lack every vestige of external sovereignty, but the limited internal sovereignty of their governments does not include freedom from interference in local affairs on fundamental issues.*

The justice of the federal constitution must be protected by sanctions which include forceful intervention to uphold the constitution in every part of the federal community. Furthermore, as the "general welfare" clause in the American Constitution shows, the federal common good takes precedence over the special interests of the several states.

The peace of a federal community remains insecure so long as all of its member states do not approximate uniformity in the practice of, not merely lip service to, the fundamental laws. Variation in the letter of the law can be combined with constancy to its spirit. But as long as there are radical antagonisms between the spirit of one locality and that of another, or as long as local interests remain paramount, civil strife imperils federal peace and even threatens to disrupt the federation.

12

None of the conditions required for perfect peace is unattainable. None demands a utopian transformation of human nature or human society.

Civil peace is nonexistent without civil government. It remains

---

* One sovereign state cannot interfere in the internal affairs of another except by acts of war or at the risk of war. Though we hold democracy to be the best form—perhaps the only good form—of government, we can do nothing to prevent other peoples from choosing inferior or even vicious regimes, inimical to the welfare of their neighbors and the world, as well as contrary to their own best interests. Only a federal constitution can effectively control the basic political choices of the various localities it unites, by setting standards for the constitution of government in these subordinate communities and by judging the constitutionality of the laws they enact.

imperfect to whatever extent the institutions of government do not provide legal means and legitimate force for remedying injustice. Its perfection does not include the abolition of all injustice, as it does not involve the abolition of crime and vice. It cannot hope to prevent the violence of men who use force to gain an unjust end; nor can it eschew the use of force to counteract such violence.

With these qualifications, which respect the limitations of human nature, political institutions and economic systems can be perfected to the point where civil peace is no longer threatened by any form of justified civil violence. That is perfect peace. And perfect peace is perpetual peace.

We speak of universal and perpetual peace. The universality of peace can be achieved only by world government. That universal peace must be perfected to become perpetual. World government can achieve this by satisfying all the conditions we have just considered. Obviously, the world may enjoy universal peace long before that peace is itself perfected by the justice and efficiency of world government.

World government must not only be constitutional, but it must also become democratic, with all the implications this has for the political status of men everywhere. It must not only become politically democratic, but it should also look to the realization of economic democracy. It should not only be just politically and economically, but it must also safeguard whatever justice is attained by adequate sanctions. More than that, it should provide effective machinery for altering any compromise *status quo,* for improving justice continually by due process of law. No form of imperialism can be allowed to remain.

A legitimate use of force and every implement of education must be directed toward achieving equality of conditions throughout the world and in reducing local deviations from the spirit of the laws, especially reactionary or intransigent subversion.

When these things are done, universal peace will become perpetual. Clearly nothing less than the perfect peace which is universal and perpetual can be our ultimate goal. Nothing less need be, for this goal is practicable, not utopian.

CHAPTER 12

A Society of Men

IT HAS NOW been proved that universal and perpetual peace is possible. Let me briefly summarize the steps of the proof.

(1) We have seen the conditions required for *any degree* of peace. These conditions are the same regardless of the size of the population and of the area with which we may be concerned. Peace exists wherever there is a political community, a society of men living together under government—in a city, a state, a nation, or the world.

If these indispensable conditions could be realized only in limited areas of the earth's surface, and only with portions of its people, then world peace would be impossible. But there is nothing in the nature of a political community and nothing in the nature of government which limits them quantitatively. History shows us a slow but steady growth in the size of political units. There is no reason to suppose that this development will reach its natural limit until the world community is formed.

The obstacles in the way of setting up world government are great. They are greater than the difficulties the world community will face after it has been instituted. But none of these obstacles is insuperable. None arises from the limitations or imperfections of human nature. All belong to the order of contingent circumstances which men can overcome. They have overcome similar obstacles at every point of signal advance in their political history.

What must be done to get world peace is, perhaps, more difficult than anything men have ever done politically. But it can be done. The difficulty of the task gives us some measure of the probable time it will take. World peace will be difficult to achieve —difficult, not impossible.

(2) The universality of peace is only one aspect of its perfection. It is the quantitative aspect. There is also a qualitative aspect which varies with the likelihood of civil strife within any com-

munity having some degree of peace. Peace is qualitatively perfect only when it is perpetual, only when the justice and efficiency of government preclude the occasions or the need for civil violence.

Political peace has developed qualitatively as well as quantitatively. With the steps of political progress from despotism to constitutional government, and from defective forms of republican government to the achievement of democracy, higher degrees of peace have been reached in particular communities. Perpetual peace may not yet be realized even in the most advanced of the world's nations, but the road ahead has no obstacles as great as those already surmounted.

Whether perfect peace will be achieved in some local community before world government arrives is an unanswerable question. We do not have to answer it in order to see that the conditions requisite for perpetual peace are as capable of being realized in the world community as in particular states. They may not be as manageable for the whole world as they are in the nations which have already come a long way. But this again is a matter of difficulty, not of impossibility.

It seems likely that world peace will be instituted before it is perfected. Yet it is conceivable that world peace cannot be made until it can also be made perpetual. In either case, the argument remains the same.

No condition required for the perpetuation of peace becomes unrealizable when we shift from a particular state to the whole world. And all these conditions are capable of being realized within particular states. It follows, therefore, that a lasting world peace is possible.

2

Let me suppose for the moment that this argument is clear and persuasive. I can still imagine a way in which it can be rejected.

I am not now thinking of the person who will confuse possibility and probability, who will dismiss as utopian what is merely very difficult. I have in mind rather the person who will say that there is an easier way to get world peace. He will not deny that the conditions set forth could procure world peace, but he will try to insist that there are other and more amenable ways to procure it.

We must be able to show this person that the conditions set forth are the minimum, not the maximum, conditions. Much more may be required both to get world government and to make it work, but nothing less than world government will solve the problem.

To make this point, we do not have to describe the precise character of world government and the way in which it will be related to all the levels of local government that must remain. We do not have to choose between the various blueprints for world political organization which have so far been offered. We do not have to defend any of these plans or projects in their institutional details.

As a matter of fact, we are still too remote from the realization of world government to be able to conceive the precise character of the institutional arrangements. Current plans and blueprints do us a disservice if they distract our attention from the indisputable principles and draw discussion into the area of questionable details. By keeping our eye on the principles, we can defend the thesis that nothing less than world government will establish world peace, even in the least degree.

The argument can be put in a nutshell. Let anyone suppose the maximum extent of political organization short of world government. Let him suppose large regional federations in place of a larger plurality of independent states. Let him even suppose the world divided into *two* regional federations and, for the purpose of illustration, let us imagine these to be an Atlantic and a Pacific community of federated states.

But one condition remains. Each of these two regional federations retains its external sovereignty. Each is an independent political organization, with its own foreign policy and its diplomats, with its defensive armaments which may have to be used aggressively, with its insistence, by right of sovereignty, that it must decide what is for its own interests.

By performing this experiment in our imagination, we can see that a state of war will not have been abolished. Nor will actual combat be prevented. In this imagined situation, actual warfare may be postponed for a much longer time than it has ever been in the world's history, especially if the two great powers are evenly matched in physical resources, industrial capacity, man power, and military prowess.

But nothing in the nature of power allows us to suppose that the balance will be forever preserved. In the scales of power, a perfect equilibrium can never be maintained, even if it momentarily happens. Furthermore, other considerations of partisan interest, which weigh heavily in foreign policy, may lead one of the regional federations to take the risks involved in the awful arbitrament of war.

We have seen this happen when a balance of power has been approximated by vast alliances and ententes. Two vaster power blocs in the form of regional federations will not change the picture.

Between a single world government and two regional federations there can be no choice, if world peace is the aim. The person who supposes the contrary confuses peace with truce. The most enduring truce is not the least degree of peace. Interregional warfare would remain as inevitable as international warfare is now.

Even if the imperfect peace established by world government did not preclude certain types of civil strife, the situation would be different. However imperfect, world peace would have had a beginning. Civil strife might interrupt it, but peace, not a truce, would be recovered when it was over; and the civil strife might lead to political improvements and economic reforms, through which a higher degree of peace might be secured.

3

This line of argument may not satisfy the person who has objected. He may claim that his position has been misrepresented.

By the maximum degree of political organization short of world government, he does not mean two or more regional federations. He means some form of international organization, such as a reconstituted League of Nations. He means a development of international law, administered through the agency of world courts, and enforced by a cosmopolitan police force.

He may envisage international tribunals as having compulsory jurisdiction over all controversies between nations, not merely those legal issues which nations voluntarily submit to arbitration. He may envisage the police force as having sufficient power to execute international law, and to enforce the judgment of its courts. The police force itself he may conceive as recruited in any number of ways.

The point at issue therefore comes to this. How far can we go in the direction of international organization without setting up world government? How shall we draw the line between world government and any sort of international organization which falls short of it? Will anything short of world government procure world peace, or will it only tend to prolong a truce?

In order to show that nothing less than world government will do, it is necessary to draw the line which divides it from mere internationalism. Until we draw that line sharply, we cannot tell whether or not the objection is based on self-deception. In the various proposals mentioned above, a man may in fact be projecting world government, though he tries to avoid the name. Or he may deceive us and himself by proposing something which approaches world government and yet is as much a miss as if it were miles away.

To draw the line between world government and all its counterfeits or approximations, we need not consider the institutional details on either side of that line. We can make the distinction by appealing to clear-cut principles.

There is nothing fuzzy or indefinite about these principles, though most of the historic peace plans and a great many contemporary books have tried to evade their implications by fudging the issues. Whether the fudging has been willful or artless self-deception makes no difference. To play fast and loose with these principles ends in contradiction.

Above all, we must defeat the tendency of language to obscure the principles, and to save us from knowing that we have contradicted ourselves. Such words as "nation," "national," and "international" are the worst offenders.

Do we mean the same thing when we speak of international law and of laws to be enacted and enforced by world government? Do we mean the same thing when we speak of regulating international affairs and when, as under the government of the United States, we speak of interstate commerce as subject to federal regulation?

Do we mean the same thing when we think of the world community as a society of nations or as a society of men belonging to different races or nationalities and living under different local governments? Do we mean the same thing when we think of a world-state and of a world-wide federal organization subordinating the polities of local areas?

4

In order to determine what our words mean and what our thoughts imply, we must have criteria by which to judge the variety of possible situations with respect to world affairs.

There seem to be only four major possibilities: (1) a plurality of independent, sovereign states which may enter into alliances with one another by treaty; (2) a confederacy or league of independent states which may or may not include all nations and which may or may not be supported by alliances; (3) a world community including all peoples under world government, federal in structure; and (4) a world state which consists of a world community under government that is not federal in structure.

We can omit consideration of regional federations. Either these regional federations will be independent political units, and so will fall into the first or second category; or they will be subordinate parts of a world community, and so will fall into the third category.

No one can confuse the first and the fourth possibilities. A plurality of independent states stands at one extreme. A single world state stands at the other.

The difficult problem concerns the two middle cases. As we have seen, these tend to be confused. Moreover, some form of international confederacy or league of nations is often proposed as a satisfactory substitute for world government, federal or otherwise. It is not satisfactory unless that *ersatz* peace, a truce, is our only aim.

There is one criterion which, by itself, draws the line between arrangements that can result only in a truce and institutions that can secure peace. That criterion is sovereignty.

If any vestige of external sovereignty remains, if there is any relic of what we call "national independence," then the plan under consideration falls on the truce side of the line. It falls there even if it speaks the language of international law, world courts, and international organization. It might even be said that it falls there precisely because it still retains all the notions connected with *internationalism*.

Unfortunately, there is much quibbling about sovereignty, and a rampant loose use of the word. We have already seen how this arises from failure to distinguish the internal and external aspects of sovereignty, or from careless talk about sovereignty as a "bundle" of rights—as if the rights belonging to *external* sovereignty could be surrendered piecemeal.*

---

* In an article in *Life* ("Our Foreign Policy"), Mr. John K. Jessup seems to contradict this by observing that for many years nations "have been surrendering bits

To circumvent such quibbling, let us use the following criteria for testing on which side of the line any proposal falls. These criteria add up to the presence or absence of external sovereignty; they permit no doubts as to whether a given proposal is a truce plan or a peace plan.

1. Will local governments need and have a foreign policy and with it the work of a foreign office or state department, diplomats and emissaries?

    If so, then even if there be some form of international organization it will be a mere league or confederacy, not a world federal government or a world state.

2. Will there be any need or room for treaties of "peace" contracted by separate political communities?

    If so, then we do not have world government, federal or otherwise.

3. Do the states which are members of an international organization have the right to secede from that organization?

    If so, then it is a mere league or confederacy, not a federal structure.

4. Must any rule or decision of an international council or assembly be adopted by the unanimous assent of all the states therein represented?

    If so, then that legislative body belongs to a league or a confederacy. It is not the congress or parliament of a federal government, in which any type of majority rule can prevail.

---

of sovereignty to international agencies, courts, and laws. . . . International anarchy has been abolished with regard to piracy, the drug traffic, the mails, copyrights, patents, diplomatic usage, fishing, migratory birds, etc." The contradiction is, however, only apparent, for Jessup adds the all-important qualification that "it is vital to remember that *these are agreements between sovereign governments, which reserve the right to enforce them on their own citizens. They are laws* . . . only in the sense that the House Rules of a country club are laws." [Italics mine.] In the same month in which Jessup's article appeared, *Time* dealt roughly with the myth of international law, pointing out that it "has worked, and can only work, as applied to those comparatively minor matters about which practically all the nations of the world are already in genuine agreement—such matters as the prohibition of piracy or the protection of diplomats and migratory birds."

5. Will there be immigration restrictions and trade barriers which affect the passage of peoples or goods across the boundaries of local communities?

   If they are the enactments of the several local governments, and not of the world government, then the several local governments are not merely local divisions of a central, federal government, but remain autonomous in their external relations.

6. Will there be, in addition to an international police force, armaments and military establishments held in reserve for some other purpose than the enforcement of federal or local laws?

   If so, the international organization does not have the power proper to a federal government, and the member states have more power than is proper for local governments. The issue here is not between total disarmament and the retention of some implements of force. The issue is rather between the status of such implements—as instruments of war or as instruments of law enforcement.

7. Will the internal affairs of the several states be entirely exempt from intervention by the international organization, even though the course of internal affairs in one state seriously affects the welfare of another?

   If so, then the several states have merely joined a league or a confederacy. They have not become members of a federal organization.

8. Will individual men have citizenship only in their local community, being represented in world affairs in an indirect manner by emissaries of the state to which they belong? Will the international organization attempt to regulate states alone, affecting individuals indirectly, only through the mediation of the state to which they belong?

   If so, then the international organization is not a federal government, and its laws and their enforcement do not operate in the federal manner.

9. Will the budget of the international agencies be met by a levy on the several states, in contrast to all methods of financing government by direct taxation upon individual citizens?

If so, then these international agencies belong to a league or confederacy. They are not the departments of a federal government.

10. Will patriotism still consist in a paramount devotion to the goodness of a local community and a desire to see it pre-eminent in any respect over other local communities, or at the expense of the general welfare?

If so, then such patriots have only a national allegiance. They are not citizens of the world, and there is no world community or workable government.

These ten criteria sharply separate every form of *internationalism* from every form of *world government*. They are so closely connected that a negative or affirmative answer to any one will mean no or yes all along the line. It could not be otherwise, since these ten criteria do no more than express concretely what is involved in the single criterion of sovereignty.

By these ten criteria we can see what it means to say that nothing less than world government will secure world peace. Anything less leaves the world composed of independent nations in a state of war, potential or actual. Any plan proposes something less than world government if it answers these questions affirmatively.*

* The reader can exercise his understanding of these criteria by using them to cross-examine the Mackinac declaration issued by the Republican Postwar Advisory Council, which advocated participation in a "co-operative organization among sovereign nations"; Secretary Hull's similar statement of foreign policy made at approximately the same time (September, 1943); the Fulbright Resolution adopted by the House of Representatives, and the Connally Resolution subsequently approved by the Senate, which recommended that the United States "join with free and sovereign nations in the establishment and maintenance of international authority with power to prevent aggression and to preserve the peace of the world," and which, as adopted, incorporated a clause from the Moscow pact calling for "a general international organization based on the principle of the sovereign

5

Let us look for a moment at international law to see why it cannot possibly meet the needs of the situation. The point is not that international law is at present defective and that, when developed or improved, it will perform the task of keeping peace. The point is that world peace requires a complete transcendence of international law.

We have already seen the respects in which international law is like primitive law. It is the kind of law which belongs to an anarchic community in which the basic legal functions are performed by individuals judging and helping themselves. But there are still further respects in which international law differs from the law of a true political community, the sort of law which manifests the operations of government.

International law is usually divided into general and particular. Its general content consists of the customs which prevail in the conduct of international affairs. It would be more accurate to say that it consists of maxims which are *sometimes* acknowledged as a matter of custom and sometimes honored as moral precepts.

It is supposed to be a matter of custom that nations respect each other's sovereignty. It is at least customary for each nation to demand respect for its own sovereignty.

It is a moral precept that nations, like individuals, should keep the promises they have made.

These two maxims summarize the general content of international law in so far as it concerns the *rights* of nations and their

---

equality of all peace-loving states"; the American Legion's recent advocacy of international co-operation on the part of independent nations; the "Six Pillars of Peace" proposed by the Federal Council of Churches; the seven-point "Declaration on World Peace" jointly issued by representative Catholics, Protestants, and Jews; and the eight-point "Pledge for Peace" recently issued by an independent citizens' committee headed by Supreme Court Justice Roberts. This latter declaration is unequivocal in its proposal for the relinquishment of two sovereign rights, a) the right to declare war; b) the right of secession from the world-organization.

duties to one another. It should be obvious at once, from the whole history of international affairs, that nations frequently violate each other's rights, and frequently fail to discharge their obligations. International law is as powerless to prevent such malfeasance or nonfeasance as it is powerless to prevent the wars which result therefrom.

It seems a little odd to describe as customary law what is more frequently breached than observed. The general maxims of international law can be regarded as customary only in the very special sense already observed. It is customary for each nation to demand that *other* nations fulfill their obligations. It is customary for each nation to demand that *other* nations respect its rights.

General international law merely *describes* the customary grounds for international conflict. It does not *prescribe* what every nation must do or suffer the penalty of law enforcement. What Bertrand Russell once said of ethics applies to general international law: it is the art of recommending to others the things they must do in order to get along with one's self.

Particular international law consists of all the rights and obligations which have been defined by specific treaties between nations. This in itself is strange. A treaty is nothing but a contract between individuals. It is not like the social compact or the constitutional convention by which individuals set up a form of government. It is exactly like a contract between private individuals engaged in some sort of transaction with one another.

A private contract cannot make public law. Even though sovereign states have the character of public persons, the treaties they negotiate are no better than private contracts between corporate personalities. And when a treaty concludes a war, it is no better than a gentleman's agreement between brutes who have been forced to their knees.

Such contracts do not make law, except in the paradoxical sense in which international law is law. Furthermore, if a private individual breaches a contract, the legal system of his community provides a way for determining who is at fault, what damage has been done, what compensation must be made. Applying the law of contracts, courts judge the controversy, and other officials use public power to enforce the judgment.

But in the international situation the only rule is the maxim that promises should be kept—*by the other party!* I do not mean to imply that nations always dishonor their treaties. Many treaties have been observed in the spirit as well as the letter. Within the last hundred years, many controversies over treaty obligations have been voluntarily submitted to courts of arbitration, and the tribunal's decision has been accepted by the party adversely affected, and voluntarily executed.

But when matters of paramount national interest are at stake, international law breaks down. The matter may or may not be submitted to an impartial tribunal, and even if it is, the party adversely affected may refuse to comply with the court's judgment, in which case the other party must help itself. This means war. That is why the members of the League did not try to save Ethiopia by enforcing sanctions against Italy.

There are still other aspects of international law which show its peculiarity. It needs the mediation of national law in order to regulate the conduct of individual men living in independent states.

It holds all the members of a state collectively responsible for the acts of its nationals. War is not made against the particular individuals who may have committed the injury which occasions a conflict; it is made against all the people of the country to which those particular individuals belong, without respect to who is or who is not at fault.

International law does not distinguish between criminal acts and civil causes, nor does it separate punitive action from compensatory remedies.

It does not attempt to make the punishment fit the crime. It does not follow the rule of justice that gradations of punishment should be correlated with the gravity of the offense. Minor as well as major offenses elicit the capital punishment of war, without violating the peculiar sort of justice embodied in international law.

6

When all these things are contrasted with the characteristics of legal systems having political foundation, we see how peculiar international law is. We see that it is a law divorced from political institutions. It is a law of *nations* living together anarchically, not a law of *men* living together under government. It is a law of *war* (potential or actual), not a law of *peace*.

Once more I quote my favorite authority on matters which are profound, but not too subtle for clear wits to grasp. An editorial in *The New Yorker* observes that

> Law is, unfortunately, not law unless it is enforceable, and the "laws" of warfare are in their very nature unenforceable, being a mere set of rules for quarrelling, which any country can disregard if it chooses. When war comes, each nation makes its own rules to suit itself. Japan makes hers, which includes murdering enemy fliers. . . . When at length Japan is punished, as she certainly will be, for having executed American aviators, the act of punishing her will not be "justice" since no court exists which has jurisdiction and no force exists for carrying out such a court's order. To call it justice is to do ourselves a disservice, because it deflects our gaze from the terrible spectacle of a world without law.

Precisely because international law is the law of a society of nations, not the law of a society of men, it can never be developed or improved to the point where it will function effectively to keep the peace. Law will function effectively in world affairs only when it ceases to be international.

When we cross the line dividing the anarchic from the political community, we experience a change of kind, not one of degree. When we cross the line between every form of international alliance (or league) and world government, the difference is again one of kind, not degree. So, too, when we pass from international law to the legal system of a world-wide political community.

Not by alterations or improvements in international law, but by its *total abolition* in favor of a different kind of legal system, will we transcend the international order—the order of battles and truces. What has always been said of treaties applies equally to the sort of law which is a creature of treaties.

The ancient Greek orator, Isocrates, said:

> It is to no purpose that we make treaties; for we do not settle our wars, but only defer them and wait for the time when we shall be able to inflict some irremediable injury on one another.

This has been echoed through the centuries. Rousseau and Kant excoriated treaties as making truces, not peace. As recently as 1917, Thorstein Veblen, in his *Inquiry into the Nature of Peace and the Terms of Its Perpetuation,* wrote:

> Peace established by the State, or resting in the discretion of the State, is necessarily of the nature of an armistice, in effect terminable at will and on short notice. It is maintained only on conditions, stipulated by express convention or established by custom, and there is always the reservation, tacit or explict, that recourse will be had to arms in case the "national interests" or the punctilios of international etiquette are traversed by the act or defection of any rival government or its subjects.

International law, like the customs and treaties which comprise its content, belongs to the present era of world history. In its time, it may serve a certain purpose, but it can never serve the purpose of making or keeping peace.

We can have no excuse for blurring or obscuring the clear-cut distinction between an international order and a world political community. If we use the word "international" to mean "relating diverse nationalities," then there are many international governments already in existence. The government of the Soviet Union is certainly international in this sense. But if we use the word "international" to mean "relating independent states or sovereign nations," then we should know that "international government" is as self-contradictory as "round-square."

The best way to remember how we are using the word "international" is by reference to *international law*. In that sense of the word, it properly applies only to battles or truces and to the anarchic community which is called a "society of nations."

It does not apply to peace or government or to the world community of the future which must be a society of men.

CHAPTER 13

The Inexorable Alternative

To UNDERSTAND the possibilities of peace is to know the minimum conditions for its realization. This knowledge should save us from pinning false hopes upon any plan or policy which reveals, by the very nature of what it proposes, that it aims at truce, not peace. This knowledge can save us from deception and disillusionment.

Truce and peace are exclusive alternatives. So long as there is merely a truce among nations, world peace will not begin to exist. When world peace begins, all the familiar aspects of the international situation—its warfare and truces—must disappear.

In the order of action and of practical thinking, it is necessary to judge the means by reference to the end in view. We cannot tell whether a course of action is prudent or expedient without considering the requirements imposed by our objective.

If we permit distinct goals to become confused, or fail to define the conditions prerequisite to each, we might just as well proceed in a trial-and-error fashion. We ought not to pretend that we know what we are doing. We ought not to talk as if we were solving a practical problem in the only way in which practical problems can be solved, namely, by calculating the means specifically adapted to a certain end.

During the last four centuries, men have been engaged in drawing up peace plans—primarily schemes for perpetual peace in Europe, though in several instances the larger problem of world peace has been considered. In almost every case, the publicist or statesman or philosopher who had a project to offer tried to evade the inexorable demands imposed by his objective.

Most of them claimed to know the distinction between peace and truce. Yet they allowed themselves, for one reason or another, to propose means which could not succeed.

For the most part, their projects amounted to the proposal of a league of nations. They tried to combine national independence with some scheme for regulating the conduct of independent nations. The fact that they aimed to regulate *the conduct of nations* shows that their plans could do no more than ameliorate the international anarchy, not abolish it. Another indication of their self-contradictory internationalism is the fact that many of these plans talked of federation, yet called for nonintervention in the internal affairs of sovereign states. Worse, they permitted one sovereign to call upon other members of the league to help him maintain the *status quo* of despotism against revolutionary forces within his own domain.

Beneath their variety in detail, these fundamental defects will be found in the plans of Émeric Crucé (1623); the Duc de Sully, to whom the Grand Design of Henri IV is usually attributed (1634-1662); the Abbé de Saint-Pierre (1738); Jeremy Bentham (1786); Henry Ladd (1840); and James Lorimer (1884). William Penn's little essay, *The Future Peace of Europe* (1693), stands out as a striking exception because of its explicit awareness of the stumbling block, sovereignty. Yet even Penn misconceived federation as resulting in a society of princes whose sovereign acts would be regulated by government.

None of these classic schemes was put into practice in its day. But the test, long delayed, came with the formation of the League of Nations after the first world war.

We did not need this historic experiment to know that it was doomed to failure. From the various ways in which it respected the sovereignty of its members, we could have known that the League was not an instrument of peace. Without trying the experiment over again—with whatever modification short of transforming a league into a federal government—we can know that the result must be the same.

It has been said that "it is not necessary to leap from a window twenty times to know that if one leaps, one falls." With knowledge of the law of gravity, it is not necessary to leap even once.

2

The practical situation is complicated by the fact that the world is not yet ready for peace. The same conditions which tell us that peace is possible also tell us the great difficulties which must be overcome. When we understand what is necessary for world peace, we know two things, not one.

We know that leagues or conferences or congresses of independent nations cannot succeed, any more than the less polite forms of power politics—alliances and treaties to establish balances of power or dominant hegemonies.

We also know that the only arrangements which can *ultimately* succeed cannot be instituted *now*.

These facts obligate us to judge current proposals by four criteria:

1. **Do they claim to provide means for peace when, according to their principles, they are at best plans for prolonging a truce?**
2. **Do they aim at both peace and truce without distinguishing these objectives and without specifying the means to be employed for each?**
3. **Do they offer a plan for peace without recognizing the great improbability that world peace can be made in our lifetime?**
4. **In offering plans for prolonging a truce, do they consider the effect of their proposals upon present efforts to promote progress toward the peace which is not yet attainable?**

So far as peace, not truce, is concerned, we must temper all our hopes by a profound respect for the laws of growth.

Men mature slowly. Misguided efforts can succeed in making an infant precocious, but without the weight of years nothing can make a child a man. Far from hastening maturity, the stimulation of unnatural precocity will usually delay or even prevent a timely coming of age. John Stuart Mill can tell us the poignant story of how he almost failed to become a whole man because his father and Jeremy Bentham succeeded in making him a prodigy.

Human society and social institutions mature even more slowly than human individuals. The natural tempo of their growth is based upon the capacity of men to alter their traditions, a capacity limited by the inertia of tradition itself. We can accelerate the development of desired social changes by awakening men to the fact that they are partly responsible for the course of human events. But we will drive them to despair if we neglect to consider that their freedom is limited by the inertia of outward circumstances.

Children do not grow into men merely by the passage of time. They must exercise their capacities in order to develop them. In this they are helped only by such education and experience as fits the stage of their growth, not by hothouse forcing.

Similarly, more than a succession of generations causes the growth of a society or a culture. At every stage of development, men are at work transforming the institutions of their social life. But they must always work upon the institutions, and within the social environment, their ancestors have bequeathed them.

This legacy of tradition limits what any generation can do, as well as providing it with a foundation on which to build. Social planning respects the laws of social growth only when it attempts to elicit and direct impulses without demanding that the inertia of the whole past be overcome in a moment.

Peace cannot be built from a plan. It is not an artificial thing like a house. It is a natural consequence of certain political institutions, and these in turn are natural developments of man's political capacity.

Peace plans should not, therefore, be like architectural drawings which project the finished house. Given an empty plot of land and the requisite materials, the blueprints envisage an orderly series of steps by which the house can be constructed. The wood and stone and steel do not grow into a house. The builder does not have to adjust his plans to their changing susceptibilities.

Peace plans should be more like the physician's policy in watching over the course of a disease. He adapts his treatment to the varying phases of the disease. He changes his prognosis from day to day, and with that he alters his therapy. He knows that the disease must run its course, and he foresees the probable turn of future events. He tries to help nature achieve its own cure, and he is ever alert for the crisis, that turning point when the medical arts may be most helpful in facilitating the natural recovery of health.

We have watched the painful course through the centuries of the political pathology that is war. We have at last begun to see signs that the disease is curable. We have observed peace grow in isolated parts of the body politic. We have noted a tendency in this healthy condition to spread, but we have also noted that the rate of growth is slow—impeded by the disease all around the healthy tissue.

We understand the causes well enough to know what we must do to facilitate the process, but we also know that our power to control the causes changes from time to time. We must proceed, then, with a flexible policy, altering our prognosis, watching for the critical points, ever ready to take advantage of turns for the better.

To shift the metaphor, peace is like a living thing. It has taken root, has grown, has flourished in local communities. We can help it take root in the world as a whole, but we must observe two cautions: we must let the world grow toward readiness for peace, and we must not try to produce world peace by a simple act of transplanting. World peace has its own seeds. These must be sown and cultivated when the soil is ready.

3

In the preceding chapter I enumerated four possible world conditions. Of these, two already exist, but only one has developed to its maturity. The other only began to exist recently, and has barely passed its infancy. The remaining two are still in the limbo of unrealized possibilities.

Let me repeat the four conditions:

(1) *A plurality of independent, sovereign states which enter into alliances with one another by treaty.* This is the primitive situation of the world.

From the beginning of world affairs, a plurality of separate communities has existed. As this situation naturally developed, the techniques of power politics became mature. This situation has a long history of growth behind it, but however long it may survive, its future does not hold out a promise for further maturation. From this point on, there can only be decline.

(2) *A league of independent states which may or may not include all nations and which may or may not be supported by alliances.* This situation began to develop at a period when the primitive condition had already reached maturity.

It is characterized by the conceptions of international law, by plans for international congresses, by the institution of world courts, and by the first formation of a working League of Nations. This second world condition had its inception in ideas that go back hundreds of years, but it did not begin to exist institutionally until the twentieth century. As yet it is far from its own fullness of growth. The basic ideas of internationalism are still novel enough to be regarded by most people as portents of the future.

(3) *A world community including all peoples under world government, federal in structure.* This third among the possible situations does not yet exist.

It seems unlikely that it will begin until the era of internationalism has worked itself out. In the natural course of growth, the maturity of internationalism will probably coincide with the institutional origins of a world community. The world community in its infancy will see the decline and disappearance of internationalism.

(4) *A world state which consists of a world community under government that is not federal in structure.* This final stage of development in world affairs cannot begin until the third phase has reached its maturity.

This plot of events is not like the growth curve of a single individual, but like the chart of an evolutionary series. Variation in an older species gradually gives rise to a new species. The rise of the new species is accompanied by the extinction of the ancestral forms. But we must not push this analogy too far. Social evolution is not biological evolution. It operates under laws peculiar to itself.

The critical point, with respect to war and peace, occurs in the transition from the second to the third world condition. The birth of internationalism is not the birth of peace. Yet internationalism, both in idea and institution, prepares the way.

When its most mature developments have worked their effect upon social traditions, weakening their inertia against a more radical change, internationalism will give way to world government. It will have run its course and done its work. With its death, world peace will be born.

4

In our effort to promote the coming of peace, we must, therefore, encourage the development of international institutions, such as the League of Nations or the World Court. We must seek to improve these institutions in their own line, giving them more power, extending their influence, and safeguarding their operation from sabotage.

For example, Professor Kelsen's proposal that states be *com-*

pelled to submit their controversies to an international tribunal, and that such a court be given compulsory jurisdiction over a wider area of problems, would be a step forward. It would not bring peace, but it would be a step toward peace, preparing for world government.

We have already noted the way in which the anarchic community of the primitive tribe develops into the political community of the civilized state. The legal or governmental functions become centralized in courts and police forces and legislatures. Observing the parallel between the primitive society and the anarchic international community, Professor Kelsen suggests that we shall probably have to go through the same slow stages of development. He writes:

> A social reform has more chance of success if it follows the tendencies hitherto exhibited by social evolution. It has less chance if it opposes these tendencies. It is relatively easy to proceed to socialism from capitalism or even from state capitalism, but an attempt to attain the same object starting from feudalism is impossible, even senseless. For the same reason it is probably impossible to proceed directly from the completely decentralized condition of the international community of today to a federal world-state.

But there is one important difference between the parallel cases. In the development of the political community out of a primitive tribe, the society remains a society of men. The status of the individuals has changed, but it is the individual man who exercises self-judgment and self-help under primitive circumstances and the individual man who submits to courts and expects police protection under government.

In contrast, the transition from the anarchic international community to world government will mean a radical transformation in the character of nations. It will not merely be a change of status—a change from self-judgment and self-help to living under law. To suppose that is to make the error of think-ing of world government as a government of nations.*

In the federal structure of a world community, the separate nations will not be the primary subjects of government. They will have ceased to be separate nations. Federal government will have transformed them into units of local administration.

Because federal government abolishes the external sovereignty of the member states, the step from anarchic internationalism to the world community will probably be more difficult than the corresponding step in the origin of the state from the primitive tribe. The way may be eased, and the progress mediated, by the formation of regional federations having larger scope than any federal governments now in existence.

Mr. Walter Lippmann speaks of the states bordering on the Atlantic Ocean as "members of the same community of interest." According to Mr. Lippmann "the test of whether a community exists is not whether we have learned to love our neighbors, but whether, when put to the test, we find that we do act as neigh-bors."

Neither is the right criterion. Not love but justice; not mutual self-interest, which leads nations to act *for a time* in a neighborly fashion, but government and law, create the political community. The so-called "Atlantic community" is strictly anarchic, a society of nations rather than a society of men.

Were this to be turned into a real political community under

---

* The coercions of government can be legally executed only against citizens, not states or nations. Applied to the latter, such coercive measures comprise acts of war. In a recent address Mr. Justice Roberts observed that "the United States could never have persisted through the 150 years of its life if the laws of the Nation had been addressed to, and binding on, the States as entities rather than upon the individual citizens of the States. . . . Enforcement against a citizen is a police function; enforcement against state or nation as an entity is war." This point com-pletely corners those who try to evade the issue by arguing that world government is compatible with so-called "limited sovereignty." If a state retains any external sovereignty whatsoever, its members are subject to the coercive force of no laws except its own; in which case, world government could not exist because the entities primarily governed would then have to be states, not men, *and this is impossible.*

federal government, we would have some experience of the death of independent states, and of the birth pangs involved in expanding local peace by freely adopted measures rather than by conquest. This local experiment might be almost as difficult to perform as federation on a world-wide scale.

5

With every increase in the size of the political community, involving the sway of centralized government over wider areas and larger populations, more careful provision must be made for the decentralized institutions of local government. The centralization of governmental functions does not do away with the services performed by local agencies. On the contrary, every degree of centralization demands a corresponding degree of decentralization as its natural complement.

We know how this has taken place in a federal structure. It happens in almost the same way in a large political community that is not federal in structure.

The chief, if not the only, difference lies in the fact that the subordinate divisions of a nonfederal state have no constitutional autonomy. The provincial governments operate under a charter granted by the central government, instead of under their own constitutions recognized by a federal constitution. In the United States, for example, the states are units of local government operating under constitutions, whereas the cities and towns of a given state are units of local government operating under charters from the state or acts of incorporation.

From the point of view of the services performed by local government, it makes no difference whether the decentralization takes one or the other of these forms. Local government can be just as effectively carried on in the nonfederal as the federal state. The difference between the nonfederal and the federal state is largely a historic matter—whether its unity originated through the accretions of conquest or through the voluntary act of federation on the part of several independent states.

When a larger political community is formed by federation, the states which give up their former independence retain their sovereignty in its internal aspects. Although they function only as units of local government, providing the necessary decentralization, they do so under their own constitutions. If they were to exchange their constitutions for a charter granted by the federal government, they would lose the last vestige of their original sovereignty. Nevertheless, that can be expected to happen in the course of time.

In the first era of a federal government, the citizens have more allegiance to their local community than to the political whole of which it is a part. But with time the local traditions weaken, and the individual gradually tends to regard his federal citizenship as primary. Communication and transport, commerce and cultural interchange, gradually weld the population into closer political unity. The impact of national life exerts greater pressure than local affairs.

There will be an effort to enact uniform legislation on important matters, the variety of state laws having become an obstacle to the free movement of people and goods from one state to another. There will be less and less talk of "state's rights" and "state sovereignty." The internal sovereignty of the state will gradually become a legal fiction that needs only a constitutional reform to abolish it in theory as well as in fact.

The history of the United States shows changes of this sort—and they are still in progress. The states were in the ascendant during the first half century or so. The federal government and national life have been in the ascendant ever since. Men ceased to be New Yorkers or Virginians and became Americans first.

This development will probably continue and reach the point where it is conceivable that a basic constitutional reform will be required to fit the realities of the situation. Decentralization of government may then be more efficiently performed by chartered provinces than by sovereign states. These provinces are likely to cover larger areas, regions having more economic and political significance, than the original states.

In parallel manner, a world community under federal government may, through the centuries, develop into a nonfederal world state. Such a change may be required by the need for a more effective administration of local affairs and a more realistic subdivision of the world into its economic and political localities. But it will not happen until it has been prepared for by centuries of experience with a world federation, under which local government is carried on by states retaining their internal sovereignty.

The inertia to be overcome in passing from the third to the final phase of world affairs may be as great as that involved in passing from anarchic internationalism to world federation.

6

So far as world peace is concerned we need not consider more than the difference between power politics and internationalism, on the one hand, and world government, federal or nonfederal, on the other. In that difference lies the inexorable alternative between truce and peace.

We have seen that planning for peace must take account of historic factors and stages of development, as well as of the basic principles which distinguish peace from truce. By reference to these principles we can understand the possibility of peace and the minimum conditions of its realization.

But that realization will take place in the future. That future is more or less remote. To plan well, and with due regard for the course of future developments, we must know more than the possibility of peace. We must estimate its probability.

We must dare to prophesy the length of time and the trend of events between now and the day when peace can be made. Prophecy is always hazardous. But it need not be guesswork or dreaming. It can be a sober prediction based upon the facts of history and the lines of growth which they reveal.

PART THREE

THE PROBABILITY
OF PEACE

CHAPTER 14

An Optimistic View of History

THE RISE of a philosophy of history in modern times is responsible for a new attitude toward the problem of war and peace. Our ancient and medieval ancestors, and even those who lived as recently as the eighteenth century, envisaged no future radically different from the present. They tended to emphasize permanence and repetition rather than change and progress.

The idea of progress is, perhaps, the most characteristic modern notion, and with it was born the insight that, though wars have always been, they need not always be. The idea of progress and the possibility of peace go together. With a view of history which allowed men to anticipate no fundamental improvement in human affairs, what hope could there have been for peace?

Our ancient and medieval forebears had knowledge of the past. They knew something of the course of events which had brought men to their present condition of life. But they did not know enough to perceive history as having an upward motion beyond their own day. For them the present was almost a dead end.

In a sense, their presumption was greater than ours, even if we dare to predict the future. They looked upon history as a prologue and a background for the action of their day. They seldom, if ever, conceived their own role as merely to set the stage for greater events.

To whatever extent they saw some amelioration of the human condition, they presumed to think that the struggles of the past had won their fullest victories. Civilization had climbed from crude beginnings, but at last the heights had been reached. They saw the future stretching out to the horizon on a long plateau. If they had any notion of progress at all, it belonged to the past. It was an account of things already done.

2

Knowledge of history does not suffice to make an epoch or a culture historically-minded. When I say that the ancients or the men of the Middle Ages were not historically-minded, I mean that they had no sense of the future. In its deepest formation, the historical sense is a sense of the future, and this comes only with a philosophical attitude toward history.

Herein lies the most important difference between mere history and philosophical history. History itself deals with particular facts, is concerned only with the past, or, at best, with the past as leading to the present. History become philosophical tries to find a pattern in the events, and a reason for the pattern; it searches for general trends beneath particular facts; it surveys the past in order to turn its eyes to the future.

The philosopher who concerns himself with history looks for the plot behind the story of mankind. He does not limit himself to particular epochs or cultures, to the rise of this nation or the fall of that. Beneath all the variety of cultures, beneath the manifest differences in human life at different times and places, man is the cardinal fact on which all history hinges. Man's capacities remain a constant factor throughout. The unity of human history lies in the simple fact that it is all human. This justifies the philosopher in searching for a history that has never been written —the history of the human race.

This philosophical quest is sometimes regarded as an attempt to construct a universal history. It would be more accurately described as an attempt to *universalize* history, to formulate the insights which give the multifarious details their most general significance. It resembles the effort to reduce all novels and plays to a few fundamental plots. Only it goes further. It hopes to find the one plot, the single plot which makes sense of all the episodes and incidents, the complications and catastrophes.

But history is stranger than fiction. It includes events which would be incredible in a romance or a tragedy; it takes turns which would be inartistic in a made-up story; above all, history is unfinished. It is a story which takes time to tell, and until time comes to an end, the story will not be finished. How can we find the plot of such a story? We have only been permitted to read a few chapters. How dare we presume to guess the rest?

There comes a point in any story when the reader does begin guessing. The direction of the plot has begun to reveal itself to him. His suspense consists in his anticipation of what will happen, anticipation qualified by doubt and on the alert for surprises. Until he finishes the story, the reader entertains probabilities which vary as the plot unfolds. The philosophy of history deals in such probabilities about the future.

The fact that men have begun to speculate about the course of history only within the last few hundred years shows how recently men have had enough knowledge of past changes to project their trends. Enough history has unfolded at last to warrant conjectures about the rest of the plot. To the extent that they are warranted by fact, they are not mere guesswork; but they are never more than probable. The philosopher who deals in such matters should speak with a modesty befitting his ignorance of what remains hidden.

3

In *The City of God,* Saint Augustine wrote a theology of history, an interpretation and a prophecy based on God's revelation of His plan. The four major dispensations which divided the epochs of human life had been set forth in Holy Writ. Saint Augustine did not need to rely on a great wealth of historical detail; nor did he need to discover, by *a posteriori* inference, the prevailing trends. As Mr. Arnold Toynbee remarks, "the author of this tale of two cities had a supramundane range of vision in comparison with which no appreciable difference is made by a few thousand terrestrial miles or years more or less."

But the philosopher as opposed to the theologian is a secular prophet. His range of vision corresponds to his knowledge of the facts—the revelations of the past rather than of God. That is why there were no philosophers of history before Giovanni Vico, Voltaire, and Hegel. Through no merit on their part, the men of the eighteenth and nineteenth centuries were less blind because they had *more* recorded history behind them, and *better* records of the past. They were born to an elevation in time which enlarged the prospect they could behold, as it enlarged the scope of what they could survey in retrospect.

This correspondence between prospect and retrospect suggests a principle which might be formulated as the law of historical optics.

In the science of physical optics, one of Newton's great generalizations concerned the equality between the angle of incidence and the angle of reflection. A beam of light striking a mirror at a certain angle will rebound from the mirror at an angle equal to the first. If you know the angle formed by a line drawn from your body to the mirror, you can tell where another person will have to stand in order to see your image in the mirror.

In the philosophy of history, the angle of prediction varies with the angle of retrospection. The centuries pile up an elevation on which we stand. This tower of time determines the amplitude of our view in both directions. The amount of future we can preview is roughly proportionate to the amount of past our position in time enables us to review.

The two amounts will not be equal. Our degree of foresight depends not only upon our historic elevation, but also on the clarity of our perspective. The law of historical optics is complicated by these two facts.

Compare our temporal elevation with that of Greek civilization in the fifth century B.C. At most the Greeks could look back upon five hundred years; and, with the exception of fairly recent events, their view was hazy and uncertain. They did not have enough recorded past, nor did their records reveal it clearly enough, for them to turn retrospect into prediction.

We have over three thousand years upon which to look back. With the exception of remote events, at the very edge of history, our field of vision is comparatively clear and precise, even in matters of detail. From our elevation in history, and under these atmospheric conditions, we should be able to see the outlines of at least five centuries of the future. A vague prospect of five centuries may seem small by comparison with the three thousand years needed to give us this perspective, but we should be grateful for this breadth of vision. Until fairly recently our ancestors had almost none at all.

Five hundred years of foresight are enough to yield a prediction our ancestors would not have dared to make. Within the limits of that period, we can foresee the coming of world peace and the beginning of its perpetuation. Our vision cannot discern the phases of the process by which these things will come about, but it can detect the general course of history's motion toward these ends. Within five hundred years, the *probability* that they will be achieved is great.

Not to become exalted about our sense of the future, we need only try to imagine the prospect from the tower raised by ten thousand, or even five thousand, years of recorded history. From the vantage point of that elevation posterity will find the twentieth century almost as blind as we do the ancients.

4

One other factor enters into the law of historical optics. We can use glasses to aid our vision. Our understanding of the past consists in penetrating beneath the particular facts to the general trends. Our view of the future depends, therefore, upon the philosophical principles *through which* we examine the past.

The two simplest generalizations about the motion of history are widely known. One is that history repeats itself. The other is that history moves along a straight line of development from inferior to superior conditions.

The first is a philosophy of despair; the second, of unbounded optimism. Both are too simple to be true. Neither can account for the facts to which the other appeals. Yet there are some facts to which each can appeal. In each of these generalizations, there is some truth which can be salvaged.

A more sophisticated form of the view that history is always going around in circles is the theory of recurrent cycles. According to this view, each great culture or civilization follows a general pattern of growth and decay.

A culture is like a living thing which has a growth curve—from birth and infancy through stages of maturation to full bloom, and then from maturity in stages of decline to decay and death. History repeats itself in the sense that each culture goes through the same cycle of phases. It cannot hold on to its moment of glory forever. It cannot escape its ultimate doom.

This theory was popularized by Oswald Spengler's *Decline of the West*. It has been vastly improved in scholarship by Arnold Toynbee's monumental *Study of History*. Toynbee has added many qualifications to account for all sorts of deviations from the general pattern. Nevertheless, this point of view remains inadequate because it concentrates attention on the history of separate cultures rather than on the history of the human race as a whole.

Within a particular society, each individual goes through a life cycle, and in this the men of one generation resemble the men of another. We distinguish the individual pattern of growth from the pattern of growth in the society as a whole. We do not identify the life history of individuals with the social history of the group. So we should not identify the life history of a culture with the social history of mankind.

The rise and fall of cultures is like the succession of generations in each of which men flourish and decline. The growth of a particular culture cannot be identified with the fortunes of individual men, through whose successes and failures the society in which they live slowly accumulates the increments and decrements of its own pattern of change. Neither should the current of civilization as a whole be confused with the ebb and flow of particular cultures. Even if Spengler were right, the doom of the West would not be the doom of mankind.

When we look at human history as a whole, we cannot compare its characteristic motion with the cycle of individual living things. The nearest parallel in nature to the pattern of historic change is found in the evolutionary development of the diverse forms of life. This includes atavisms and regressions as well as advances to more complex and better adjusted organisms.

Limited by environmental circumstances and by the accidents of breeding, living matter tends to develop all the potentialities latent in its germ plasm. Inferior types sometimes succeed more highly developed forms. The evolutionary picture is one of progress, but not of progress in a straight line. The ascent follows a winding and tedious path which often falters, often dips down before it climbs again.

Seen in this light, the path of history is neither a circle nor a straight line. It combines the directions of both. It goes around in the course of going upward. The motion of history follows a spiral path.

But there are many relapses and retrogressions to interrupt and qualify the slow progress upward. In its cyclical phases history often takes a turn for the worse—downward instead of upward. The most vivid image of the course of history is provided by a bent spring, some of its coils crushed into others.

This evolutionary view of history is usually attributed to the German philosopher Georg Wilhelm Friedrich Hegel and, after him, to Karl Marx. Both saw the conflict of opposing forces throughout the recorded past. They saw how, at every stage of history, some tentative resolution is reached, and some advance is made to a higher level of development, on which conflict recurs in a new form. But in their enthusiasm for the particular line of progress in which each of them was most interested, they tended to describe history as moving toward a single goal. Aiming at the universal, each allowed himself to become provincial. Hegel presents the sorry spectacle of a philosopher who could deceive himself into thinking that history had labored to give birth to the Prussian state. Marx at least suspected that communism, even the world communism of the future, might be the beginning of a new turn in human affairs.

Without passing judgment on the ideals of Hegel and Marx— false or true ideals—we can see the truth they failed to disengage from the prepossessions of their own political or economic views. That truth consists in understanding history as the working out of man's potentialities for social and cultural development.

The general pattern of social evolution is affected by all sorts of contingent circumstances which prevent it from moving in a straight line. It includes errors and failures as well as successes. Men have the capacity to brutalize and degrade their life as well as to humanize and civilize it. Nevertheless, in the course of time, the achievements of progress do become more stable and secure. Above all, human history, unlike natural evolution, must be viewed as only partly determined by physical factors. For good or for evil, it also represents the work of man's free will.

Both Hegel and Marx tended to overlook the contingencies in history, and to minimize or deny the role of individual freedom in the making of social choices. Both made necessity their idol, in whose worship men must immolate their will. Man's only freedom lies in recognizing his fate, in accepting the fatalism of the wave of the future.

5

We are saved from these errors by a purified version of the fundamental truth that history is a tragicomedy.

Its plot, in so far as we can discern it in the unfinished story, leads us to anticipate success for man's deepest aspirations, a success achieved against all sorts of obstacles by the persistence of man's free striving. As a fallen-away Marxist has recently observed, there are heroes in history as well as social forces.

At times the obstacles are overwhelming; at times man's will weakens, compromises, or succumbs. There are the tragic moments of bitter failure and dismal ruin when no hope seems left. Yet it is always reborn. The struggle is renewed. Achievements lost are rewon, and new progress is made. History is a heartbreaking success story.

This optimistic view of history was held by Immanuel Kant. He developed it in a book which has significant connections with his later work on *Perpetual Peace*. Ten years earlier, in 1784, he wrote a treatise entitled *Idea of a Universal History from a Cosmopolitan Point of View*. Its fundamental thesis was that human capacities are "destined to unfold themselves completely in the course of time, and in accordance with the end to which they are adapted."

The attainment of the highest level of civilization is the goal of the race, as the attainment of happiness is the goal of the individual life. But whereas the individual may fail to achieve the full good of his being, the race will succeed in fulfilling the promise of nature's endowment.

Human civilization is a work of reason and of freedom, not of instinct. Since men use their freedom for evil as well as for good, the motion of history will not be in a line of steady progress. The struggle of many generations is needed for the predominance of good and for the increments of progress by which the human race gradually perfects its civilization.

Kant saw that the perfection of civilization depended upon the establishment of a civil society, the political constitution of which embodied the justice needed to fulfill man's social nature. He also saw that the internal well-being of particular societies is profoundly affected by their external relations with one another. The state of war between nations continually works against the tendency toward civilization within communities. Universal and perpetual peace is, therefore, the goal toward which man's striving tends.

Here Kant's optimism was seriously qualified. He looked upon lasting world peace as an unattainable ideal. It has practical significance only in the sense that it regulates the direction of our efforts. It remains a goal, in that progress is determined by motion toward it, but history is doomed to fall short of its realization.

I think we are in a position to be more optimistic than Kant. Though less than two centuries have elapsed since his day, a slightly superior historic elevation has altered the prospect within our range of vision. What for Kant could be no more than a regulative ideal has become for us a practicable objective.

But the fundamental basis for optimism remains the same. Optimism rests upon a philosophy of history which interprets the past in the light of two fundamental beliefs—a belief in the beneficence of nature or in the goodness of Divine Providence and a belief in human freedom as able to choose between good and evil. These two beliefs are not incompatible. A man can say, "There but for the grace of God go I," and also act on the principle that God helps those who help themselves.

Long-run pessimism is incompatible with religious belief. It is incompatible with the religion of the naturalist; how much more so with faith in God.

Short-run optimism fails to take account of human freedom. Nature does not necessitate every turn in the course of history; nor does Divine Providence exclude the individual's free choice between good and evil. The individual man is free to work with or against his nature, with or against God. Yet, since freedom is part of his nature, since he enjoys freedom under God, it is not an unlimited freedom man exercises. It is a freedom conditioned by natural circumstances or by God's will.

Believing in freedom and in freedom's destiny, the philosophical optimist neither despairs of the future nor relies on the present. He thinks there is a tide in the affairs of men, but one that is deflected by all sorts of unpredictable eddies. He thinks that men themselves exert a decisive pressure at every turn in their own fortunes.

He believes in progress without resigning himself to any wave of the future. He lives in hope that history will march forward, but not without fear that it will suffer many temporary retreats. Above all, philosophical optimism does not make any concrete predictions without the benefit of history. That is why men who share the same fundamental belief in progress will, according to the historic outlook of their time, differ in their projection of the future.

What they know of the past, how they understand the present, determine what they anticipate. That is why we differ from Kant in our concrete image of the future. That is why our posterity will see other goals *beyond perpetual peace,* goals of which we cannot even dream.

CHAPTER 15

The Future of Democracy

THE PREDICTION of world peace within five hundred years acquires its probability from the facts of past history and from the emergence of certain tendencies in the reality of the present. Apart from the philosophical tenets of optimism, no set of facts might encourage such a prediction. But even with an optimistic frame of mind, we must still go to the facts to estimate probabilities and to talk in terms of eventualities which have a date.

Considering particular communities rather than the world as a whole, we have seen that the motion from despotism to constitutional government, and beyond that to democracy, is a progressive development of local peace. We have seen the bearing of such progress on the future formation of a world civil order.

It may be objected, however, that no such progress has occurred, that despotism is just as rampant in the world today as it ever was.

No one can deny that large portions of humanity still live under despotism. Despotism may have changed its face through the centuries, but its essential character has remained the same—an absolute dominion by some over others who are subjected to their will and unprotected against their violence.

No one can deny that despotism still exists. But once *most men* suffered in its toils. Today a larger number of men than ever before enjoy the happy auspices of constitutional government. And within the last century, constitutions have been slowly amended in the direction of democracy. Earlier than that not even the best republics were legally democratic, much less so in actual practice.

Though we have seen constitutional government threatened by a particularly virulent form of despotism, we have also witnessed its strength in self-defense. When the latest reversion to absolutism is squelched, there is some chance that constitutional government will spread to lands where it has never existed, or where it has never prevailed long enough to take firm root. If the United Nations lose, juridical institutions have less chance of surviving anywhere, and more chance, if they win, of extending their domain. Constitutional government in itself is far from being the optimal condition, but it is the condition prerequisite to further developments—political democracy and a just economy.

2

There has been political and economic progress during the last twenty-five hundred years. This truth is not altered by the fact that atavisms have also occurred, that advances have been punctuated by temporary defeats and throwbacks.

Who would dare to say that the future of slavery, even in its milder forms, looks the same today as it did in the fifth century B.C., or even in the fifth or fifteenth century A.D.? The struggle against chattel slavery has slowly prospered: first, by legal protections to ameliorate the slave's condition; then by the spread of Stoic and Christian ideas which regarded slavery as unnatural but necessary under certain circumstances; then by the unqualified condemnation of slavery in principle, accompanied by efforts to abolish slave trading and slave markets; finally, by the actual abolition of the institution in an ever-increasing number of communities.

True, within our generation men have lived in slavery under the tyranny of totalitarian regimes; but today a large part of the world condemns the German idea as barbaric, especially the brutality of its labor battalions and its concentration camps. Twenty-five centuries ago, and even less, civilized as well as barbaric communities deprived countless men of human status. The abolition of bondage had not yet become the first credential of civilization.

True, even in the so-called democracies, a milder and subtler form of slavery is still the lot of the proletariat. But peonage and industrial exploitation are not chattel slavery. Furthermore, the abolition of these injustices has become for us another milestone of civilization.

3

The story of political progress is more complicated. It contains many more scenes of defeat, many more episodes of reversion and degradation.

In twenty-five hundred years the battle for constitutional government has been fought many times, and lost almost as often as it has been won. But each time that it has been lost, the efforts which men will make for liberty and justice have brought about a rebirth of constitutionalism; and in each new incarnation the principle of constitutionality has been better understood and embodied with greater practical wisdom—hence more firmly established and more surely protected against dissolution from within, if not from external assault.

Each time that constitutional government has emerged again after an eclipse, it has found new ways to safeguard itself. It has profited from the experience of its weakness against undisciplined force. It has learned how to protect its justice by efficiency, how to support duly constituted authority by sanctions.

Most important of all, it has spread from isolated spots to cover large areas of the earth's surface. Twenty-five hundred years ago, constitutionalism was nothing but a revolutionary movement. It had to fight to begin, and fight to continue, in a world of despots. Today, though it is still fighting, and still menacing despotism with its reforms, constitutional government has become an established order within which further revolutions can take place.

There is no longer any chance of stamping it out entirely, as the Persian kings almost succeeded in doing, or as the Macedonian conquerors did. And now there is a chance that despotism can be completely extirpated. Less than a century ago, Lincoln dared to prophesy with calm assurance that constitutional government "shall not perish from the earth." In a funeral oration with which Lincoln's is often compared, Pericles, speaking in 431 B.C., could exalt the Athenians with the nobility of their civil life, but he could not have persuaded them that it had more than a fighting chance to endure.

4

Constitutional government was the great invention of the Greek cities. All its rudimentary notions and basic institutions were the work of Greek political genius. The conception of citizenship as the primary political office and of all other public offices as open to citizens, by lot or by election, was one of the great seminal ideas in the world's history.

With all due respect to Confucius, it is a much more important idea than that of government by music and courtesy. It is the one idea of government which properly fits the political nature of man.

Though it originated in one small historic culture, it belongs to all men everywhere, in the Orient as well as in the Occident. The Greeks, with their contempt or pity for the barbarians, may not have understood this, but the American constitutionalists centuries later proclaimed the fundamental truths of good government with a deep feeling for their universal significance.

Because constitutional government was so new and strange a thing, so radical a departure from all that had gone before and from everything in the surrounding world, the Greeks were naturally impressed by the difference between themselves and the peoples they called "barbarian." Herodotus, the historian of the war between the Greeks and the Persians, could not help but betray the political self-consciousness of a Greek writing about the customs and institutions of people who still lived under kings or despots. And Aristotle looked back upon Homeric civilization as a semibarbaric period when even the Hellenes still lived under kings—the absolute dominion of a tribal chieftain.

Glorious in its brief day, Greek constitutionalism did not flourish long. Tainted by the imperialism of the leading cities after they had repelled the Persian, weakened by almost continuous war on the islands and mainland of the Hellenic world, and torn by revolutions resulting from the conflict for power between the wealthy oligarchs and the laboring classes, constitutional government had little strength left to resist Philip of Macedon.

Even apart from Philip, it might have succumbed to the civil strife for which constitutional remedies had not yet been found. In any case, the world of Alexander's empire saw little trace of it left.

5

This cycle of rise and fall is repeated many times in the next two thousand years.

The Romans expelled the Tarquin kings, and replaced their tyranny with a republic which embodied the fundamental principles of Greek constitutionalism, but which was vastly superior in its legal devices and its institutional structure. The old fight between rich and poor continued. The Roman Republic could not entirely avoid the ordeal of civil war, but its political parties could often compete for power without overthrowing the constitution. The institutions of the senate and the tribunate afforded means for political debate which elevated factionalism above the level of mob violence.

The imperialism of republican Rome paved the way for an imperialism which killed the republic. After a brief century or two, the swing back to absolutism occurred again. For a short time, the Roman emperors pretended to retain the statutes and customs of the republic, as if they were discharging the duties of a constitutional office. After that the Caesars recognized no limits to their power. All that remained of the constitution was the legal fiction that the people had transferred all their law-making authority to the emperor. The senate became a rubber stamp.

Constitutional government does not arise again until it reappears transformed by the feudal character of medieval life.

The feudal system involved reciprocal rights and duties as between inferior and superior at every level. It also gave custom, the customs of the manor or of the realm, the authority of law, binding alike upon ruler and subject. To this extent, the medieval kingdom had a constitutional aspect.

When custom could not keep pace with social and economic change, representative assemblies or parliaments became at least advisory to the king in the enactment of laws. Yet the king retained absolute power in the executive sphere of government, in the administration of internal as well as foreign affairs; and by his appointment or discharge of judges, he controlled the judicial process as well.

This mixed character of the medieval kingdom is well described by two great commentators on English law, Bracton and Fortescue. They speak of it as "royal *and* political government," using the word "royal" to signify the absolute power of the king in administration, and the word "political" to signify the constitutional aspect of customary law and legislative assembly. It was not constitutional monarchy in the nineteenth-century sense of a true republic which retained the legal fiction of a throne.

Toward the end of the Middle Ages, the only pure form of constitutional government existed in the free, and extremely wealthy, commercial cities. Outside the political sphere, the universities and the monastic orders also operated under charters or rules which were models of constitutional practice.

From these areas or aspects of medieval life, constitutionalism might have grown and spread. But it was to meet another setback by a new revival of despotism on the part of kings.

6

Beginning in the fifteenth century, and with increasing success in the sixteenth and seventeenth, the leading dynasties of

Europe nullified the medieval limitations upon the crown, and arrogated to themselves the absolute power which the Roman emperors had seized. Using the fictions of Roman law and speaking the language of "divine right" provided by their apologists, they strove once more to turn back the clock.

Absolute monarchy succeeded in reducing constitutional practices to empty forms, in such countries as England, and in effacing them entirely elsewhere.

Once more the clock would not stay turned back. With Cromwell's rebellion in England and with the much more significant, though bloodless, revolution of 1688, the revival of constitutional government occurs. In the eighteenth and nineteenth centuries, the struggle occurs in France and is won and lost several times. It occurs in the North and South American colonies of the European empires, and here, for the most part, republican institutions, once adopted, have prevailed. It occurs throughout central Europe in 1848 with varying degrees of success. As late as 1905 it spreads to Russia, with the first Duma as some check upon the absolute power of the czars.

By the beginning of the twentieth century, constitutional government, whether in the pure form of a republic or in the modified form of limited monarchy, had been adopted by most of the civilized nations of the world. At the end of the First World War, thrones tottered and republics multiplied. But we know sadly and too well how soon that bright new world tarnished and spoiled.

Only in some countries was constitutionalism firmly rooted in the traditions and spirit of the people. Only in some countries had the justice and efficiency of constitutional government been perfected to the point where due process of law afforded peaceful means for social and economic change.

Elsewhere constitutional government had not yet succeeded in bringing the people to political maturity; nor was it able, without this maturity, to deal effectively with internal disorders.

The anarchy and inequity of the international situation aggravated the difficulties and, fusing foreign and domestic policy, opened the way for the latest reversion to despotism—to fascism, the dictatorship of a faction and its leader.

Yet who would fear to predict that constitutional government will gain new ground, as well as regain old, during the next few centuries? Who cannot see, in its long and checkered career, the sign that it will continue to spread until it covers the earth? Observing that with each revival its strength increases, who would deny that the day will come when constitutional government can flourish without interludes of despotism?

7

The second great step in the world's political progress did not begin until the nineteenth century.

Though the rights of suffrage were discussed as early as the seventeenth century (for example, by a group in Cromwell's ranks who called themselves "the Levelers"), the movement to extend the franchise did not effect significant constitutional reforms until the middle of the last century. As a matter of fact, there are today only a few countries in the world which are constitutionally democratic—in which universal suffrage exists *by law* and in which privileged political classes have been at least *legally,* if not actually, abolished.

Apart from the principle of constitutionality in government, democracy is impossible. But the reverse is not true. Constitutional government which is not democratic is quite possible and has, in fact, been the best form of government that men have known and fought for in all but the last century of political history. In fighting to defend constitutional government today, we seek not merely to preserve a political heritage, but to bequeath one which will be the beginning of a new fortune in human affairs. We have reached a turning point in history as epochal as that one in the remote past when men first fought for constitutional government.

As a form of government, democracy belongs to the future. It has so recently taken shape in the affairs and in the minds of men that it is still but a shadow of what it will become. Moreover, it is a form of government which will not exist in fact until social and economic, and even cultural, changes that have not yet occurred take place. Though he is the Vice-President of a government which operates under a written constitution which is *almost* perfectly democratic, Mr. Henry Wallace speaks of the century of the common man—the democratic century—as a thing of the future. It has been well said that "the reason men feel that the democratic world must survive is not that it is perfectly realized, but that it is scarcely realized at all."

Even in those countries in which democracy has been constitutionally enacted, it is still more legal than operative, more in the letter of the constitution than in the spirit of its performance. Economic disadvantages, racial and religious discriminations, the privilege of wealth and position, inequality of opportunity, and educational failures, all these things make real democracy a thing of the future.

Yet who can doubt that democracy will be realized where it has already been instituted, and instituted where constitutional reforms are still needed? There is a new struggle in the world today, a new striving which reinforces even as it transforms the age-old effort to set up and preserve constitutional government. From the point of view of the common man, the defense of constitutional government now involves higher stakes than ever before, because now as never before the promise of democracy, whether in its bare beginning or in its progressive realization, means justice for all, not for some.

By its very nature, constitutionalism tends toward the legal adoption of democracy. Its fundamental notions of citizenship, of political liberty, of equality before the law, cannot be defended as applying to some, not all, men. Once these notions are understood, "the people" who possess inalienable rights cannot be restricted to any portion of the population less than the whole.

For the same reason that constitutional government rather than despotism fits the political nature of men everywhere, despite their differences in race or culture, democracy must perfect the constitutions of all governments. "The people" must become coextensive with mankind.

Wherever and whenever democracy becomes legally enacted, it will begin to assert itself in practice. The obstacles it must overcome to realize itself are many and difficult. But everything in the history of man's economic, social, and political emancipation justifies confidence in the people's ultimate conquest of the people's rights.

8

The spread of constitutional government and, more than that, the gradual democratization of the world are phases in the progress toward lasting world-wide peace. These things are inextricably connected.

The international anarchy, the imperialism it permits, the wars it necessitates, the armaments it requires, the banditry of the cartels it cannot control, the secret diplomacy and the deceits of foreign policy with which it demoralizes domestic politics—all these things weaken constitutional government, wherever it exists, and impede the growth of democracy.

The institution of world peace and the beginning of a world republic will come together or they will not come at all. The improvement of world peace and the democratization of that republic will follow parallel courses.

Either the history of the last twenty-five hundred years has no meaning at all or its meaning indicates that men can do what must be done to complete the progress so far accomplished. The growth of world peace is inseparable from the political developments which history makes probable in the next five hundred years.

CHAPTER 16

Progress Toward Peace

IN THE FIELD of political history, there seem to be two laws of growth. One formulates the tendency of *political development* from despotism to constitutional government and, under the auspices of constitutional government, from oligarchy to democracy. The other formulates the tendency of *political expansion* from communities small in area and sparse in population to states which embrace vast territories and populations, heterogeneous as well as numerous.

Both of these laws are merely probable generalizations from the facts of history. Both have predictive significance.

They signify the probability of further changes which will continue in the direction of the historic tendencies already observed. They signify the probability of peace, predicting its event as dated by the time it will take to reach the next stages of growth.

That time cannot be precisely estimated. Unforeseen contingencies and the use men make of their freedom may either speed or delay the event. Men may have to adjust to environmental conditions for a time but, unlike other animals, they can usually master circumstances and adjust their environment to themselves.

Any prediction we make must, therefore, be in round figures. The best we can do is to venture a maximum and a minimum estimate of the time. From a practical point of view, it is not crucially important whether five hundred years is the maximum or minimum. What is important practically is that we understand the present century as a turning point.

Five hundred years is an intelligible period of time. It is not, like infinity or even fifty thousand years, a span totally beyond our comprehension, except for astronomical or geological reckoning. The special characteristics of the present in which we live began to take shape five centuries ago. The shape of things five centuries hence may be shadowy now, but the shadows we perceive are being cast by events in our lifetime.

In addition to the hazards of prediction, discussion of the future involves other pitfalls we must avoid. Philosophizing about history so readily becomes a speculative enterprise divorced from practical interests. We assume that it emancipates us from history.

Whether we believe in progress or are pessimists, we sometimes assume an Olympian detachment and survey the course of human events throughout the whole of time—*as if* we were not human, living at a particular time, and engaged in turning the course of events this way or that. We are men, not gods. We cannot see things under the aspect of eternity, much less can we act as if we did. The historic elevation from which we survey the past is not an ivory tower, but a promontory from which we must leap into the future.

Discerning the laws of historic growth enables us to understand our present situation. It helps us to participate intelligently and purposefully in the struggles of our day. Their outcome will hasten or postpone events we can foresee.

But neither our understanding nor our foresight entitles us to remain on the side lines. Along the path of history there are no innocent bystanders.

2

The two laws of historic growth—the law of political *development* and the law of political *expansion*—do not stand in the same relation to the coming of peace.

The development of constitutional government and of democracy has a bearing on the degree of peace which obtains in any political community. When a world community exists, the protection of its peace from civil strife will depend upon the character of its political and economic institutions.

But progress in the development of these institutions within particular communities does not by itself signify the emergence of a world community. That event is forecast by the historic tendency of local communities to expand.

Throughout history communities have grown quantitatively, as well as improved qualitatively. This law of political expansion bears on the probability that a world community will be formed, just as the other law of political development bears on the probability that world government will be so instituted that civil strife can be minimized or prevented.

We hope for a peace that will be universal and perpetual. Its universality will result from achieving the natural limit of political expansion—a single community embracing the world. Its durability will be assured to whatever extent world government is just and efficient.

3

The law of political expansion can be expressed in terms of degrees of anarchy. The amount of anarchy in the world is measured by the number of independent political communities. Relative to the total population of the world at any time, the number of independent communities will be correlated with their average size. Though the earth may be more populous at one time than another, the number of separate communities may be less.

Let us take the history of one continent to exemplify this process. In the course of European history, the degree of anarchy has varied from period to period. One need only turn the pages of an historical atlas to have a moving picture of the waves of expansion as the political boundary lines shift from map to map. But here, as in the case of the qualitative developments, progress does not occur in a straight line.

We are not concerned for the moment whether larger communities are formed by conquest or by union, whether they are dissolved by rebellion from within or aggression from without. The point to be observed is that in the course of centuries larger communities have been formed out of smaller ones, only to be again broken into fragments, and again re-formed along new lines.

When the Roman Empire reached its widest extent, anarchy had been reduced to a minimum. When it crumbled, the European world fractured into a multitude of kingdoms and principalities. The empire of Charlemagne, later the empire of the Hohenstaufens, and still later the Austro-Spanish dominions of the Habsburgs reassembled some of the pieces for brief periods.

So long as feudalism persisted, the anarchy of Europe could not be substantially reduced except by the temporary overlordship of powerful men or dynasties. The Holy Roman Empire of the Franks or of the Germans was never an international organization. At its best, it was a suprafeudal confederacy.

The frequency and character of war vary with the degree of anarchy in any era. One further condition must be added: if independent communities are *totally isolated* from one another, anarchy does not place them in a state of war which intermittently turns to fighting. But in the European world, no geographical barriers produced such total isolation. Economic factors, whether in the form of commerce or plunder, the desire for land or resources, added motives for conquest to the opportunities provided by the geographical situation. When anarchy is in the ascendant, the number of relatively simultaneous wars may increase, but these wars will be local and trivial.

At the height of feudalism, many wars were going on almost all the time, but they were fights between neighboring landowners—between local barons and counts, supported by their own retinues, the friends they could solicit, the mercenaries they could engage. When the brigandage of the robber barons turns into the dynastic struggles between kings or emperors who have accumulated vast dominions, the wars become more extensive and more serious. The larger the political units which predominate in any area, the larger the wars and the more drastic their depredations.

In view of all these facts, it may well be asked how the law of political expansion points toward peace. On the one hand, political communities seem to shrink or break up as often as they enlarge or amalgamate. On the other hand, the gravity, if not the frequency, of wars seems to increase as the anarchy diminishes.

There are two answers to the question. On the second count, we must remember that nothing but the abolition of anarchy can prevent war in any area. On the first count, we must look beneath the apparent seesaw motion from small to large to small again, in order to find how the underlying tendency toward political expansion prevails in the long run.

4

At the beginning of political theory, Aristotle described the first stages of political expansion. He went back to the primitive beginnings of the city-states which seemed to him the ultimate in political growth.

The primitive social unit was, according to Aristotle, the family. The family group must be large enough to provide for the daily wants of its members. He refers to the members of a family group as "companions of the cupboard" or "companions of the manger."

When several families unite, a larger community is formed which Aristotle calls the village and which we would call a tribe. The village or tribe is said to be "a colony from the family" in the sense that intermarriage and consanguinity bind its members together. It is "composed of children and grandchildren suckled with the same milk." Because of this fact, despotism is the natural form of government in the village community. Just as the paterfamilias is a despot, so the headman of the village or the tribal chieftain rules the enlarged family group in a paternal manner.

The economic aspect of village life differs from that of the isolated family by reason of its larger population and greater capacity for division of labor. The village is able to provide for more than the daily needs of its members. It can accumulate stores. It can organize in advance for defense or aggression.

Aristotle had in mind the sort of society which is described in the Homeric poems. Such kings as Agamemnon or Menelaus or Ulysses were tribal chieftains who ruled small villages and went to war with small bands of personal retainers. The difference between these petty principalities and the great cities of Athens and Sparta, Syracuse and Carthage, must have seemed to Aristotle a tremendous increase in the magnitude of civil life—as tremendous as to us seems the difference between the little Saxon kingdom of Alfred the Great in one corner of the British Isles and the United Kingdom of today.

The third step in political expansion is that from village or tribe to city-state. The city-state was formed by the amalgamation of villages or tribes. Aristotle called this community simply a "city," meaning thereby the truly political community, large enough "to be nearly or quite self-sufficing" and able to develop the arts and sciences which elevate human civilization above the animal plane.

The Greek word *polis,* which means "city," is also the root of the word "political," which signifies a new departure in government. Political government, the government of a city, is naturally constitutional, whereas family and tribal government is naturally despotic or paternal. Living in a city and under constitutional government, men are able to realize their political natures by becoming citizens, which means participation in *civic* affairs.

When we refer to the Greek cities as "city-states," we do so in order to contrast the *size* of these political communities with the *size* of the nation-states in the modern world. Both the ancient cities and the modern nations are *states* in the sense that they are truly political communities, not families or tribes, even when despotism temporarily degrades the quality of their civil life.

The Old Testament history of the Jews gives us another example of this line of growth. The patriarchs, Abraham, Isaac, and Jacob, were the heads of large family groups which later developed into tribal units under the sons of Jacob. After their exodus from Egypt, these tribes united in the Promised Land to form the larger community which ultimately divided into the kingdoms of Israel and Judah.

The kingdom of Judah was a city-kingdom, with its life centered in Jerusalem. Similarly, the peoples against which the Jews fought—the Philistines, the Chaldeans, the Assyrians—belonged to the city-kingdoms of Tyre, Babylon, Nineveh. Even the great kingdom of Persia consisted of a large agricultural domain dominated by a single metropolis, Sardis.

Yet another example of this stage of growth is the development of the city of Rome from the tribes who lived upon the Seven Hills. Even after the Romans conquered the Etruscans and the Sabines, the kingdom or the republic, which had extended its power northward and southward over the whole peninsula, remained a city-state. It was no less a city-state than Athens had been at the height of its imperial expansion.

5

These facts show us that the mere amount of territory ruled and the gross size of the population involved do not by themselves define a stage in the expansion of political life. It is necessary to consider the economic characteristics and the way in which the political life is concentrated or diffused.

In the agrarian and commercial, but nonindustrial, societies of the ancient world, political life was concentrated in one or, at most, a few great cities. To be exiled from the metropolis, to be rusticated, was to suffer political ostracism.

In this sense, we can regard the Roman Empire at its greatest expansion as a city-empire. Counting both its slaves and subject peoples, as well as Roman citizens, this empire was many times larger in area and population than such states as Belgium or Holland, Portugal or Switzerland, are today. Yet, with or without colonial empires, they are nation-states and Rome was always a city-state both before and after it acquired a vast empire.

In the transition from family to village, from tribe to city, and from city to city-empire, the enlargement of the community did not occur as the result of deliberate decision to obtain the advantages of greater size and more efficient division of labor. Aristotle describes the process as if that were the only factor. It may have played a part, especially when larger communities were formed by voluntary union; but, for the most part, war and conquest brought about the consolidation of peoples.

Family units living in proximity to one another and competing for subsistence on the same terrain engaged in wars of aggression or defense. Such family wars could not be avoided until families ceased to be independent units. But then tribal wars supplanted them, inevitably occurring for the same reasons.

When by conquest or agreement the tribes formed cities, inter-city wars resulted from the anarchy of neighboring cities whose affairs brought them into conflict with one another. This is followed by wars between the great city-empires, such as the Peloponnesian War between Athens and Sparta and Corinth, each of which dominated a confederacy, or such as the Punic wars between Rome and Carthage.

Thus the type of war changes with the character of the political units involved. What matters here is not whether they are internally organized as kingdoms or republics, whether the people live under despots or under constitutions. What matters is the stage of political expansion that has been reached. The size and gravity of the wars are determined by the economic, social, and geographic structure of communities, not by their forms of government.

That is why Thucydides began his account of the Pelopon-

nesian War with the statement that it was "more worthy of relation than any which had preceded it." He did not even make
an exception in favor of the war between the Greek cities and
the Persian kings. After reviewing the events of remote antiquity,
and even those which immediately preceded the war, he came to
the conclusion that, before the struggle between the city-empires,
"there was nothing on a great scale, either in war or in other
matters."

For the same reason that the city-states of Greece were new
and remarkable political formations, the war between them was
an event of unprecedented magnitude and importance.

6

Within the three thousand years of western history which we
are considering, only two more stages of development follow the
rise of city-states and their empires. Of these two, the first is
partly a reversion to more primitive conditions.

The feudal organization of society resembles the tribe more
than it does the city. But in part the feudal system contained
within itself the seeds of the national state. It is this latter development which carries us to a new level of political expansion.

If we regard the feudal period as a transitional phase in the
process of political growth, then there is only one stage beyond
the city—the nation-state and, correlated with it, the nation-
empire.

Under the feudal system, the social hierarchy was built upon
an agrarian economy naturally rooted in the land. Political rank
and power, as well as the complex network of allegiances, could
not be separated from landownership. The feudal manor or
demesne was the primary political, as well as economic, unit.
Under these circumstances we find the maximum decentralization of political life.

Feudal warfare naturally took a form which differed from
territorial conquest in the ancient world. As one baron or count

overcame another in local contests, he not only enlarged his landholdings, but became the feudal overlord who could claim the allegiance of new vassals. It would then be these great peers who engaged in conflict with one another.

Some of the early medieval kings were merely feudal overlords who had gained supremacy and acknowledged no one in their immediate neighborhood as a peer or a superior. In other cases, the king had political authority without real feudal power. The early kings of France owned little land outside their ancestral estates in the county of Paris.

The development was complicated by foreign conquests, such as the Danish and Norman conquests of England, or the Saxon and Hohenstaufen invasions of central and southern Europe, not to mention the incursions of the Saracens and later the Turks which required the consolidation of defensive forces.

Still another factor in this development was the survival of kingdoms and dynasties which traced their lineage back to the dismemberment of the Roman Empire in the west, such as the Ostrogothic kingdom of Lombardy, or the kingdom of Burgundy.

Because the same factors were not operative everywhere at the same time or to the same degree, the rise of nation-states did not occur throughout Europe in any one characteristic manner, and certainly not simultaneously. The process of national unification took place by conquest and by dynastic marriages which affected the succession, by the merging of principalities and by the struggle of kings against feudal prerogatives which dwarfed their authority and sapped their power.

It took place earlier in England than in France and Spain, and it took place as late as the nineteenth century in the case of Germany and Italy. City-states had survived longer in northern Italy than elsewhere on the continent. They exist nowhere today.

In some cases, such as England and France, the process of unification occupied many centuries. In other cases, such as Italy, the event was consummated in a brief period, though it had been the object of aspiration for three hundred years.

In most cases, the unification was accomplished under the auspices of royal government, but the federation of the Swiss cantons and the formation of the United Netherlands were constitutional unions. Just as it made no difference to the characteristic unity of the city-state whether it existed under a despot or a constitution, so it made no difference to the typical formation of the nation-state whether it was a kingdom or a republic.

7

The various national states which now exist have had quite diverse origins. They differ in extent of territory, in the character of their population, and in their forms of government. Yet we should be able to find what is common to all of them in so far as all embody a new stage of political expansion beyond the city-state. The study of a single example—the unification of Great Britain—may help us to discover the difference between city and nation.

After the Roman civilization receded, the Britons remained in approximately the same tribal condition in which the Roman conquerors found them. They offered feeble resistance to the first English invaders who came to settle and who succeeded in displacing the original inhabitants.

The Anglo-Saxons landed on the island in A.D. 449. For the next four centuries, the settled part of the island was divided among a half-dozen kingdoms—of Kent, Wessex, Mercia, Northumbria, Essex, East Anglia. Among these there was almost continual warfare until, in the ninth century, they were united under Wessex by the leadership of Alfred the Great, who played, in the English development, a role similar to that of Charlemagne in the French.

During the next century, this unity was harassed by provincial revolts, border warfare, and the beginnings of the Danish invasions. After the Danes had conquered all the English lands, the Danish dominion was rent by civil strife between rival claimants to the throne; and it was under these circumstances that, in the eleventh century, William the Conqueror made himself king of all England.

The power of the Norman kings subdued the English feudatories and accomplished national unification much sooner than did the Capetian kings of France after the dismemberment of Charlemagne's empire. In the Frankish lands, the feudal powers and prerogatives of the great duchies and counties gave the king little more than nominal sovereignty outside of his own estates.

The English nation-state existed in the eleventh century. Its development for the next seven hundred years consisted in the gradual extension of its territories, largely by conquest, though in one exceptional instance by an act of union. Ignoring the wars of the Plantagenet kings to increase or consolidate their French dominions, we must observe the slow process by which all the peoples on the British Isles came to live under a single United Kingdom.

At the time that the Norman-English people had formed a nation, the Welsh and Cornish, the Irish and Scottish, were still living in tribal or clan formations. Warfare on the Norman marches bordering Wales led in the twelfth century to an invasion of that western territory, but its spirit of clannish independence took five hundred years to overcome. Conquest and revolt alternated during these centuries.

The invasion of Ireland was also begun in the twelfth century, but not until the Tudor effort in the sixteenth century did military conquest succeed. As we know, the pacification of Ireland and its incorporation into the United Kingdom were never really accomplished.

The wars between the English and the Scotch began in 1296, but the English never gained more than a temporary advantage for many hundred years. Not until 1707 did the English and Scotch form a single nation by a constitutional act of union.

Even the peace thus established continued for some time to be threatened by the clannish separatism of the highlands. Nevertheless, the least degree of peace did not begin to exist in the limited area of the larger of the British islands until the national unification was completed.

Though it began later, and fought against different obstacles, the national unification of France was accomplished sooner by Henry of Navarre's suppression of such great independent estates as Burgundy and Brittany, Anjou and Provence. That occurred toward the end of the fifteenth century. In the next two centuries, national solidarity was perfected by the work of Richelieu under Louis XIII and by the supremacy of Louis XIV.

In Germany and Italy national unification was long delayed by a variety of factors—most important of which were the survival of feudal divisions in the German lands, and the jealousy and warfare between the city-states of Italy. On the continent only the Swiss Federation begun in 1291 represents a continuous national unity from the Middle Ages to the present day.

8

In what does national unity consist? How does the nation-state or national state differ from the city-state?

Both are properly called "states" as opposed to tribes or families. Both are political communities, whether they exist as kingdoms or as republics. Difference in form of govenment, such as that between despotism and constitutionalism, will not distinguish them.

Both can become empires. Far-flung colonial possessions and dominion over subject peoples are not peculiar to either.

The difference lies in the kind of political unity which characterizes the nation-state. It combines centralized government with diffusion of political life and with subordinate decentralized agencies. The best way to grasp this unity is by reference to its origin and gradual formation.

Almost all of the great modern nations came into being and grew by overcoming feudalism. Feudalism naturally tended in the opposite direction—toward the anarchy of territorial division and the extreme of political decentralization. But feudalism also harbored another tendency from which nationalism emerged. Though himself a feudal lord, the king at the apex of the feudal hierarchy gradually became the pivot of political life. *Decentralized* in so far as it was *feudal,* and *centralized* in so far as it was a *kingdom,* the feudal kingdom was the modern nation in embryo.

Yet the spirit of locality was unquestionably the dominant spirit of feudalism. Local customs and local magnates prevailed. There was often no common law or single government even for peoples speaking the same language, belonging to the same racial stock, and having cultural traditions sufficiently similar to provide a natural basis for community.

It happened, therefore, that in overcoming feudalism, the rising nations also succumbed to it. They could not help incorporating its most characteristic trait. Though national kingdoms set up centralized governments which abolished the independence or external sovereignty of the feudal domains, they did not wipe out the feudal divisions or destroy the institutions of local government. They subordinated these. They modified them. But they retained them in fact and principle, as part of their own organization.

In consequence, national government is both centralized and decentralized. It is concentrated, but it is also diffused throughout the entire territory of the nation, by means of a hierarchy of local subdivisions into provinces and departments, counties and towns. In this hierarchy we have the vestige of decaying feudalism, of feudalism transmuted into national unity.

The political life of the nation-state is diffused throughout the entire realm. It is not concentrated in a single city, governing outlying provinces. The center of a nation's political life is institutional, not geographic. The central government may have its headquarters in a single capital city, but rural sections and small towns live under that central government as much as the residents of the capital. The residents of the capital live under local government as much as all other inhabitants of the nation. Centralized and decentralized government belong to both.

It is also true that the growing nations tended to include populations diverse in racial stock and heterogeneous in culture. Almost all the great nations—England, France, Spain, and Russia, no less than the United States—have been melting pots, having to assimilate the customs and dialects of conquered areas in the course of their enlargement.

But this is a secondary fact. The process of assimilation could not have been accomplished apart from the counterprocess of political diffusion. Though modern nations usually have a common language (not always so, as the case of Switzerland or Russia makes evident), and though they have wrought a certain cultural homogeneity out of diversified materials, the primary unity is political.

That political unity, by which the nation is distinguished from the city-state, results from the combination of centralized and decentralized government. We find this true even in the case of the United States, as well as other colonial establishments which have become independent nations, despite the fact that these growths have remote feudal origins. It remains true regardless of whether the nation is formed by federation, as in the case of the Swiss or the Dutch lands, or by territorial expansion through conquest.

The city-states of antiquity were formed out of tribal units. Since the nation-state is the next stage of political expansion beyond the city-state, it might be supposed that it would be formed by the amalgamation of city-states, as these originated from tribal groupings. *But that is not the case historically. If it had been, the nation would not have the characteristic unity it possesses.*

The modern nation is formed out of counties and duchies, out of border marches and ecclesiastical principalities, out of manors and villages and towns. These are all feudal units. The cities which it includes within its domain originated for the most part from military camps and walled castle areas. It is only later that the rising commercial centers, which remained for a long time free cities, were incorporated as local units of the nation.

The political unity of a nation is coextensive with the geographical unity of its domain, excluding from consideration all foreign colonies or imperial possessions. That is why we speak of a nation as "a country." Its political life is the life of the whole country, rural as well as urban.

In contrast, the political life of the city-state is not diffused throughout its whole area, again excluding from consideration its colonial settlements and conquered peoples. The outlying countryside of a city-state provides economic support for the political life of the city, but does not share in it equally with the city dwellers who engage in commerce and politics.

9

With the economic changes produced by the industrial revolution, all the tendencies implicit in nationalization received new impulse.

The industrialized nation became more unified politically than an agrarian and commercial nation could ever be. This was not due merely to the fact that the technological advances of the industrial era included improved facilities for transport and communication. These did, of course, augment both the diffusion and the centralization of political life. But in addition the industrial economy required a balance between agriculture and trade, mining and manufacture, which rendered all parts of a country much more interdependent.

Nationalization proceeds more rapidly, and departs further from feudalism, under industrial conditions. Crompton's invention of the spinning mule and Adam Smith's publication of

The Wealth of Nations, both in 1776, are unrelated events which become related in their consequences for the future course of national development.

Because of its special type of political unity, the nation-state can be larger in territory and population than the city-state. This is especially true under the conditions of an industrial economy. Excluding the empires each may have and which, of course, can be equal in size, the city-state can never reach the dimensions of a nation-state.

The fact that the great city-empires of antiquity were not as large, or as far-flung, as the British Empire in the nineteenth century must be explained by improved facilities of transport and communication, not by any great difference between city and nation with respect to imperialistic ventures.

We see, therefore, that the transition through feudalism from the polity of the city to the polity of the nation constitutes an integral step in the process of political expansion, as radical in its consequences as the shift from family to tribe, or tribe to city.

The fact that some nations are larger than others does not alter the point that *by their very nature nations are larger than cities.* Nor is it affected by the fact that, in the course of international wars, with the rise and fall of dynasties, and as waves of conquest spread out and recede, individual nations expand and contract. These are surface phenomena.

Underlying the apparent seesaw changes in the size of political communities, there is a progressive motion in one direction only —expansion. The nation-state tends to replace both feudalism and the city-state everywhere in the world. That fundamental change is now almost completed.

We have reached a new stage of political growth. It might almost be said that that stage of growth has reached its own maturity.

Even if one nation were, by conquest, to become the imperial master of the whole world, that by itself would not carry us beyond the nation-state to the next stage of political expansion.

That will occur only when a radically new political formation takes place, differing from the nation-state in its characteristic unity and its geographical dimensions as radically as the nation-state differs from the city-state.

10

It should certainly be obvious that the nation-state is only the *latest*, not the *last*, stage in the process of political expansion.

To suppose any such thing would make us as blind as Aristotle, who understood the process, but thought it stopped with the city-state. His limited historical retrospect excuses his lack of foresight. But we have no excuse for thinking, as Hegel did in the nineteenth century, that the nation-state must be the ultimate stage of political evolution.

We should be able to understand the process well enough to perceive factors now at work which will eventually precipitate the next advance. At any rate, we should be able to see that the process will go on until the limit is reached.

The only limit to political expansion is the world-state. Nothing less than that can stop the process. The world-state is the natural limit of expansion, the last stage of political growth in which two fundamental unities coalesce: (1) the unity of the planet as the territorial basis for man's political life, and (2) the unity of human nature, underlying all racial and cultural differences, as the psychological basis for universal citizenship.

These two unities together will determine the political character of the world community when it is formed. The increasing economic interdependence of all parts of an industrialized world will facilitate this last stage of unification. Nations will become units of local government, just as counties and cities became local centers in the process of nationalization.

The most obvious marks of this truly ultimate stage of political development will be the total abolition of imperialism or any other form of territorial aggrandizement, the complete absence of "foreign affairs," the cessation of wars which transform diplomacy into shooting.

Writing during the First World War, the English economist and political philosopher, J. A. Hobson, challenged the prevalent notion that "the national state is the final product of social evolution." He pointed out that, in addition to running counter to the facts of history, this idea is based on a false theoretical assumption.

What is the worth of this assumption that the associative instincts and interests of men, which have gradually built up the fabric of the national state from smaller units by fusion and co-operation, are precluded from carrying the process any farther by some absolute barriers of sovereignty and independence. Were not the smaller social units, which have in the past grown together into the present national states, once themselves little states, often as sovereign and independent as the great states of today? If once separate tribes, cantons and provinces, widely divergent from one another in economic structure, in civilized development, in language, and in political government, have been able to coalesce or to co-operate in a larger political union, why should not nations be able to do the same? It may, indeed, well be admitted that wide differences of political institution render federation difficult. But they do not render it impossible.

If Professor Hobson's statement be discounted as the appeal of an advocate for world federation, it can be supported by the disinterested views of a student of medieval history who saw in the rise of nations out of feudal anarchy the portent of a greater event—the emergence of the world-state from international anarchy.

In his *Civilization during the Middle Ages,* written in 1894, Professor George Burton Adams, of Yale, forecast what to his mind the whole historical process implied.

As in the opening age of civilization of which history tells us anything—not by inference backward but by record—the unit was the family, and later the tribe was formed by a union of families, later still the city-state by a coalition of tribes, and all ancient history centered about the strife of city-state with city-state . . . so by the end of the middle ages another stage in this line of progress was reached, and in modern times the unit of all political and public life and the acting force in what we call "international" politics has been the nation . . . a higher organism than any which had existed in the classical world.

To this statement, Professor Adams adds the following footnote:

If we could venture to put any trust in the apparently regular and natural character of this progress, the next step logically would seem to be the formation of some kind of an international federation, or possibly even a world-state.

This is more than the next step logically. It is a transition already discernible in forces now at work in the world of national states and due to its anarchy.

Professor Adams had observed how feudalism contained the seeds of nationalism, concealing "in its bosom the weapons with which it would be itself one day smitten." To point out that a similar transformation has already begun, he quotes this comment from the French historian M. Monod:

As we can follow through the feudal epoch the development of the monarchical idea which was to destroy feudalism, and as we can follow through the monarchical epoch the development of the national idea which was to throw dynastic interests back into second place, so we can follow across the history of the last two centuries the development of economic and industrial interests, the social idea, which is destined to overthrow the national.

The operation of the great international cartels is one way of seeing this point concretely. Community of interest on the level of economic advantage literally compelled the great baronial corporations in different countries to erect a new feudal system which cuts across national divisions for the sake of monopolistic efficiency. In consequence of their strictly nonlegal modes of combination, the cartels escape from, rather than transgress, the restrictions imposed by any country's laws. They must, therefore, remain outlaws so long as the world of nation-states persists. To put an end to this brigandage we must go beyond the present order.

Another way of seeing the same point is by observing the changing character of war. Feudal wars replaced city wars. Local and limited international wars replaced feudal wars. But now international wars have become world wars, and from this point on all wars will naturally tend to expand to the circumference of the earth. This is a sign that the political community must now expand to the circumference of the earth.

The probability of that expansion is the probability of world-wide peace, the universal peace of the world-state supplanting the local peace of the nation-state. The fact that civil strife may still remain to disturb world peace in no way lessens the radical character of this future transformation of both war and peace by political growth.

Once existent, world peace can be perfected. From being universal, it can become perpetual.

CHAPTER 17

The Physics of Peace

In our day the word "geopolitics" has come to be associated with the business of planning conquests for world domination. That is because the word has gained currency through much learned and popular discussion of the work of Karl Haushofer's Institute at Munich. Whether it be science or pseudo-science, Haushofer regarded his work as a contribution to the counsels of the German General Staff.

But political and economic geography was not a German invention. The fundamental notions of geopolitics were developed by Sir Halford Mackinder as early as 1904 in technical papers and later popularized in 1919 in his *Democratic Ideals and Reality.* The English version does not differ essentially from the German. It, too, deals with world strategy, with conquest and war, though it makes some pretense at being concerned with the future of freedom and democracy.

This is an unfortunate limitation. Economic and geographical considerations should not be applied to war only; nor even restricted to problems of the balance of power among independent nations. Peace has its geopolitics—its physical conditions—as well as war.

The physical conditions of world peace are geopolitical in the sense that the geography of the planet and the distribution of natural resources affect the formation of a world political community.

Every type of political community, whether it be tribe or city-state, nation or world-state, covers a certain territory. It involves an area of the earth's land, as well as the people dwelling thereon. The size of the area and the means of subsistence it provides have a bearing on the size of the population and upon its mode of life.

Political institutions must be adapted to these physical conditions. Fundamental changes in the political forms of society must accompany fundamental changes in its material conditions. The form must fit the matter. Politics must be adjusted to economics and geography.

The fact that physical conditions underlie political development does not mean that a radical political transformation will take place as soon as the material aspects of human society are ready to take on a new political form. There are overlying as well as underlying factors.

The moral and cultural atmosphere in which political institutions must live influences their development as much as the ground on which they must be built. As physical conditions affect politics from beneath, so spiritual forces affect it from above. Political thinking and action must mediate between these two conditioning realities. The intangible factors are as real as the things we can touch.

Progress occurs only when both sets of conditions can be harmonized. Sometimes it is necessary for spiritual aspirations to wait for certain physical changes in order to become practically feasible. Sometimes it is necessary for advantageous physical conditions to wait until the human spirit is ready to take advantage of them.

In the progress toward world peace, the physical conditions have outrun the spiritual. In terms of economics and geography, the formation of a world community and the institution of world government have much greater probability than they have in terms of moral and cultural conditions. The fundamental obstacles to peace in the immediate future are spiritual. The fundamental opportunities for peace in the immediate future are physical.

The time it will take for education to overcome the obstacles and for technology to perfect the opportunities measures the remoteness of peace from the lifetime of our children and grandchildren. Instead of one century, it may take five.

2

Oceans and deserts, rivers and mountains, and above all, distances, determine the lines of division or connection between people. But how they determine the boundaries of a neighborhood depends upon the available means of transportation and communication. The time it takes for men to travel from one part of the earth to another, and the ease with which they can communicate without traveling, alter the social significance of the physical terrain.

Within the period of recorded history, no remarkable changes have taken place on the earth's surface. Its main features have remained constant. Oceans have not shrunk. Mountains have not dwindled. But within that same period, the techniques of communication and transport have made ocean barriers into avenues, have scaled mountains and bypassed deserts—in short, have contracted and transformed the social spaces of the world.

To think of geography politically, we must measure distances not merely in terms of space, but also in terms of time. The same physical distance changes socially according to the time and effort required to traverse it, or to make contacts across it. Historical space, the space of political activity, is a function of geographical time, the time of acting through or across the earth's distances.

Using the word "technology" in the familiar sense to mean the tools and techniques which men have devised to master their physical environment, we can say that every important technological advance alters the geopolitical situation.

Technology also changes the economic face of things. The modes of production and distribution will vary with the tools and techniques by which men turn the earth's resources into consumable goods, and by which they bring raw materials to the producer, and his product to the consumer.

Since we are here concerned with the physical conditions of

peace, we can ignore the moral aspect of the economic process. The feudal economy may be less unjust than the slave economy of antiquity, but both differ in the same way from an industrial economy. The injustice of capitalism may be the same in the domestic as opposed to the industrial system of production, or under the auspices of mercantilism and free trade.

For our present purposes, the question is not which is the most just or the most efficient system but rather, how do the physical aspects of an economy condition the institutions of political life?

That technology should be central to both the geographic and the economic foundations of politics is of the greatest importance. The rate of technological progress gives us some measure of the probability of political change. But we also know that invention is, of all things, the most unpredictable.

We can, perhaps, estimate the speed with which existing tools and techniques can be perfected, and we can even foresee something of the improvements which lie ahead. But some genuinely novel inventions, such as the telephone or wireless, were not even vaguely anticipated by the great prophets of new skills and apparatus, even by those who dreamed of man's flying through space.

To the extent that political progress depends upon technology, there are unpredictable contingencies which may affect the rate of change—usually in the direction of hastening a growth already begun. On the physical side, we may be nearer to world peace than cautious estimates now indicate.

3

There are two things which limit the size of any community of men.

One is the size of the earth. That is the natural limit of political expansion. Communities can be smaller, but they cannot be larger, than the spinning globe. We need not consider the possibility of interplanetary war and peace, though we must remember that not so long ago world wars fought in the air were regarded as a Wellsian nightmare.

The other thing which limits the size of a community is communication. A community consists of men whose lives interact and who can establish contacts with one another. The interaction may be direct or indirect. The contact may be face-to-face or through messages and intermediaries. But certainly government can go no further than it can reach physically. The political community may be limited by the physics of communication to boundaries much narrower than the earth's surface.

It is necessary to observe certain qualifications of this point. Communication is not merely a physical matter. The physical means of communication must also be used for the purposes of a common life. Linguistic and cultural barriers and conflicting purposes can nullify the opportunity for political community which the physical means of communication provide. In consequence, we find throughout history that physical communication is almost always wider than the political community. The Balkan situation is the rule rather than the exception. Were this not so, wars (or truces) between separate tribes or states would have been impossible.

Despite these qualifications, the negative significance of the point remains. Just as wars are impossible between groups which have no way of making physical contact with one another, so it is impossible for men to form a political group unless they can communicate. Without physical contact, neither cultural nor political community is possible.

Of these two physical factors which limit the size of a political community, the first remains invariable. From the beginning of history, and before it could be conceived, it was always true that nothing on earth could be larger than a world-state. But the second factor varies from time to time. It varies with the facilities provided by technology.

4

The Greeks thought the size of a city to be limited by the carrying power of a man's voice. The citizenry should not be larger than the forum can accommodate. Citizens must be able to acquaint themselves with each other's opinions; all must be able to participate in the discussion of public questions.

As John Stuart Mill points out:

> In the ancient world . . . there could be nothing like a regulated popular government beyond the bounds of a single city-community; because there did not exist the physical conditions for the formation and propagation of public opinion, except among those who could be brought together to discuss public matters in the same agora. This obstacle is generally thought to have ceased by the adoption of the representative system. But to surmount it completely required the press, and even the newspaper press, the real equivalent, though not in all respects an adequate one, of Pnyx and the Forum.

Quite apart from the distinction between direct and representative government, the communities of the ancient and medieval world were limited in size by the physical facilities needed to operate the machinery of government. Mill goes on to say:

> There have been states of society in which even a monarchy of any great territorial extent could not subsist, but unavoidably broke up into petty principalities, either mutually independent, or held together by a loose tie like the feudal: because the machinery of authority was not perfect enough to carry orders into effect at a great distance from the person of the ruler.

The great empires of Persia or Egypt, of Alexander or of the Caesars, of Charlemagne or of the Hohenstaufens or the Habsburgs, could reach no farther than transport by horse and sail, and communication by courier. At this stage of the physical facilities, oceans, mountain ranges, and deserts usually represented impassable barriers—except to the elephants of Hannibal or to the hard-riding legions of the Great Khan.

The Roman pacification of the world was stopped by the Atlantic to the west, by the German forests of the north, by the African deserts in the south, and by the distances, as well as difficult terrain, to the east.

It is interesting to observe how the ancients used the word "world." When Alexander wept over the fact that there were no more worlds to conquer, he did not know how small was the part of the world he had overrun. The great world conquerors of antiquity lacked a veridical image of the world.

In western history, the world image has gradually enlarged from a Mediterranean world to a European world, with fringes in north Africa and west Asia. Only recently has it become a world of the five continents.

For all practical purposes, either of conquest or of government, Orient and Occident belonged to separate worlds as late as the eighteenth century. Napoleon would have considered himself an unqualified success as *world* conqueror had he subdued the European continent and its Mediterranean fringes, the British Isles, and the American colonies. But much more than half the earth's surface and peoples would have remained beyond his grasp. Could he have succeeded in his European world, Napoleon would have dismissed this vast residue as readily as if it were on Mars rather than on this earth. China and Japan, most of India and the great islands of the Pacific, not to mention darkest Africa, belonged to another world.

But today world conquerors, whether they be Oriental or Occidental, mean the whole planet when they say "world." At last men have attained a veridical image to accompany the word. This fact has as much significance for the future of peace as it has for the future of war. Its significance was first realized within our own lifetime as a result of technological developments in transport and communication which began to make their social effects felt during the nineteenth century.

5

The first glimmering of the present world and the future will be found in the literature of schemes for peace rather than in plans for war and conquest. This is not an astounding fact. Peace planners can always afford to be a little less realistic than military strategists. But it is none the less a good omen.

Writing in 1786, Jeremy Bentham begins his *Plan for an Universal and Perpetual Peace* with these words:

> The object of the present essay is to submit to the world a plan for an universal and perpetual peace. The *globe* is the field of dominion to which he aspires. . . .

I have italicized the strange word which had political significance for none of Bentham's contemporaries or predecessors, and which, along with its derivative "global," is regarded by many persons today as journalistic jargon. Most of the classical peace projects, both before and after Bentham, talked of "universal peace" but meant little more than Europe. In fact, until our own century, only Kant joined Bentham in thinking of the problem in "global" terms.

Kant conceived world peace as involving what he called a "cosmopolitical right"—

> The right all men have, of demanding of others to be admitted into their society; a right founded upon that of the common possession of the surface of the earth, whose spherical form obliges them to suffer others to subsist contiguous to them, because they cannot disperse themselves to an indefinite distance, and because originally one has not a greater right to a country than another. The sea and uninhabitable deserts divide the surface of the globe, but the

ship and the camel, that vessel of the desert, re-establish the communication and facilitate the right which the human species all possess, of profiting in common by its surface.

When Kant wrote these words in 1795, the cosmopolitical right had an insecure foundation on the back of a camel or the decks of a sailing ship. Today the technical achievements of aviation and radio give it wings to soar on, and an indivisible air ocean through which to encompass the globe.

6

The physical conditions which raise the probability of world peace, far beyond the most optimistic estimate which could have been made by Bentham or Kant, have developed so recently that many do not yet recognize their significance. Let us, therefore, go back one step to observe a comparable effect of technology on the expansion of the national state.

Toward the close of the eighteenth century, political writers debated the question of how large an area and population a nation could cover or include. They were not thinking of a nation's colonies or imperial possessions. Their question applied only to the homeland of the nation.

They knew enough about the characteristic differences in political form between city and nation to know that the modern national state could be much larger than the city-states of antiquity. But living before the era of railroads and telegraphy, they could not guess the true limits of national expansion.

In the controversy over the Federal Constitution as opposed to the Articles of Confederation, such proponents of the Constitution as Hamilton, Madison, and Jay argued that the geographic extent of the thirteen colonies did not prevent them from becoming one nation. Today it is hard to realize that the opposition could make out a very strong case against the attempt to set up a single government over so small a domain. But it was not a small domain in 1787.

In that year, the traveling time from Boston to New York was six days, from Boston to Savannah twenty-five. The mails, and with them the newspapers, traveled by stagecoach or sailing packets. The report of events in the nation's capital would be long delayed in reaching all its citizens, and many would seldom be informed at all of what political actions had been taken until their remote consequences began to be felt. The people's representatives in Congress would have great difficulty in keeping in touch with their constituents, and the national administration could hardly keep its finger on the pulse of the nation.

Under such physical conditions of transport and communication, it was certainly debatable whether the geographical extent of the thirteen colonies could be embraced by a single political community under efficient government. To give the question its full force, suppose that the Federalists could have known in 1787 the true geography of the American continent. Suppose that they could have imagined the possibility of migration westward across the Great Plains and the mountain ranges to the Pacific Coast.

Let them imagine that as a result of colonizing and settling these lands, new territories would seek admission to the union as states until the original number more than tripled, and until the population grew to be more than thirty times as large as the three million of 1787.

But with this foresight of what was going to happen within a hundred years, let them remain totally oblivious of the possibilities of transport by steam and messages by wire. Would the Federalists have dared to defend the practicality of a single nation covering so vast an area and with such a huge population, even though it were to be divided into more than two score states, each providing local government?

To have so dared would have been a degree of fanaticism uncongenial to the reasonable mentality of Hamilton, Madison, and Jay.

Yet within that hundred years, the traveling distance between

New York and San Francisco became much less than that between New York and Savannah in 1787. And by the turn of the next century, fast trains reduced that time to little more than the six days required to go from Boston to New York. Telephone and telegraph wires brought the two coasts into daily conversation. Important events in any locality, as well as affairs of national interest, within twenty-four hours became known to anyone who could read a newspaper or have it read. The United States was a more compact political community in 1900 than it was in 1789.

Steamboats and steam trains, telegraph and telephone wires, had worked a transformation in the physical condition of political life. In little more than a hundred years, they had created new facts which killed old theories about the limits of national expansion. But the miracle they performed is dwarfed by comparison with the transformation we have witnessed in the last quarter century.

7

Today no spot on the globe is more than sixty hours away from anyone's local airport. That is very much less than the travel time in 1787 between New York and Savannah, much less even than that between Boston and New York.

Today, world news is the hourly possession of men who read newspapers, and the almost instantaneous possession of those who listen to radios.

Today the radio makes it possible for all men everywhere to participate in the discussion of political matters, international as well as national.

Today the motion-picture screen enables men to witness events which happened yesterday, or perhaps the day before, in some remote corner of the world.

Physically the world has become a single neighborhood. There are no longer any geographical barriers. There are no longer any people who need to remain unacquainted with the visible actions of their fellow men anywhere else.

Encompassed by a single air ocean which is magnificently navigable in all directions, enveloped by an atmosphere through which the human voice and pictures of human action can be transmitted with the speed of light, the world is one in a physical sense which has profound political significance. No one can challenge Mr. Wendell Willkie's vision of the oneness of the world, *so long as it is rightly interpreted to mean that no physical impediments remain to restrict the size of the political community.* The only limit now is the natural limit of the globe itself.

It may take some time for men to see that the unity of the human race is the psychological fact which fits the physical fact of the world's unity, just as the unmitigated diversity of races and cultures belongs to a world of impassable geographic barriers, forbidding distances, and unbroken silences between isolated peoples.

However long that time, we can be sure of one thing. Technological progress will be accelerated and distances will shrink accordingly. Air speeds will make global circumnavigation a daily affair. The radio and motion picture will make the world's events as local as those on a village Main Street. The perfection of television may increase the vitality of radio and telephone as mediums of communication. Individuals anywhere in the world may be able to talk face to face.

These are not Wellsian daydreams. These things belong to the easily predictable future. It would take the imagination of an H. G. Wells to conjure up fantasies of the really novel inventions which have as yet no foundation in scientific discovery or technical wizardry.

CHAPTER 18

The Economic Community

THE FUNDAMENTAL geographic fact which bears on the probability of a world community is the shrinkage of space-time by all the means of communication. The fundamental economic fact which has similar bearing is the increasing interdependence of the various industrialized societies.

The economic self-sufficiency of a social group varies with two different sets of circumstances. On the one hand, the size of the group and the extent of territory it occupies tend to increase its economic self-sufficiency, making possible a more efficient division of labor and making likely a greater abundance of natural resources. On the other hand, the technological development of the economy increases its need for a wider variety of natural resources and so makes societies in different localities dependent on trade and commerce with one another for the exchange of materials indigenous to the territories of each.

The ancients observed the first of these factors at work. The larger group of the tribe not only could satisfy the daily needs of its members, but could also accumulate reserves. The city was even more competent to solve the economic problem; it was "nearly self-sufficing." But that it was seldom *quite* self-sufficing should have been apparent from the facts of trade and commerce in such city-states as Athens and Corinth.

In this connection, we should observe the difference between the Athenian and Spartan mode of life. What we would call the "standard of living" was much higher in Athens than in Sparta. Sparta was primarily an agricultural and military society. In Athens, the arts, both useful and fine, had reached a much higher stage of development. The useful arts and crafts had multiplied the conveniences and refinements of life. In consequence, Athens was much more dependent than Sparta on foreign trade. Both

221

exports and imports were indispensable to the maintenance of its more complicated economy.

In the *Republic,* Plato distinguishes between the "piggish" state and the "luxurious" state. The "piggish" state lives at an economic level which satisfies only the basic biological needs. When men seek the comforts and refinements of life, when their arts enable them to have amenities in addition to the bare necessities, they tend to develop the economy of the "luxurious" state. This involves a greater division of labor, foreign trade, and foreign wars.

2

Foreign trade and foreign wars are related aspects of the same fundamental fact of economic interdependence between communities. In the pastoral life of the tribe which subsists by hunting and fishing, the only economic occasion for conflict with other tribes will be a dispute over hunting grounds or fishing preserves.

Commerce between separate communities requires certain conventions to be observed. Commercial practices must be regulated. The rules of trade between independent communities cannot be determined by the separate laws or customs of either. They must consist of customs commonly recognized by the various groups which engage in commerce with one another.

Commercial interchange thus creates an economic community in the absence of a political community. That is why economically interdependent societies, which are at the same time politically independent, make treaties with one another, not only to terminate fighting for a time, but also in order to resume trade, and to regulate it by explicit agreements.

Where two politically independent states do not belong to one economic community, there is as little likelihood of either explicitly contracting a truce with the other as there is of either making overt war on the other. Both "shooting war" and "peaceful commerce" signify that the same situation obtains between two groups, a situation which must always be described by the two facts of *economic interdependence* and *political independence.*

3

Economic interdependence increases in proportion as technological advances lift the economy above the "piggish" level.

The agricultural, as opposed to the hunting, society requires salt to preserve its food stocks and iron to make its implements. The community which is fortunately situated with respect to these natural resources may trade or hunt for slaves to man its mines. With the development of the arts of weaving and metalwork, manufactured goods become marketable commodities in exchange for agricultural produce and mineral deposits.

In any area of the earth's surface where distinct communities have established communication with one another, the differences in their natural situation with respect to the fertility of the earth, the possession of valuable ores, the availability of water ways and land routes, will determine the various ways in which they are economically counterbalanced.

Each will profit by its natural advantages. Each will suffer from its natural deficiencies. Economic inequality will usually be a many-sided affair, for without some superiority no group is in a trading position.

What is most important of all, the economic level attained by the technologically most advanced society will affect the relation of all the societies which belong to the same economic community. The general tendency to improve the physical conditions of life and to raise the standard of living will cause each society to seek the level reached by the state having the most fortunate natural endowments or the greatest technical skill.

Working against this tendency will be two other factors: the desire on the part of each state for the nearest approximation to self-sufficiency, and the economic inequalities which determine the deficiencies as well as the surpluses of each state. As a result of these factors in combination, the degree of economic interdependence will usually tend to increase in proportion as one or a few of the societies in an economic community enjoy the advantages of technological superiority.

When *machino*facturing replaces *manu*facturing, the multiplication of goods and services creates the conditions for an economy of abundance. The industrial revolution changes agriculture and mining, and the transport facilities for foreign trade, as much as it changes the number and variety of the tools and consumables available for exchange.

The industrial economy of the modern world increases many times the interdependence of separate communities. The fact that all parts of the world are not yet industrialized is offset by the fact that, under modern conditions of transport and communication, no part of the world remains unaffected by the industrialism of the rest.

Furthermore, we can expect industrialization to spread from the economically more advanced to the economically more backward peoples. When this happens, the unalterable inequalities with respect to natural resources will tend to increase rather than diminish the interdependence. It seems unlikely that synthetic substitutes will ever make any industrial nation truly self-sufficient.

4

There are those who deplore industrialism. Committing the fallacy of identifying the old days with good days, they try to argue that the agrarian, and less commercial, economy enables a society to develop a more truly human culture, and puts fewer obstacles in the way of leading the good life. They see in the expanding economy of industrial production manifold temptations to vice, a debasement of the arts, and a dehumanization of both society and civilization.

Their fundamental error consists in failing to separate the use of machines from the abuse of men, for which men, not machines, are responsible. They fail to see that the machine can liberate as well as enslave, and that men can master machines as well as make them.

The virtues of the simple life are not more, but less, admirable precisely because they represent the solution of simpler problems. Leisure, freedom from degrading poverty and brutal labor, are indispensable to a good life, a characteristically human life, and these things become possible for more men in an industrial economy than ever before.

The injustices and exploitations which have not yet been corrected do not alter this fact. Culture and civilization can reach a much higher level when machines work for men than when men must do the work of machines. Historians of the future will regard the emancipation and enlightenment of the Russian masses as an inevitable consequence of the industrialization of Russia. The Communist revolution will be credited with initiating that process and with bringing it to its socially desirable fruition with less hardship and misery than accompanied the industrial revolution in England, and in less time than England took to accomplish the social and political reforms which industrialism makes possible.

All moral judgments aside, no one can doubt that the machine is here to stay. Whether or not anyone advocates it, we can no more go back to the preindustrial economy than we can return to the political structure of the city-state or feudalism. And as industrialism intensifies and spreads in the future, the economic interdependence of all the world's peoples will increase.

5

All the peoples of the earth now belong to a single economic community. That *present* reality, like the shrinkage of space-time, is a physical factor determining the probability of world peace. On the physical side, the probability will grow as these two factors come to exert a deeper influence on both war and peace.*

The very notion of the politically independent state carries with it the idea of economic self-sufficiency.

The individual human being cannot be a sovereign precisely because of his individual insufficiency. Under extremely primitive conditions, the family can retain the external sovereignty of an independent group, but it surrenders its sovereignty for the sake of joining a larger and more self-sufficient society.

Every stage of political expansion is accompanied by a new level of economic organization, aiming to combine political sovereignty with economic adequacy. When modern nationalism became politically self-conscious, it also favored the economic theory that a nation should try to subsist in independence of its neighbors, in order to exercise its sovereign right to act independently of them. But even under the brilliant administration of Colbert, the mercantilist system could not render France economically autonomous.

The shift from mercantilist principles to those of the physiocrats was favored by colonial expansion, the rise of new manufactures, and, with that, the competition for raw materials as well as foreign markets. According to the physiocratic theory, as adopted and modified by Adam Smith, the wealth of nations in an expanding world economy depends upon free trade—both within countries and between them. An industrial expansion

* We must observe that the world-wide economic community is still in the process of growth, and that it is still too recent a development for most men to recognize its existence or to understand its implications. In his essay "Toward World Order" (in *A Basis for the Peace to Come*), Mr. John Foster Dulles points out that "interrelation and interdependence, while often existing on a world-wide scale, fall far short of being universal. There is, to be sure, a world-wide stratum of interdependent activities. But it is a thin stratum when measured in terms of the activities of humanity as a whole. Even to the extent that interdependence in fact exists, there is no such general awareness of it as to lead people generally to accept world government in replacement of their national governments. People are still largely uneducated as to interdependence which they cannot see with their own eyes." Because of these facts, Mr. Dulles believes that we cannot yet "wholly supplant national government by world government."

Adam Smith could not foresee has given new meaning, as well as greater force, to his strictures against monopolies and tariffs. Under industrialism nations have long ceased to be capable of an isolated economic life. Without economic autonomy, their retention of political sovereignty is all the more anomalous. As Mr. J. A. Hobson remarked,

> If nations were in point of fact self-contained, materially and morally, living in splendid or even in brutish isolation, the doctrine of [sovereign] States or Governments might be tenable. But they are not. On the contrary, their intercourse and interdependence for every kind of purpose, economic, social, scientific, recreational, spiritual, grows continually closer. Hence the doctrine of State sovereignty and independence grows continually falser.

For nations to try to remain politically independent when they belong to one economic community runs counter to natural tendencies, as much as for individual men to try to live anarchically while participating in a division of labor.

6

That the whole world now forms a single economic community can be amply evidenced. By listing the principal exports of forty nations, Harry Scherman, in his striking essay, *The Last Best Hope of Earth*, showed "the incontestable truth that there is a clear planetary indivisibility of production and employment." Another significant fact is that

> Since 1750, about the beginning of the Age of Steam, the human population of the earth has more than tripled. It was then about 660,000,000; it is now well over 2,100,-000,000. . . . The true import of this great fact is plain: 1,500,000,000 more human beings can remain alive on the earth's surface, can support themselves by working for others who in turn work for them. . . . This extraordinary tripling of human population in six short generations finds its

final explanation in the rapid progress toward earthwide economic unification which took place during the same period. . . . If it were conceived that tomorrow the infinite variety of goods that men produce had to be confined within the national boundaries where they were produced, tens of millions of men, women, and children would swiftly die of starvation; hundreds of millions more would be in the last extremes of destitution and misery.

These facts point to the political development which must take place. They stimulate its occurrence. They almost demand it. As Mr. Scherman says, this economic unification "must be matched by a world political organization which, by some general limitation of sovereignty, will allow that union to function and progress without the deep conflicts of interests that end in war."

Despite the lag of centuries, we can expect the political expansion to reach the stage where it fits the economic realities. Until it does, foreign wars and foreign trade will give us rapidly alternating periods of shooting and truce. The degree of interdependence has become so great that all foreign wars will henceforth tend to become world wars, as foreign trade has become world trade. What happened during the First World War will happen again: commerce will continue between the combatants in order that they may have the wherewithal for their arsenals.

Physical conditions, both geographic and economic, have unified mankind. The world's physical oneness is a forerunner of the political community it demands, as that in turn will be the forerunner of the cultural unity to which the diversity of races will be assimilated when they all share in a common civil life. But until political institutions match the economic realities, and conform to the true dimensions of social space, the physical conditions we have been considering will exert their influence in the direction of war.

As Mr. Emery Reves has recently pointed out in his *Democratic Manifesto,* the technical developments which render the world smaller and its parts more interdependent can have two consequences: "(1) a political and economic rapprochement, or (2) fights and quarrels more devastating than ever, precisely because of the proximity of men to each other. Which one of these two possibilities will occur depends on matters essentially nontechnical."

Both will occur within the next great historic epoch, but the second before the first.

If world peace depended only on essentially technical matters, it could be brought to pass within our lifetime. That event is highly improbable because of the obstacles to peace, all of which are moral or spiritual.

The next phase of progress toward peace must be devoted to overcoming these impediments. We must shift from physics to psychology, from technology to education.

CHAPTER 19

The Obstacles to Peace

MEN WANT peace, said Eric Gill, but they do not want the things that make for peace. To desire an end, but not its requisite means, is obviously self-defeating. Obvious but not uncommon: men frequently want things for which they are unwilling to pay the price.

Attending the peace conference at Versailles in 1919, Lincoln Steffens heard a story which epitomized such contradictoriness. Clemenceau had turned to Wilson, Lloyd George, and Orlando and asked them whether they really meant what they said about seeking "permanent peace." They assured him they did. He asked them whether they had counted the cost of such a peace. What cost? Clemenceau replied that he meant such things as the relinquishment of empire and all claims to empire, the tearing down of tariff walls, the removal of all immigration restrictions.

When the others quickly told him that they did not have all this in mind, he said: "Then you don't mean peace. You mean war."

Steffens' comment on this rumored conversation was: "Wilson did not want peace, not literally; nor do we Americans, nor do the British, mean peace. We do not want war; nobody in the world wants war; but some of us do want the things we can't have without war."

Both Eric Gill and Lincoln Steffens had in mind the evil things men want which they cannot have without war, which they will not sacrifice for peace. They were thinking of the economic maladjustments which profit some men and nations, injuring others. They were thinking of imperialism and exploitation, of white superiority, and that higher standard of living which must be protected by tariff and immigration barriers.

But there are also good things which men rightly desire more than peace, and for which they will always fight. Peace without liberty or peace without justice is a doubtful blessing to those who are enslaved or exploited. And, be it added, there are men to whom peace is a doubtful blessing because their empty lives crave the excitements and excursions of war. Peace is no good to men unless they seek goods which are unattainable without it.

Peace is not an ultimate end, an absolute good in itself. Political peace, like the very existence of a civil society and its welfare, provides the conditions men need to lead a good human life. Peace is a means to happiness, and the pursuit of happiness requires both liberty and justice.

We see, therefore, that world peace cannot be made if men will not give up the things which stand in its way. Even if it is made, it cannot be perpetuated if the terms of its making demand the sacrifice of the very goods which peace should serve.

We see one further point. If men misconceive their happiness to consist in money, fame, or power, they do not really want peace even if they delude themselves into thinking that war disturbs their pursuit of these things.

There is nothing intrinsically evil in money, fame, or power. What is evil is the infinite lust which seeks to possess them at all costs—the desire to have them in unlimited quantities, and before anything else.

Men who place their happiness in such goods, pre-eminently or exclusively, not only defeat themselves, even in the short run of a single lifetime; they also jeopardize the common good of the society in which they live. No one—man or nation—can seek unlimited wealth without impoverishing others, without increasing rather than diminishing the inequitable distribution of the material factors in human welfare. No man or nation can wield unlimited power without enslaving or subjugating others.

The simplest test of a true conception of human happiness is that it should be attainable by each individual *without in any way impeding or preventing an attainment of the same goods by others.* Anyone who regards the pursuit of happiness as a competitive enterprise, in which first come first served and the devil take the hindmost, is doomed to discover that the first shall be last in the devil's accounting.

He is also self-deluded or a deliberate hypocrite if he thinks he wants peace. He really wants war, potential or actual, for anarchy, not peace under a just and efficient government, will help him get ahead by beating his neighbor and by despoiling the common good.

2

All of the moral obstacles to peace arise from disordered desires, desires for things in the wrong order, or *unlimited* desires for things which are good in their place and under some limitation of quantity which respects the needs of others.

The habit of wanting the right thing in the right order in the right quantity and with due regard for the social context of the individual life is moral virtue. To whatever degree men lack moral virtue, which is nothing but a reasonable discipline of desires, they frustrate their own happiness and invade the welfare of others.

The moral obstacles to peace thus arise from what individuals want. But though all desires must be traced back to individual human beings, we can speak of group desires and national wants.

Within a community, different groups of individuals may want different things. Some may want peace and the things which make for peace. Some may want peace because they want the benefits peace yields. Some may have desires which militate against peace, even when hypocrisy or self-deception leads them to pretend otherwise.

Since most nations will be divided on such fundamental matters, how can we speak of what a nation wants?

We obviously cannot construct a fictitious desire for the whole community by some kind of compromise between irreconcilable aims. Nevertheless, what the community as a whole does or is prepared to do in relation to other communities represents its dominant desire, the desire which dominates its course of action. Neither Hitler nor Roosevelt could declare war without such popular support.

For all practical purposes, we can regard a nation as wanting the things for which its members are either willing or compelled to act. This is determined by the dominant group in the population. It need not be the numerical majority. It may be the group which, through wealth or position, exerts a real, if not a nominal, control of the government; or which influences the cast of articulate public opinion by an organized campaign employing all the techniques of propaganda.

There is no need to go to the extremes of cynicism. Under the conditions of constitutional government, and especially under constitutions which permit the practice of democracy, the desire of the majority will eventually prevail. It takes time for it to reach a decisive clarity and to become sufficiently articulate.

In the absence of constitutional democracy, it will take more time for the majority opinion to become a public force, and still more time for that force to overcome whatever faction controls the nation's destiny.

With these things in mind, we can see that the moral obstacles to peace are both individual and national. Their ultimate source is in the individual. But at any time their effective expression will be found in the national will, however that is resolved.

When we come to enumerate the various moral obstacles, we shall therefore have to consider both individual and national differences. All nations will not have the same reasons for opposing peace. They will vary, just as individuals do, according to their character and the peculiarities of their situation. We may, however, expect to find some impediments which are common to all nations, and which are at present inoperative only in the case of certain individuals or minority groups.

There is another group of obstacles which have nothing to do with individual desires, group wants, or national interests. These arise from the present condition of the human world as a whole.

Men are divided into diverse races and belong to different cultures. Sometimes biological diversities and cultural differences fall within a single political community. Sometimes these lines of division and differentiation roughly coincide with the political lines by which nations are separated from one another. In some cases, one group of separate nations will be distinguished from another group by all these alignments.

Two other factors must be mentioned here. The first is connected with racial or cultural differences—the diversity of human languages. The second consists in radical inequalities in the level of civilization reached by the various nations of the world.

Human beings are not given the same educational opportunities in all parts of the world, nor is the education they are given equally conducive to participation in civil life.

Starting from different historical origins, and developing under the influence of different environments, the nations of the world have not marched abreast in the path of political progress. Some communities are politically much more advanced than others. In the backward countries or among the more primitive peoples, vast numbers of men lack the sort of political experience which comes only with a long tradition of constitutional government and which can be universalized only by democracy.

Let us call these factors the cultural obstacles to world peace. The fundamental difference between the cultural and the moral impediments should be obvious at once.

The moral obstacles can be overcome only by changing the wants of men and nations. Furthermore, the moral obstacles will vary in force and character from nation to nation. But the cultural obstacles belong to the world as a whole. They are realities which every nation must recognize, quite apart from what it does or does not want for itself.

Taken together, these moral and cultural factors comprise the spiritual difficulties in the way of world peace. They more than overbalance the physical conditions which promote the coming of a world community. To the extent to which they postpone it, they render world peace improbable in the near future. Its probability within five hundred years amounts to a calculation of the time it will take to bring about the necessary spiritual changes.

3

With one exception, the cultural obstacles are of almost negligible importance. Of these, only the existing inequality in level of civilization presents a real impediment to the formation of a world community. But by itself it is quite sufficient to bar the way for many centuries.

As for the rest, the plurality of races and cultures, the diversity of languages and religions, do not seriously matter. To suppose that they do would be to suppose, quite contrary to fact and principle, that a political community requires racial and cultural homogeneity, that it cannot exist unless all its members speak the same language and unless all adhere to the same religious faith.

History affords numerous examples which show that political unity requires none of these things. Political principles explain why association for a common good can embrace men of diverse biological stocks and coming from different cultural traditions; why the communication needed for civil life does not necessitate the adoption of Esperanto; and why the separation of church and state permits, in fact demands, that a plurality of creeds be tolerated, as well as nonparticipation in any religious communion. If anyone thinks that perfect spiritual unity is required for political community, he should also be honest or realistic enough to admit that world peace is impossible, or at least improbable, until the end of time.

It is certainly unlikely that migration and cross-breeding will totally obliterate the biological strains which manifest themselves in skin color, physique, and temperament. Let us not ask whether such biological uniformity would be desirable. That is beside the point. The point is simply that such uniformity would be hundreds of centuries off even if all peoples were to belong to a world-state tomorrow.

If the earth's peoples continue to live under conditions of political separation, then its improbability is multiplied a hundred times. Hence those who falsely regard racial homogeneity as a precondition for world government must be forced to an utterly pessimistic conclusion.

The same holds for local customs, language, and religion.

Even if all members of the human race belonged to a single political community, most of them would still continue to live in particular neighborhoods the greater part of their lives. They would adopt the customs of their locality. Diverse localities would always tend to differ in custom because customs arise from racial differences in temperament and from the peculiarities of different physical environments, such as climate and the conditions of livelihood.

Economic interdependence and the shrinkage of space-time may increase the number of practices which are world-wide customs. This growth of universal as opposed to local customs may be further augmented by the formation of a world-state. But it is neither likely nor necessary that local customs be entirely transcended.

Men do not have to dance to the same tunes, sing the same songs, dress in the same way, have the same table manners, or indulge in the same ceremonials, in order to live together in the same political community.

Nor need they speak the same tongue in order to communicate for political purposes. The Swiss Federation has existed for over six hundred years, though its united cantons are divided into three language groups. The Soviet Union includes a much wider diversity of languages. In such communities, one language has usually been adopted as the official medium of political utterance and government documents, but even that does not always obtain, as is shown by the bilingual practice of French Quebec.

The ultimate fact here is that all human languages are suffi-

ciently capable of translation into one another so that interpretation can always establish a meeting of minds. Those who do not
try or *want* to understand one another will remain incom-
municado even if they speak the same language.

Differences in religion can be regarded either from a secular
or from a religious point of view.

To the unbeliever, creeds are like other elements in the mores.
Local variations in belief and ritual are like local variations in
other customary matters.

To the devout, religious differences sometimes represent
schism and heresy, or worse, the pagan worship of idols or false
gods. Sometimes they represent the variety of ways in which
Divinity has revealed itself at different times and to different
peoples.

For the deepest spiritual brotherhood to obtain among all men,
it may be necessary for all to recognize the fatherhood of one
God. But that is not necessary for political comradeship among
citizens of the same state. For the peace of God, nothing less than
the theological virtue of charity will do. But justice—political
and economic—is sufficient for civil peace.

In a recent article on the possibility of a European federation,
the distinguished French philosopher, Jacques Maritain, wrote
that economic interdependence and

> . . . it alone would be altogether insufficient. . . . A com-
> mon idea of the general ends of political life and of the com-
> mon task to be undertaken is needed—in brief a common
> idea and a common spirit of civilization.

It is not necessary, he went on to say, for the state to be limited
to a single "nation" in the strictly biological sense of that word.
Diversity of nationality, and even of culture, is no obstacle. The
state, and especially the federal state, "can gather in its unity
different 'nations' and even different cultural heritages."

From these principles, M. Maritain drew the unwarranted
conclusion that *world* federation is barred by factors he does not

find operative in the *European* situation. Unless he has in mind the greater religious diversity in the world situation, unless the common though attenuated tradition of Christianity is prerequisite for political unity, the greater plurality of races and cultures does not make a substantial difference in the two situations.

M. Maritain is right in thinking that there must be fundamental agreement in the sphere of political ideas or principles. But the idea of liberty and the principle of justice are not peculiar to any one race or culture, certainly not to the European group of races and cultures. The statement by the Chinese philosopher Mencius that "there is a common heart in man" is equivalent to the Christian statement that the natural moral law is implanted in the human heart, and is therefore the same for all men everywhere.

One further point must be observed. There is a prevalent tendency to overemphasize cultural differences, and to minimize or neglect the profound similarities between diverse cultures. These common elements lie deep, because they are rooted in the underlying humanity of men everywhere. The differences, being accidents of place or breeding or history, are necessarily superficial.

In short, cultural community is as real a possibility as the existing cultural diversity is a real fact. But the realization of this potential cultural community must follow, not precede, political unification.

Just as in the past the cultures of particular communities have resulted from the mingling of races and traditions within their borders, so in the future a world culture will develop from the mingling of all peoples in a universal political community.

Certain elements of world culture already exist. Neither science nor technology admits provincial boundaries. International commerce and international law have required at least lip service to concrete principles of justice and fair dealing. And the motion picture has become an art enjoyed all over the earth, despite the fact that cinematic productions are still far from universal in their conception. Essentially art for the masses, and speaking the language of pictures which all men understand, the narratives of the screen have been able to touch the emotions of common men in every country, and to create a world-wide community of enjoyment.

4

Let me be sure I have made my point clear. I am not saying that cultural and racial differences do not present obstacles to world peace. They do, indeed, but only through the intervention of such moral factors as race prejudice and cultural antipathy.

There is a significant distinction between saying that these differences create emotional barriers which prevent men from wishing to join hands politically and saying that a political community cannot be formed until these differences are obliterated. The latter statement is simply false. The former is as obviously true.

Racial and cultural differences are not in themselves obstacles, but they do create serious obstacles in the moral order—in the sphere of what men love and hate, what they want or are willing to do.

This distinction has great practical significance. The moral obstacles are genuinely surmountable by education and by enlargements of experience. Race prejudice can be overcome. Cultural antipathies can be reduced. But the diversity of races and cultures cannot be removed, certainly not in advance of world government. If that diversity were in itself an obstacle, it might effectively bar the way forever, or for an indefinitely long time.

This brings us to the one cultural factor which makes world peace improbable in our century.

A federal government of the world requires political homogeneity among its component states. A world federation would have to be constitutional. In consequence, all the federated states would have to be republics. None could be dictatorships or absolute monarchies.

Despotisms and constitutions cannot federate. To this extent, at least, political uniformity is required in a set of federated states, even if all are not equally democratic in their constitutions. But all the peoples of the world are not yet prepared by tradition or experience for constitutional government. There are nations in which constitutional government has never been tried; and others where it has been a papier-mâché affair, concealing a succession of dictatorships.

These facts have long been claimed by imperialism to justify itself as a kind of benevolent despotism. The white man has discharged a burden as well as pocketed a profit. He has paternalistically ruled peoples who have not been fit or ready to rule themselves.

It makes a great difference whether one says "fit" or "ready." To say of any people that they are by nature not *fit* to rule themselves is to deny their human dignity, to deny that they are men, for the nature of a political animal is to be self-governing. To say that they are not yet *ready* may be a true observation of their condition, but the imperialist usually forgets that children are not made ready for adult responsibilities by being kept children.

Nothing but education for citizenship and the concrete experience of civil life will produce political maturity in a people. This seldom happens under imperialistic domination, precisely because it defeats the purpose for which the imperialist is willing to be paternal. He indulges in benevolence not as an act of charity, but as a condition of efficiency in gaining his own ends. Otherwise he ceases to be an imperialist and becomes a missionary.

The backward nations of the world will have to remedy their own defects. They can be helped by others only to the extent that imperialism is renounced; and, perhaps, by advice and example. But in the main task of achieving political maturity, they will have to pull themselves up by their own bootstraps.

History indicates that the process is both long and painful. Starting with some natural advantages, the English people took at least four hundred years to rid themselves of despotism. Under present conditions of communication and with increasing industrialization, other nations which still have to go through the same process may be able to succeed in a somewhat shorter time.

5

We are accustomed to think of the grades of civilization in terms of the degree to which the fine arts are developed or manners are refined. We forget that the fine arts can flourish in a society in which most men are slaves or peons, leading an almost brutal life. We forget that when politeness and civility grace the life of the privileged few, the rest live in a swinish manner outside the pale of civilization.

The aristocratic measure of civilization judges the quality of a culture and the height of its characteristic attainments without regard for the number of men in the society who have been cultivated. The aristocrat would rather see the treasures of the Louvre safe from pillage and fire than risk them to revolutionary violence which might liberate the vulgar horde.

He weeps over glories which have been swept away with an ancient regime; he seldom has tears for the monstrous deprivations of culture suffered by the masses under it. Nor does he understand that those rare and precious refinements which can be enjoyed only by the gifted few are merely the embellishments of a civilization, not its substance or soul.

To the democrat, level of civilization is measured primarily by the quantity of men who enjoy its benefits and by the extent to which all men, *not some,* are cultivated.

The equalization of educational opportunity becomes indispensable to raising the level of civilization. Equal educational opportunity is usually inseparable from political equality. Only those who are admitted to the status of free men will be edu-

cated for freedom. Only those who deserve to be admitted to
citizenship deserve as much education as befits their native
talents. But liberty and suffrage belong by right to all normal
men. So do all the advantages of education and all the benefits
of civil life.

Through education and enfranchisement men participate in
the activities of civil life. Through being cultivated, they become
contributors to culture. By democratic standards, the primary
growth of civilization is at its base—in the life of common men.
The special attainments or contributions of the gifted few must
be valued primarily as a leaven working to raise the level of the
mass.

In view of the political conditions of world peace, only the
democratic standards are relevant. World federation requires a
basic equality in the civilization of the federating nations, which
means an equality in political status and in educational opportunity for their several populations. Such equality does not now
exist at the base of civilization in the world's communities, however they stand with respect to the embellishments which the
aristocrat values for their own sake.

The peoples who have been deprived must fight and struggle
for their own improvement. They cannot be given political experience on a platter any more than they can be fed freedom
through a tube. But except for those who still think that some
men are born to be the permanent wards of their betters, if not
for complete servility, no one can doubt that what some peoples
have already won for themselves other nations will eventually
achieve in the same way.

6

I turn now to the moral factors which make world peace
highly improbable in the immediate future.

Before we examine a rough classification of these obstacles, it
is necessary to meet an objection which may be raised against

the sharpness of the distinction between the moral and the cultural aspects of the problem. It may be said, for example, that a people who want to preserve their economic advantages, who do not wish to sacrifice their higher standard of living, belong to a culture that is essentially materialistic. This, in essence, is Lin Yutang's whole case against the West.

To call a culture "materialistic"—using the word in a derogatory sense—is to point out a fundamental moral disorder in the life of a people. The majority, or the predominant group among them, want things in the wrong order; or they want too much of certain goods to the detriment of others.

How, then, can we separate the moral character of a nation from the moral character of its culture?

For certain purposes the separation cannot be made. A culture includes moral standards as well as intellectual or artistic attainments. It includes what a people are in the habit of wanting as much as it includes all the rest of their social practices and customs—what they are in the habit of doing and believing. Cultural diversity will, therefore, be determined in part by differences in morality.

But for our purposes the distinction is justified. We are interested in the obstacles to world peace. There are many aspects of cultural diversity which do not present impediments. The one serious cultural obstacle—the basic inequality of the world's nations with respect to political maturity—would remain for a long time even if the exploiting nations renounced their imperialistic aims. Unlike the other cultural factors, it does represent a difficulty, but along with them it also represents a situation which cannot be attributed solely to the conflict of desires on the part of different groups of men.

It seems reasonable, therefore, to classify under one head all the impediments which have the same ultimate source. Such procedure has practical significance, for in overcoming impediments we must know their origin. The probability of their being mitigated or removed will also depend on the causes from which they flow.

If the materialism of Western culture is the chief moral fault which obstructs the coming of peace, the political deficiencies of the civilizations of the Far East constitute the chief cultural obstacle.

Dr. Lin Yutang does not understand, in the first place, that peace requires more than right moral attitudes, it requires political institutions. Failing here, he fails to see that the political inequality between East and West is just as serious as the moral discrepancy in the other direction. For world peace East and West must meet, but each in the line of its own defect has just as far to go.

7

We can divide the moral obstacles into four main types. Let us examine each of these briefly.

(1) *Race prejudice.* In a world community under federal government, racial discriminations would have to be obliterated.

Those who think there are inferior and superior races usually turn this prejudice into a policy which calls for political inequality, with obvious consequences for economic and educational opportunity. Hence, wherever men in any country base their fundamental policies upon race prejudice, they also take a position inimical to the foundation of world peace.

Race prejudice creates another line of opposition to world government. Federal institutions normally provide for the free passage of people from one state to another. Anyone who has federal citizenship can change his domicile and with it his local citizenship. This means that the migration of peoples can take place without immigration or emigration restrictions. It may not mean that such matters go without any regulation, but it would certainly involve drastic alteration in the prevailing policies of nations which erect barriers either against the ingress of foreigners or against the egress of their own people.

Barriers against immigration, like barriers against imports, are supposed to protect a country's standard of living from being lowered as a consequence of having to compete with cheap foreign labor. Race prejudice thus tends to be reinforced by economic considerations.

(2) *Economic nationalism.* The nations of the world are unequal with respect to the possession of natural resources and with respect to technological developments. We need not inquire into the historic circumstances of this inequality, nor need we here pass moral judgment on the means the wealthier nations have employed to obtain their present advantages.

The significant moral fact is that the peoples of the wealthier nations wish to retain their advantages. This holds not only for the upper economic levels in the population, but also, though to a lesser extent, for the laboring classes who identify national prosperity with the maintenance of their own standard of living.

The great industrialists want a favorable tariff policy for the same reason that the great labor unions want protection against immigration. Furthermore, both groups have a stake in the profits of imperialism, though they do not share equally in the gains.

The wealthier nations are, therefore, strongly averse to most of the economic implications of world federation. To the extent that it involves free trade among the members of the federation, they think it would jeopardize their present advantages. They usually forget that the great exponent of the wealth of nations, Adam Smith, held free trade to be the bulwark of a nation's economy. But even if they understood his point, the wealthier peoples would dislike the economic equalizations involved in world government.

Whole nations, like individuals, want to preserve their vested interests. If the economic conditions of world peace require that world prosperity take precedence over national prosperity, economic nationalism will lead the wealthier nations to reject the conditions indispensable to world peace.

(3) *Political nationalism.* Under the prevailing international anarchy, people either live in an independent state or belong to a dependency, whether that be a colonial settlement or a conquered nation.

Colonies usually try to throw off the mother country and set themselves up as independent states. Conquered peoples usually seek to regain their national independence. In all the more fortunate communities, men treasure their national freedom almost as dearly as their own individual liberty.

As long as the world situation remains anarchic, national independence will remain an unquestionable ideal. In this situation, the only alternative to independence is the subjugated status of a political dependency.

Here we find an ideal which, through a natural misconception, leads men everywhere to oppose world government.

While it is true that national independence is incompatible with even the federal institution of a world community, *it is not true that federated states become dependencies.* The members of a federation are not subjugated provinces or exploited colonies. With respect to each other, all the states in a federation remain equally independent. None falls under the dominion of the other. Nor are the states dependencies of the federal government, but rather its subordinate units of local government, each retaining internal sovereignty in its own locality.

As long ago as 1693, William Penn, appealing for federation to preserve the peace of Europe, faced the objection

> . . . that sovereign princes and states will hereby become not sovereign, a thing they will never endure. But this . . . is a mistake, for they remain as sovereign at home as ever they were. . . . The sovereignties are as they were, for none of them now has any sovereignty over one another. And if this be called a lessening of their power, it must be only because the great fish can no longer eat up the little ones, and that each sovereignty is equally defended from injuries, and disabled from committing them.

But the confusions about sovereignty still persist, especially the failure to distinguish between its internal and external aspects. This prevents men from seeing that *subjugation or political dependency is not the only alternative to national independence.*

They do not see that if they give up external sovereignty in order to establish a world federation, they necessarily retain the internal sovereignty of their government in local affairs. They do not see that the choice between national independence and subjugation arises only in the anarchic situation.

If they were to decide against international anarchy in favor of world government, they would be avoiding the possible loss of national independence at the hands of a conqueror, at the very same time that they would be surrendering external sovereignty for federal status. This most men do not see.

In consequence, most men the world over find themselves emotionally opposed to world government. As Mr. Walter Lippmann has observed,

> The world we live in is a world of many sovereign national states, and for purposes of practical action this condition is given and is unalterable. . . . If there is to be peace in our time, it will have to be peace among sovereign national states, and the makers of foreign policy can be concerned with no other kind of peace.

Mr. Lippmann is saying, of course, that in our time there cannot be world peace at all, but only a temporary truce. In this view, a great many other observers concur, notably Herbert Hoover and Hugh Gibson, Carl J. Hambro, Lionel Gelber, Hans Kelsen, Edward Hallet Carr, Halford Mackinder, Edwin L. James, Arthur C. Millspaugh, John Foster Dulles, and John K. Jessup.*

* In a "Background for Peace" to which I have already referred, the Editors of *Time* ask whether men are ready for world government, and conclude: "The hold of nationalism is still deep in the people. In no nation on earth—least of all in any powerful nation—are the people yet prepared to trade their precious nationality for true world citizenship, to trust their welfare to the other peoples of the globe."

These men, who have thought and written about the aftermath of the present war, regard any plans which call for the abolition of national sovereignty as totally unfeasible in our time, which means that world peace is also unfeasible now. The reason they give is always the same: in the name of national independence, the great majority of people everywhere are deeply opposed to world federation.

These writers unfortunately fail to note that this true ideal is a false motive when the choice is between national sovereignty and world government. As a result, they do not see that what is improbable now under the prevailing confusions and misconceptions will become more and more probable in the future, in proportion as enlightenment about these matters becomes a widespread public possession.

(4) *Patriotism.* Like national freedom, patriotism deserves to be idealized.

In its pure form, patriotism consists of loyalty to the welfare of one's community. The well-being of a community is the common good for which individuals must work if they seek the benefits of community life.

Without patriotism, which is nothing but a willingness to serve the common good, no community could long survive, even if unmolested by foreign aggressors.

But like other ideals, patriotism suffers the admixture of impure motives.

Because of the fact that patriotism usually becomes most intense and articulate when a nation is engaged in foreign wars, it tends to adopt the slogan, "My country, right or wrong!" From being a proper devotion to the common good of one's own community, patriotism becomes a violent antagonism to everything alien.

Since independent nations are always potentially at war, the patriot will usually maintain the same attitude during periods of truce. He is willing to die for victory when the shooting begins.

When the guns are silent, he wishes to see his own country supreme in all the so-called "peaceful pursuits." As Mr. Emery Reves recently pointed out,

> If a man says loudly and publicly five times daily: "I am the greatest man in the world," everybody will laugh at him and believe him mad. But if he expresses the same psychopathological impulse in the plural and says publicly five times daily: "We are the greatest nation in the world," then he is sure to be regarded as a great patriot and statesman, and will attract the admiration not only of his own nation, but of all mankind.

But to charge patriotism, even in its pathological extreme, with being the cause of war or national rivalry is to put the cart before the horse. The misdirection or excess of patriotism results from the international anarchy. So long as nations remain independent, and hence always potentially at war, it is impossible to dissociate the proper from the improper aims of patriotism.

One might even go further and say that there can be no rational limit to the partisanship of the patriot so long as his patriotism must remain partisan.

In his collection of essays, *War—Patriotism—Peace,* Count Tolstoi charged patriotism with being the cause of war and the stumbling block to peace. With a similar point of view, Thorstein Veblen, in his book on peace, defined patriotism as

> A sense of partisan solidarity in respect of prestige . . . a spirit of particularism, of aliency and animosity between contrasted groups of persons. It lives on invidious comparison and works out in mutual hindrance between nations. . . . It makes for national pretensions and international jealousy and distrust, with warlike enterprise always in perspective; as a way to national gain or a recourse in case of need.

What both writers fail to observe is that nationalism precedes patriotism. It does not follow it.

Under conditions of national independence, patriotism may facilitate the making of overt war, but it does not cause it. Nevertheless, patriotism will remain an obstacle to peace as long as men fail to separate the pure motive of allegiance to the common good from the impurities which arise from a plurality of conflicting common goods.

Like charity, patriotism begins at home. But like charity, it need not and should not end there. Love of country will remain antagonistic to love of one's fellow man as long as one's country does not include all men in a single political fellowship.

Just as men will someday learn that the only alternative to national independence is not life in a subjugated dependency, so they will learn that the only alternative to national patriotism is not treason or disloyalty. They will come to see, on the contrary, that world government is needed to purify patriotism—to make it impeccable as the loyalty to a common good in which all men share.

Such universal patriotism will in no way diminish the devotion men will always have to their local community. They will always have a natural affection for their hearth and land, a natural affinity for their place of birth and the companions of their youth. Universal patriotism will merely extend the range of their allegiance, and properly subordinate the narrower to the wider loyalty.

The clarified understanding of these matters may take education a long time to achieve. During that time, the world will be full of provincial patriots. All questions of blame aside, the simple fact is that the misconceptions underlying such patriotism bar the way to peace.

8

To exemplify these obstacles at work, I quote from an editorial in an influential American newspaper, the *Detroit Free Press*.

This paper opposes world federation. Its editorial can be taken

as the prototype of predominant public·opinion in all the powerful and wealthy nations of the world. In many particulars, though
not all, that will resemble the public attitude in the weaker or
poorer nations.

The editorial puts the following questions to its readers:

1. Are you willing to exchange our Stars and Stripes for any
   other flag?
2. Are you willing to have the United States of America lose
   its rights as an independent nation?
3. Are you willing to have any man world ruler, for life,
   with unlimited powers?
4. Are you willing to have unrestricted immigration from
   all countries?
5. Are you willing to risk bringing the American standard of
   living down to the average of the rest of the world?
6. Are you willing to encourage the transfer of our great
   industries to foreign countries where labor is cheaper?

The writer obviously thinks the questions are rhetorical. He
thinks that most Americans would readily answer them all in
the negative. He is quite right.

In August, 1943, the national commander of the American
Legion delivered a speech in which he said:

I am only interested in a national defense force, an American
army and navy that will fight for the dictates of our American
judgment, regardless of what any international court or society may decide. . . . [I do not want to] let some other
foreign group of governments decide what America's policy
shall be, what America's financial interests shall be, whom
America will feed, supply, and support.*

* In September, at the time of electing a new national commander, the Legion
unanimously adopted the report of its foreign-relations committee, which recommended "that our nation can best serve and protect its national interests, com-
mensurate with its power and responsibilities, by participation in the establishment
and maintenance of *an association of free and sovereign nations,* implemented with
whatever force may be necessary to maintain world peace and prevent a recurrence
of war." [Italics mine.]

If anyone is tempted to dismiss this because of its source, let him remember the remarks of the late Senator Borah when he was Chairman of the Senate's Committee on Foreign Affairs:

> There are some things in this world more to be desired than peace, and one of them is the unembarrassed and unhampered and untrammeled political independence of this republic. . . . If peace cannot be had without our surrendering that freedom of action, then I am not for peace.

The third question of the six listed by the *Detroit Free Press* confuses the issue by directing its attack against world despotism, not world federation. With that one exception, these questions elicit the four major attitudes which constitute the moral obstacles to world peace.

We must observe that two of these four attitudes—political nationalism and patriotism—are common to men in every part of the world and in every type of state. The other two—race prejudice and economic nationalism—are either peculiar to, or at least stronger in, certain nations than in others. Certainly, concern about national prosperity and standards of living does not motivate the *have-nots* in the same way that it does the *haves*.

Of these four attitudes, the two which are common to all nations are also the two which arise from fundamental confusions or misconceptions concerning the alternatives to national liberty and national allegiance. The other two are more deeply rooted in obdurate emotions and unreasonable desires.

It will take much more than intellectual enlightenment to bring about their cure. Reason can argue the case against political nationalism and partisan patriotism. With the help of experience provided by a rapidly altering world, reason may effect a re-education of the minds of men, which in turn will slowly change the color of their emotions.

But in the area of race prejudice and economic nationalism, the heart of man must first be changed. On these matters, reason cannot touch the passions until the watertight compartments which separate logic from desire and impulse are first broken down. This task belongs to moral reformation, not to merely intellectual education.

9

When in the course of centuries all these obstacles are removed, one more will still remain. It consists in the apportionment of representation in the federal legislature of the world. Unlike all the others we have so far considered, this one is a purely political difficulty. Whereas the others lead men to oppose the very idea of world government, this difficulty will remain to confront men after they are willing to favor world federation, and ready to undertake it. It, too, has its roots in the moral attitudes engendered by centuries of national independence in an anarchic world. But it cannot be solved by education, intellectual or moral.

Let us suppose, for the moment, that a bicameral system must be adopted in order to provide representation both for the states as states and also for their populations. Since the number of small states exceeds the number of large ones, the small states will be able to form a ruling majority by coalition in the upper chamber. Since the larger states are the more populous, the more numerous representatives of a few great powers will be able to dominate the lower house.

Both of these situations will seem objectionable to people and statesmen who are still thinking in terms of national sovereignty and political minorities.

To some extent, the difficulty can be satisfactorily solved only after the existence of a world federation has transformed the relation of peoples. Nevertheless, some solution must be found in the transitional period when the world is slowly passing from one stage of political development to another.

CHAPTER 20

Revolution for Peace

WHEN, AT THE beginning of the eighteenth century, the Abbé de Saint-Pierre outlined his project for perpetual peace in Europe, Cardinal Fleury said to him: "You must begin by sending a troop of missionaries to prepare the hearts and minds of the contracting sovereigns."

In his own comment on Saint-Pierre's plan, Rousseau acknowledged the Cardinal's point. "To prove that peace, as a general principle, is a better thing than war," he wrote, "is to say nothing to the man who has private reasons for preferring war to peace; to show him the means for securing a lasting peace is only to encourage him to work against them."

Cardinal Fleury's educational program, in intent more ironical than serious, would have had to be undertaken with fewer than a hundred men. These were the sovereign princes or potentates to whom Saint-Pierre had addressed his plan. Saint-Pierre was asking them to surrender, said Rousseau, "the right of doing themselves justice; that is to say, the precious right of being unjust when they please . . . the power of making themselves great at the expense of their neighbors."

How shall they be persuaded to forfeit such possessions? Rousseau's answer to this question *seems,* at first glance, to differ from Cardinal Fleury's missionary proposal.

He claimed not to assume that men could be made "good, generous, disinterested, and devoted to the public good from motives of pure humanity." He argued only that if the sovereigns of Europe could be made to see what was *truly* for their own self-interest, they would come to understand that "the establishment of such a peace would be profitable to them in all manner of ways, and that, even from their own point of view, there is no comparison between its drawbacks and advantages."

But when men "have understanding enough to see their own

[*true*] interest, and courage enough to act for their own happiness," they have attained a proper conception of happiness as the perfection of their common human nature, not as an enrichment of their private and peculiar individuality.

In this sense of happiness, what is truly for a man's own interest will also be for the best interests of all other men. One man's happiness will not be gained at the expense of misery to others, or by sacrificing the common good to individual profit.

If men could understand this and had, in addition, the virtues of courage and temperance, prudence and justice, whereby to act accordingly, they would be morally reformed. Asking for no less than this, Rousseau really agreed with Cardinal Fleury that "the hearts and minds of the contracting sovereigns" must be prepared for peace.

If the Cardinal's proposal was ironical, Rousseau's real conclusion was pessimistic. He did not believe the sovereigns could be educated. A half century after Saint-Pierre's original memorandum, he observed that "the project remains unrealized . . . not because it is utopian . . . [but] because men are crazy, and because to be sane in a world of madmen is in itself a kind of madness."

2

In the twentieth century peace also depends on education, but the educational task has become more difficult and greatly enlarged.

It has become more difficult because no eighteenth-century plan, such as Saint-Pierre's, called for the complete abolition of external sovereignty. In most of the classic schemes for peace, both before and after, the decrees of an international congress had to be approved by a unanimous vote; sovereigns could not be compelled to arbitrate their differences; resort to force remained their legitimate prerogative. We have at last come to understand the crucial differences between a mere league of sovereigns or independent nations and a truly federal organization. We know that only the latter can keep the peace of the world.

The task is greatly enlarged, first, because it is world peace, not simply the peace of Europe, which concerns us; and second, because it is no longer a handful of sovereign men who require education for peace, but the hundreds of millions of people who comprise the sovereign nations of the earth.

If Rousseau had little hope that princes or potentates could be taught what was for their own true interest and could be inspired to voluntary action in accordance therewith, should we not yield to greater despair? If Cardinal Fleury did not really believe that a troop of missionaries, however competent in the arts of conversion, could succeed in reforming the hearts and minds of a few contracting sovereigns, how dare we postulate a mission to mankind, with confidence that our educational effort will succeed?

Unless we can give reasons for our hope and confidence, we have no basis for optimism *even in the long run*.

Should education be unequal to the task, the obstacles to peace would be more than present impediments; they would be forever insurmountable. It is not enough to prove the possibility of peace by showing that a world-wide political community *can* be formed by federal institutions. Men must also be willing to adopt the means indispensable to world peace. Should that be beyond all reasonable expectation, then world peace is just as impossible as if the notion of federal government were self-contradictory— intrinsically as unreasonable as perpetual motion.

There is always the danger of proving too little or too much. The obstacles we have been considering were offered as reasons for thinking that peace is improbable in our century. But unless they are genuinely remediable, they prove much more; they prove that peace is impossible. The remedies we must now consider do not go far enough if they merely show that peace is possible, *given infinite time*. They bear on the real prospects for peace only if we have some assurance that, beginning now, education and other factors can gradually clear the way. Thereon rests any definite probability of world peace within so short a finite time as five hundred years.

3

For the last time, let us face the question whether peace is possible.

It is certainly impossible if the obstacles to it reside in any unchangeable features of human nature. If peace required men to be angels, or even most men to be saints, it would be a human impossibility. But the requisite changes in moral attitude and intellectual outlook do not entail superhuman aspirations or counsels of perfection.

Attitudes and opinions are both matters of habit. How men feel toward certain things, and what they believe about them, are consequences of nurture, not endowments of nature.

Were this not so, cultures could not differ from one another in fundamentals of belief or desire. The variety of cultures and historic changes in the growth of any single civilization show plainly enough that men vary in their habits of emotion and thought.

If the moral obstacles to peace were founded on something as instinctive as the impulse to self-preservation, then an unalterable aspect of human nature would forever prevent peace—at least for men so long as they remained men. But the moral failings and the intellectual misconceptions which seem to be the chief impediments are not instinctive.

They are habits of character and of mind. They have been acquired in the course of history and under certain cultural influences. These habits can be changed in the course of time and by means of the same factors which originally formed them—education and experience.

The intellectual habits are the easier to change. Men have outgrown superstitions as profound as the belief that loss of national independence *always* amounts to political subjugation. The conquest of false opinion has been accomplished not only in the fields of physics and medicine; it has also taken place in the sphere of social and political ideas.

Most men once thought that subjection to a despot was the natural condition of the majority. Most men no longer think so in some parts of the world. That is quite sufficient to show that, in the future, most men everywhere can become enlightened on this point.

We can argue similarly in the case of peace. Some men in the world today—however few relatively—do understand that world federation would in no way deprive nations or their people of any degree of true human liberty. This fact shows that the prevalent notions about national independence are not innate ideas which all men have from birth, and from which they cannot free themselves. Inculcated by miseducation, the confusions about sovereignty can be removed by sound teaching.

In these matters, formal schooling usually needs to be reinforced by the lessons of experience. Experience supplemented teaching in bringing large numbers of men to understand their natural right to self-government—the right which despotism violates. In the same way that the whole atmosphere of political thought has been changed on this point, it can and will be changed with regard to the false notion that absolute sovereignty belongs to nations by natural right.

4

There is, in short, no intellectual impediment to peace which sound education, supported by some experience, cannot cure. But the moral difficulties, ultimately due to emotional disorders, may be less susceptible to such remedies.

Waiving for the moment the question of how they can be handled, we must first consider whether they are utterly incorrigible. Is race prejudice, for example, a natural human attitude, so emotionally ingrained that friendship can never cross the color line? Is hatred of other races as natural an endowment as the complexion and other physical characteristics which mark a man as belonging by birth to a particular race?

There are two sets of facts which prove the negative answer. In the first place, there have been and are many groups of men who suffer so little from race prejudice that miscegenation does not seem abhorrent to them. They do not harbor the familiar shibboleths about race purity and inequality; nor do they feel any emotional repugnance to an unlike strain of human blood.

If race prejudice were as natural or instinctive as the antipathy of the quadruped for the snake, the blending of human stocks which has occurred all over the world could never have happened.

In the second place, we have seen within the last hundred years the salutary effects of education. Both by what is taught in the schools and by the spiritual and emotional training given at home, some children have been freed from a race prejudice which still prevails in sections of the society to which they belong. The fact that the numbers are comparatively small does not affect the point that children *can* be reared without race prejudice.

If it can be done in some cases, it can be done in more. The educational influence can spread from generation to generation.

Where it exists in its most virulent forms, race prejudice is usually conditioned by political and economic fears. When diverse races inhabit the same locality in sharply unequal numbers, the minority which has monopolized certain political or economic privileges fears race equality as a threat to its advantage, and hates the people whose very being embodies this threat.

The hatred can be as fierce when it is the minority which suffers from political restrictions or economic deprivations. And regardless of whether the domineering group is the majority or the minority, those who do injustice usually hate their victims as much as those who suffer it hate their oppressors, though the hatred springs from dissimilar fears and pains.

The problem of underprivileged groups is a problem of political and economic justice. The problem is complicated when the underprivileged group is biologically differentiated from the rest of a population. It is further complicated by a numerical inequality which, were it to be combined with social equality, would shift the balance of power.

This problem, however complicated, can be solved. It is fundamentally no different from problems of justice which have already been solved.

To the extent that race prejudice rests upon political or economic conflicts, it can be cured by removing the conditions responsible for such conflicts. Fair treatment of minorities and protection of majorities against the specially privileged few will present problems to world government, as it now presents problems to particular communities. The principles for solving this type of problem are the same in both cases.

When those whose work it is to formulate the institutions of world government show what concrete steps can be taken to solve this type of problem, they will do much to overcome the emotional difficulties connected with the diversity of races.

5

The intellectual solution of a problem of justice remains a purely theoretical achievement until men are willing to put it into practice.

The crux of the matter, therefore, lies in moral education—in the redirection of human desires. How shall those who now seem to profit by injustice be brought to feel, as well as to see, that their gain is spurious, their loss real?

This question is especially pertinent to that moral obstacle to peace which arises from existing economic inequalities, whether between races or nations. Economic nationalism obstructs peace to the extent that the wealthier nations oppose any interference with their present advantages or opportunities. How can they ever be made willing to sacrifice their favored position, in view of the fact that the nations who would benefit by their sacrifices could not requite them by an exchange of favors? Are we not asking for the purest and most disinterested generosity?

This was Rousseau's problem: how could the sovereign princes of Europe be made to see and feel that European peace was to their *real* advantage?

We have a better chance of solving this problem now and in the next few centuries, for the simple reason that world peace depends ultimately on the action of common people everywhere, not upon the decisions of sovereign men, or even of government officials temporarily in power. Paradoxical though it may seem at first, the educational task is easier when we are dealing with the great mass of mankind than when we contemplate changing the minds and hearts of a few great potentates.

One might despair, with Rousseau, of ever bringing the crowned heads of Europe to their senses; but one need not feel nearly so hopeless about the common man's adoption of common sense. Those whose *apparent* advantages are very great always find it more difficult to recognize that they are *only apparent*. Precisely because they seemed to enjoy unlimited power, the peerless sovereigns of Europe might never have been able to understand how their true interests could be served by subordinating themselves to law and government.

The parallel today will be found in the situation of the wealthier classes of the wealthier nations. Economic nationalism is much more intense on the part of the upper classes, because the *apparent* advantages they derive from national prosperity are so much greater than those of the proletariat and the petty bourgeoisie. The poor people, of whom God made so many, will find it much easier to understand that their true interest is served by world peace, even though world peace may require certain economic adjustments which appear to benefit the poor people of other nations.

It might be supposed that the economic royalists in the more prosperous nations would gradually come to their senses as world war succeeded world war. Each world war tends to confiscate some portion of their wealth and to increase their burden of taxation. But so long as their relative position remains unchanged, so long as they continue to be the wealthier class in the wealthier nation, they probably will not be able to undeceive themselves about their personal or national advantages.

So far as economic matters are concerned, the motivation which must prevail can be simply expressed. Individuals in each nation must ask, not how do we want world affairs arranged so that we are better off economically than others, but how do we want world affairs arranged so that we can live better, more human, lives, *even though we live no better than men do elsewhere*.

To the wrong question, how can we be better off at the expense of others, *any* answer will oppose world peace. To the right question, how can world affairs be arranged so that all men are better off, the *only* answer will stipulate the political and economic conditions of world peace.

The real choice men must make is not between the answers, but between the questions. Which question they ask will depend upon what they want: to retain the economic advantages they now have, or to improve the spiritual conditions of human life. In either case, they can be selfish, for they will be seeking their own good; but in the second case, what is genuinely to their self-interest will also be equally to the self-interest of everyone else.

When they recognize that it is not great wealth which makes for happiness, when they understand that happiness depends on a decent sufficiency of external goods, not upon wasteful surpluses, they will see that they are not really disadvantaged by other men having *enough*, so long as they themselves also have *enough*. They will see that they are humanly better off in a world in which they are neither humanly nor economically *better off than other men*. They will understand the truth of R. H. Tawney's insight that "if a man has important work, and enough leisure and income to enable him to do it properly, he is in possession of as much happiness as is good for any of the children of Adam."

These are not difficult matters to teach or learn—so far as the great mass of mankind is concerned. The great mass of mankind consists of poor men. The choice between God and Mammon is less difficult for poor men, not because they are morally superior by nature, but because they have had the good fortune to be neglected by Mammon.

Under the prevalent materialism of certain western nations, such as the United States, England, France, or Holland, children who are not born with silver spoons in their mouths learn soon enough that Mammon is a fickle god whose favors can be won. The rich are corrupted by Mammon, and the poor by envy and emulation of the rich.

To the extent that men pursue such paths, education has failed, morally and intellectually. The schools have failed. The churches have failed. The home has failed. These educational failures are a matter of record, but the record is not an indelible portent of the future.

In proportion as education becomes more democratic, both in intention and execution, it will become morally and intellectually sounder in content. When, following government, education becomes for, of, and by the people, it will be able to teach doctrines now regarded as subversive.

Now they are subversive—but only of the existing inequities, of the perversion which is materialism. Then they will not be subversive; social and economic reforms will have already turned the tables; revolution will have already blasted the way for the sort of education that is now revolutionary.

6

In the sphere of economic morals, education by itself cannot do what is required for peace; but when, with or without violence, the economy is revolutionized, education can save later generations from relapsing into the error of identifying happiness with wealth.

Education cannot cure what R. H. Tawney called the sickness of an acquisitive society. More drastic remedies are needed for that. The struggle for economic democracy of the sort Tawney describes as a functional society must take place, as did the earlier struggle for political democracy, in the arena of social action. The prior achievement of political democracy may enable it to effect the necessary transformations more gradually and with less violence.

Educational reforms will follow, not precede, these fundamental social changes. Especially in the field of moral matters, education leans heavily on the supporting social context. As Plato pointed out, the community itself is the most influential teacher of youth. The schools cannot effectively teach justice in a society which permits, and even rewards, injustice.

If the probability of peace depended on the likelihood that education—whether by church, home, or school—could gain a singlehanded victory over the moral obstacles, it would not be great. The fairness of the prospect arises from the expectation that a combination of factors will progressively and reciprocally support each other.

Social changes will redirect and reinforce education; sounder education will consolidate and extend economic and political reforms. And, what is most crucial, the decision to make peace, to institute world government, will gain its ultimate force from the resolution of common men all over the world.

The prediction that peace is probable within five hundred years is equivalent to the prediction that during this period the real and effective democratization of the world will have progressed far enough to overcome the moral obstacles. They will not be entirely removed. Men will not have become saints. But with the ascendancy of the common man in the various nations of the world, a real convergence of interests will be as likely as it was unlikely when the interests of sovereign princes had to be consulted.

CHAPTER 21

Education for Peace

DEMOCRATIC EDUCATION has just begun in the politically advanced nations.

Less than a hundred years ago, popular education existed neither in fact nor in idea. By the middle of the nineteenth century, only a small part of any population received adequate schooling. Liberal education, supposedly given by the colleges and universities, was reserved for gentlemen, which meant, of course, those who could afford the expense. The rest of the population was economically disfranchised from the educational rights of man, whether or not it was also politically disfranchised from the civic rights.

Within a hundred years or less, that situation has changed remarkably in the more advanced nations. Eight or twelve years of public schooling have become the normal opportunity or requirement for most children. The colleges, which should provide the basic disciplines of liberal education, now enroll a larger proportion of the nation's youth. State institutions, scholarships, and other devices have removed some of the economic impediments to the completion of what should be, for every child, its minimum education.

We know how great has been the quantitative achievement resulting from the multiplication of schools, teachers, and students. But we also know how far below a just equalization of educational opportunity the present achievement still is, certainly in some of the larger democracies, such as England or the United States.

The definite and clear progress of the last hundred years must, and probably will, be completed during the next century, by removing every economic and social impediment to making liberal education as universal as suffrage and citizenship.

In certain quarters, it is still supposed that the real impediment to the extension of liberal education lies elsewhere. It is supposed to be the limited mental capacity of at least half of the population—the half below the mid-point in the distribution of intelligence, the half that some of our self-styled "democratic educators" regard as fit only for vocational training, not for liberal education. Intelligence being a natural endowment, social and economic reforms can make liberal education available to all, but it cannot, according to the vocationalists, make all able to take it.

This supposition contradicts the fundamental tenets of political democracy or, worse, leads to a hypocritical espousal of them, and to a travesty on the fundamental notion of citizenship. A citizen must be competent to exercise critical judgment on civic affairs. He must be capable of acting under leadership by rational persuasion, and under the auspices of public debate of public issues.

Leadership ceases to be democratic when it must resort to propaganda, when it pushes or pulls political donkeys around by means of the stick applied to the rear or the carrot held under the nose. Democracy exists only on paper and in the legal provisions of the constitution so long as its leaders maneuver donkeys; and its followers are domesticated animals, not free men.

The freedom of citizenship can be legally granted and protected, but it cannot be actually realized, apart from the development of free men through free minds. Men are by nature born for such freedom, but nothing less than liberal education can discipline men for the political use of freedom which is the meaning of citizenship.

The dilemma we face is as onerous as it is inescapable. *Either* all men who do not have to be put into asylums for their own and the public welfare can be liberally educated, *or* all men do not have enough intelligence to discharge the duties of citizenship.

If we choose the second horn of the dilemma, we must either honestly repudiate the democratic faith that all normal men deserve citizenship, or we must become hypocrites, affirming democracy while believing that large numbers of men can never be competent citizens.

The facts do not compel us to choose the second alternative. Only *appearances* lead many of our self-styled democratic educators to suppose that the nation must always remain half free and half slave, half educated for citizenship and half vocationally trained for economic services and political puppethood.

The *appearances* are due to the fact that *we have not yet begun to try* to give liberal education to all grades of intelligence above the feeble-mindedness which warrants hospitalization. We have not yet devised the pedagogy and the curriculum needed to perform this great educational task.

2

The quantitative extension of general education has been incompletely accomplished in a hundred years. That it can and will be completed in another century is a matter of little doubt. But the qualitative improvement of popular education remains to be initiated.

Not only must our colleges cease to be largely vocational rather than liberal institutions, but we must find ways and means for giving a truly liberal education to *every* future citizen.

No one ever thought of this problem until the present century. Before it was understood that all men deserve equal educational opportunity, no one even faced the problem of educating all men liberally. Now that the problem has at last appeared, it will become more and more the dominant concern of democratic societies.

The beginning of a solution may wait for two or three centuries of experimentation with all the educational devices that human ingenuity can invent. But we have every reason to trust that the problem will be progressively solved. The nature of man as a political animal warrants the confidence that normal human nature is susceptible to the kind of education a political animal needs. In the course of time, properly directed efforts will create universal citizenship in fact, as well as in law.

The most important part of the problem is the continuation of public education for adults. Liberal discipline can be begun in schools, but the trained mind must be helped to complete its education during the years of adult life.

Mature moral and political insights, and the very substance of human wisdom, cannot be possessed by children in school or college. The youthful mind can be trained in all the arts of social discourse and, perforce, of thinking—but only the adult who knows *how* to think can really judge *what* to think about the serious problems which confront responsible men and women.

Children can be prepared for citizenship in school by the training of the mind; but adults, who have already entered upon the duties of citizenship, must be kept intellectually alive by the consideration and discussion of the fundamental ideas which illuminate economic and political problems. This is the main task of adult education. It is the ultimate educational task of democratic societies.

In the advanced nations of the world, democratic education has begun, quantitatively if not qualitatively. Yet enough has been accomplished to permit the assurance that the rest will follow in the coming centuries. In the backward nations of the world, basic political and economic revolutions must first take place. Only then can democratic education begin. If the politically more mature nations provide sound educational models to follow, other peoples will be able to adopt these exemplary programs, and adapt them to their own circumstances, even as they must adopt and adapt the basic principles and practices of constitutionalism.

Truly democratic education, as well as actual experience of democratic life, must become world-wide before men everywhere can become citizens of the world, in addition to being citizens of their local community. In view of the progress that has been made so far, and in view of the further developments which it portends, it seems reasonable to predict that the members of the human race can be made ready for world citizenship within five hundred years.

3

Most men today, even the well educated by prevailing standards, tend to misconceive freedom as freedom from government. They confuse anarchic with civil liberty. Only the anarchic individual or nation enjoys the doubtful blessings of absolute independence, doubtful because they run counter to the nature of both men and nations. Men living in a civil society can have nothing better than liberty under law; but nothing better should be desired, for such civil liberty perfectly fits the political culture of man.

Civil liberty is not unlimited freedom. It is a freedom bounded by maximal and minimal conditions. In a just society, no man should have more liberty than he can use justly, nor less than he needs to live a good life. More liberty than this becomes criminal license. Less deprives men of dignity, degrading them to slavery, which consists in their being used as means to the happiness or, more strictly, the selfish interests of other men.

It should be obvious that civil liberty is not incompatible with law and government. A man is no less free because he must obey a just law, even if he is not the author of that law, or would have wished to see it formulated differently in some particulars. Political freedom does not mean self-determination or self-government in that anarchic sense which recognizes no authority except one's own will—or whim—and hence yields obedience only to superior force.

Men are not self-governing through the possession of absolute autonomy without also being isolated individuals subject to all the predatory forces in their environment. They may enjoy anarchic liberty, but they cannot have freedom from want or fear; and though they have free speech, they have no use for it.

As members of a political community, and hence bereft of their autonomy as of their isolation, men are self-governing to whatever extent they have civil liberty. Self-government or self-determination means no more than having a voice in one's own government. The man who enjoys the status of citizenship has self-government in this sense. He participates in the determination of all public affairs by which he is affected; but that does not mean that he is free to reject any determination which others judge to be for the common good and which he thinks contrary to his own interests.

If he wants that sort of self-government or self-determination, he must abdicate his citizenship in favor of anarchic liberty.

What holds for individual men holds for nations. Yet national independence and self-determination are ideals for many persons who would not think themselves anarchists.

They must be helped to see that the political liberty of a people is augmented rather than lost when their nation loses its independence and becomes, along with other states, part of a federation. Emery Reves has put his finger on the prevalent fallacy:

> The total independence of nations, as we understood it until now, does not guarantee the freedom of nations for the simple reason that total independence of nations means not only that a nation can do whatever it wants, but that other nations are also completely free to do whatever they want.

While the federated state ceases to have the sort of self-determination which is incompatible with superior government, it retains self-government in the sense that its people, and even its own political entity, are represented in all the departments of the federal government.

Self-government through representation is better than self-government through autonomy, for the same reason that civil government is better than anarchic liberty. Men and nations, not being fit by nature for absolute independence, increase rather than diminish their freedom from want and fear by joining with others to form a community, and by submitting to its laws and government.

In doing so, men give up savagery for citizenship and civilization; nations give up sovereignty for justice and for peace.

4

When these things come to be generally understood, political nationalism will not be able to defend itself in the good name of liberty.

Until world government is instituted, men will rightly continue to regard national independence as preferable to political dependency. But when they understand that national independence deserves to be safeguarded only against conquering aggressors, they will also see that national self-determination should be sacrificed for a better political life and more political liberty than international anarchy can ever afford.

They will understand and see these things when the theory of world peace—of world community and world government—become common knowledge everywhere in the world. To teach this theory, both in school and through every medium of adult education, by radio and motion picture as well as by printed page, becomes the great intellectual task which future education for peace must perform.

Until the nineteenth century, there was no general public discussion of the problems of peace. By the end of that century, over four hundred "peace organizations" had been formed, distributed over fifteen countries, and over one thousand international peace congresses had been held. We are now prepared to go beyond these rudimentary stages of public education for peace.

Both the First and the Second World Wars of the twentieth century have been accompanied by great intensification of popular and academic interest in the problem. Whereas almost no one in the nineteenth century really understood the difference between mere internationalism and world government, today there are many men, however relatively small the number, who see that leagues of nations, world courts, and world congresses will not work so long as they are accommodated to the external sovereignty of states.

Today there are many plans for world peace which insist upon federal government as a minimum condition. Though some of these are still confused on the point of sovereignty, speaking of its limitation rather than its abolition, further and wider discussion will certainly result in the necessary clarifications.

The discussion will eventually find its way into the schools and colleges of every country. Up to the present, a boy or girl could complete formal schooling without ever having faced the problems or come to terms with the principles of its solution. For the most part, collegiate debate has centered around the issue between pacifism and militarism, and even that has been largely extracurricular.

From now on, and increasingly in the future, world peace will become, along with democracy and the just economy, one of the great themes which tie together many of the fundamental subjects in the liberal curriculum—history and social science, enlightened by moral and political philosophy, informed throughout by a proper understanding of the rational animality and the social individuality of man.

Within several centuries, both formal and adult education will have undermined the fallacies of political nationalism, and shown that it presents a false ideal because an uncompromising one. The understanding of these matters which a few men now have will become the general possession of educated men; and since men will be generally educated in larger and larger numbers, we can easily foresee the day when the now prevalent confusions about sovereignty and liberty will have been deprived of serious influence upon the course of public actions.

The prevalent opinion will then be that peace is possible, that the conditions requisite for it are practically realizable in a near future, and that it is within the power of human effort to make that future nearer still.

These educational accomplishments will be reinforced by an enlarging experience of, and participation in, the work of all sorts of international agencies. The League of Nations and the World Court we have known so far are merely the beginnings of international organization. Though every form of international organization falls short of world government, and hence remains inadequate for peace, such agencies and institutions are truly intermediate and evolutionary steps between unregenerate nationalism and the world polity. They will be more useful educationally, in the way of the concrete experience they provide, than in preventing the wars which will occur during their regime. They will bring about a gradual, almost imperceptible, change in the outlook of men on world affairs.

If, as seems quite possible, these international agencies should include a permanent constitutional convention, engaged in drafting specific provisions for world federation, then men everywhere will become acquainted with the concrete terms of peace.

5

Under the impact of changing world realities, and freed by education from its traditional blinders, patriotism will also undergo a gradual transformation. Whereas the fallacy underlying political nationalism must be exposed and corrected, the truth at the heart of patriotism must be given unlimited generality.

In a book dedicated to Marcus Aurelius, who first dreamed of world citizenship, Edward J. Byng distinguished sharply between *inter*nationalism and *supra*nationalism.

Supra-nationalism is true cosmopolitanism. In ancient Greece, the teachers of the Stoic school of philosophy coined the term *Cosmopolis*. It denoted the ideal of a world community of free and equal peoples. In other words, *cosmopoli-*

tanism is democracy on the supra-national plane—world democracy, one and indivisible.

In the cold light of reality, I cannot agree with Mr. Byng that his or any other five-year peace plan can be put into operation now, or at any time in this century. But I do most certainly agree with his educational insight. "Our children," he writes, "must learn that *a constructive patriot and a good cosmopolitan are two terms for the same thing. . . . Only a good cosmopolitan can be a constructive American.*"

These are profound truths, but it will take centuries before patriotism becomes constructive, before Americans or any other people become genuinely cosmopolitan in emotion as well as mind. At present, the word "cosmopolitan" generally means a man of the world on the convivial rather than the political level. A patriot is anything but cosmopolitan in the good sense. Good Americans, or good Englishmen, Russians, and Chinese, put America first, or England, Russia, China—not the world.

If Mr. Byng will extend his view from five years to five hundred, he can expect education and experience to accomplish, gradually and imperceptibly, what no present blueprint for peace can create by fiat overnight.

In the past, human allegiances have shifted and grown. Feudal loyalties were slowly transmuted into national patriotism. Men who were Scotchmen or Englishmen *first* became citizens of Great Britain; men who were Vermonters or Virginians *first* became Americans first. The transition from Great Britain or America *first* to primary world allegiance will be a similar transformation of national into cosmopolitan patriotism.

Any man who arose today and campaigned for world peace under the slogan "America second!" would be lynched. As a creature of my time, I myself shudder when I realize that this is exactly what I am advocating. But so, too, would any man have been lynched in the 1780's who called for Vermont or Virginia second. As late as 1861, Robert E. Lee, a man who loved his country, as he had served it, well, put Virginia first. Even in 1943, you can get into a good fight in the state of Texas by saying "Texas second!"

We must all discipline our emotions so that we can face the facts without passion or prejudice. Englishmen must learn to say, "England second!", Russians, "Russia second!", Americans, "America second!" The true patriot can become reconciled to, perhaps even enthusiastic about, these difficult words if he but realizes that *peace requires no nation to be second to any other, but only to the world.*

Devotion to the common good, which is the constructive part of loving one's country, will remain as genuinely patriotic when the common good is the welfare of the world's federated states. The essence of patriotism, like the essence of charity, is not affected by the number or proximity of one's fellow men, or by the size of the community in which all share.

The theologian tells us that we naturally feel a stronger love for those to whom we are more closely related by ties of political fellowship or blood. But as the boundaries of political fellowship enlarge, the universal brotherhood of man will become a concrete reality instead of an ideal.

Without changing in essence patriotism will widen in scope. In its political significance, charity will apply, like justice, to *all men equally.* Political peace is primarily the work of justice, but on the world-wide, as on the national, scale, it must be vitalized by the political aspect of charity, which is patriotism. True love of one's country is generous love, love which gives without asking requital.

Patriotism, therefore, can hardly be viewed as an obdurate obstacle to peace. It is itself a creature of changing conditions. The emotions and ideas which it expresses can be molded to fit changing political realities. Already some men have the insights and feelings which make their patriotism constructively cosmopolitan. In the course of a dozen generations, the intellectual and emotional atmosphere in which children will grow up will be pervaded by the elements of a new and better patriotism.

6

Of all the things which must develop before peace can be established, only one need be *completely* accomplished. A world federation cannot be instituted until all of the federating nations have manifested their capacity for republican government.

But with respect to all the other obstacles, the beginning of world peace need not wait for their *complete* removal. They must be overcome just enough to permit the predominance of a favorable attitude toward world government.

To some degree, economic and political nationalism will survive the day when a world federation begins to function. It will survive in the form of natural tensions between the federal government and the several states, and even among the states themselves. There will be doctrines of "state's rights." In world affairs, political parties will oppose one another on platforms stressing local or federal welfare.

Race prejudice will remain a problem for world government to solve by adequate protection for minorities, and by sustaining the positive values in cultural diversity. All men will not love one another with the love of God, nor will the lion lie down with the lamb. World patriotism may have taken root, but actual experience of world political life will be needed for its full flowering. The cosmopolitan spirit cannot be expected to flourish before the cosmopolis exists as an object of loyalty.

At one extreme, there is the error of supposing that peace can be established by world political institutions *prior* to any of the moral and intellectual changes needed to make those institutions *sufficiently acceptable* to *enough people*. At the opposite extreme is the error of supposing that the heart and mind of man must be completely ready before the necessary institutions can be initiated.

The institutionalist and the moralist fail to see that two sets of factors are everywhere interactive. Men must be morally and intellectually ready for political institutions—*but only to some degree.* Once the institutions exist, they will condition the whole social environment, and produce further moral and intellectual changes favorable to their own operation.

The moralist underestimates the educative influence of political institutions. The institutionalist does not pay enough attention to the psychological soil in which institutions must take root. It has been said, for example, that international institutions will not work until an international conscience exists. This strains the truth. The truth is that an international conscience will not be *robust* until international agencies become operative, and that international institutions will not work *well* until an international conscience matures. At an earlier stage, the weakest strain of international conscience may be sufficient to permit the tentative and halfhearted adoption of international institutions.

There is continual play back and forth between the moral and the institutional factors; they are mutually supporting and reciprocally related as cause and effect. As each develops, it strengthens the other, but each in developing draws some strength from the other.

What has been said about the moral and institutional aspects of internationalism applies equally to the moral and institutional aspects of supranationalism. If world peace could not be established until moral readiness for its institutions and arrangements had been perfected, it would never be realized in this world of men, for the attitudes and ideas of men do not change in a social vacuum. They take their color and impulse from the social environment which institutions create. If the moralist were right, we would have to conclude that peace is as remote as the end of time.

If, on the other hand, world peace could be established in a psychological vacuum by the blueprints for the necessary institutions, it could be established within our lifetime. Nothing but the soundness of the plans would be needed for their practical success. If the institutionalist were right about this, we would have to conclude that peace is highly probable in the present century.

A more reasonable conclusion follows, it seems to me, from recognizing the truth in both extremes. The prospect of peace within five hundred years does not overlook the moral obstacles which arise in response to the very nature of the institutional requirements; nor does it underestimate the role which institutional factors will play in perfecting the moral and intellectual development of men born into a world at peace.

PART FOUR

THE PRACTICALITY
OF PEACE

CHAPTER 22

Ends

THE ISSUE between the pessimist and the optimist can be resolved. The resolution turns on two predictions: first, that a lasting world peace will be made, but not in our time; and, therefore, second, that we can expect more wars, even world wars, in the interim. This may not appear to be a resolution because it seems to adopt the pessimistic position and to reject the major claim of the optimist that we can do something *now* about perpetual peace. But it has also rejected the extreme pessimism which denies the possibility of a durable peace; and even though it makes the probability of peace more remote than the extreme optimist likes to admit, it agrees with him that the probability justifies us in regarding peace as a practicable objective *now*.

The balanced character of the resolution will be seen more clearly in terms of objectives than in terms of predictions. The pessimist tends to be the sort of realist who dismisses, as impractical, any undertaking which cannot be realized immediately. The optimist tends to be the sort of idealist who disdains, as undesirable, such immediate goals as a prolonged truce. But we are not compelled to choose between these false extremes any more than we must resign ourselves to extreme pessimism or excite ourselves to extreme optimism.

The issue between the idealist and the realist is a false issue because it creates two false positions—the man with his head in the clouds and the man with his feet on the earth. Not all the relevant facts lie at our feet. Some can only be seen if we raise our heads. The idealist can be a man with his feet on the ground, but he does not have to keep his head there also; nor need the realist fear that lifting his head a little will transport him wholly into airy spaces.

2

We must agree with the pessimist that there are going to be more wars, general as well as local. Wars will continue to occur until we succeed in making peace. Since there is only one way to make peace on earth, and since the pessimist is right in his judgment about the realities of our century, we must agree with him that it is highly improbable that we will see the beginning of world peace.

We must agree with the optimist that a perpetual and universal peace is entirely possible and, what is more important, that it is highly probable within a short finite time—even if not short enough to suit the impatient. What for our ancestors was merely a dream has become for us a future reality and a practical objective. Marcus Aurelius and Tom Paine could talk of being citizens of the world, but they were merely recommending a frame of mind. We can foresee the existence of a world community in which our posterity will actually live as citizens.

I am fully aware of the hazards of prophecy when I predict that, under the accelerating conditions of technical progress, economic revolution, and social emancipation, five hundred years is enough to allow. Within that time, perhaps even in half of that time, all the conditioning factors will have matured to the point where no external impediments will remain. Within that time, educational progress and the spread of education to the common people in all lands will have instructed men everywhere concerning the institutions it is within their power to erect, *if they want peace*.

I am not supposing that men benighted by ignorance or deceived by their erstwhile masters want peace. The human passions mislead men, and they can be used to mislead them. But it is also true that knowledge and understanding direct the passions of *some* men; they can be used to direct *all* men in the free pursuit of what is really for their good. This is the work of education, moral and intellectual.

In the past, education has been hampered by economic slavery and by social inequalities. Worse than that, education itself has been a tool of the privileged classes. It has been misused to safeguard the status enjoyed by the few. In consequence, it has not merely been an instrument for oppressing the many; it has even failed to enlighten the few.

But a social revolution lies ahead—wider and more drastic than any the world has ever known. The names "citizen" and "comrade" are the most revolutionary words in any language. They will sweep the world free when "*all* men" finally comes to signify each and every human person.

It may take several centuries or more for this to work itself out. The industrialization of the so-called backward parts of the world will facilitate it. Economic upheavals will provide the occasions for economic reforms. Social and economic emancipations will make a reality of the fine words in the historic documents which have proclaimed the natural rights and sacred liberties of man. Political democracy, long in the process of development, will perfect itself by constitutional amendment in those countries blessed by constitutions, and it will spread by revolution to those where despotism must first be downed by force. As these changes go forward, education will operate as a cause to accelerate them, even as the reform of education will itself be an effect produced by them. When *all* men have become citizens in the fullest sense of that word, they will constitute themselves citizens of the world under a government which unites rather than divides their allegiance.

Hence, by avoiding the extremes of cynicism and naïveté, it is quite possible to be both an optimist and a pessimist—a pessimist for the short run, an optimist in the long run. When the same man is both an optimist and a pessimist, he can begin the running of both races *now*. He should not derive so much comfort from his optimism that he sits back to let time do the work; nor should he be so disheartened by his pessimism that he would rather do nothing than the little he can do.

3

In that little word "now" lies the key to a genuinely practical resolution of the problem of war and peace.

It refers to the present: not merely to the passing moment, but to the immediate future, that whole period of our lifetime in which we who face practical problems have both the opportunity and the obligation to act. In the sphere of practical problems, time is of the essence. We can *think* about eternal truths, but when we contemplate *action* we must remember what time it is.

The remote future is all the rest of time after "now." It is like the past in that neither the past nor the remote future provides us with occasions for action. But unlike the past, which cannot in any way be affected by our actions, the remote future will most certainly be affected by what we do. Yet we cannot *solve* that future's problems. They do not belong to us. A practical problem belongs to us, to the immediate as opposed to the remote future, only if we can begin to solve it now, by what we do in the days of our life.

Unlike theoretical problems, practical problems can be solved only by action. Thinking is practical rather than theoretical when it aims at action; and, for that very reason, practical thinking never suffices to solve a practical problem. An *intelligent* solution requires thinking about courses of action before we undertake them; but no thinking by itself, however intelligent, constitutes a solution. That comes into being only when we start to act.

The man who begins to act must begin in the situation in which he finds himself, not on a stage set by his imagination to suit his hopes. Practical thinking is, therefore, required to anticipate the circumstances by which action will be circumscribed at every stage of its development. That is why the distinction between the immediate and the remote future is of such crucial importance.

When we consider the probability of future wars and the probable future of peace, we see that we have two practicable objectives, not one: the longest truce that can be made to postpone another world war, and the lasting peace which can eventually be instituted to prevent all wars.

4

The shortsighted realist says that perpetual peace is *not* a practicable objective *now*.

We must disagree with him if what he means is that this problem belongs *entirely* to the future; that the only problem which deserves our attention now is postponing or controlling the occurrence of the next world war. But if he means that prolonging the truce is the only objective we can fully realize in our lifetime, he is right.

The idealist says that perpetual peace *is* a practical objective *now*.

We must agree with him if what he means is that we can begin now to promote policies and take steps which will hasten the day of its realization. But he is wrong if he supposes that this objective can be encompassed in our lifetime; if he impatiently proposes that we should discard all plans which have as their lowly aim the mere postponement of another war.

An objective warrants our practical interest if it satisfies *one* or *both* of two distinct conditions. The first condition is that the goal be something toward which we can *work* now. This is a necessary condition. Any goal toward which no steps can be taken *now* is *now not practicable at all*. The second condition is that the goal be something which we can realize during our lifetime. This is a dispensable condition. An objective toward which we can take definite steps now, but which we cannot reach in the immediate future, is practicable to some extent, though not as completely as the objective which satisfies both conditions.

Let us call the goal which satisfies both conditions an "immediate objective." Let us call the one which satisfies the necessary condition alone a "remote objective." It follows then that an immediate objective belongs *wholly* to the immediate future, both as to effort and as to attainment; whereas a remote objective belongs *partly* to the immediate future, *as to effort,* and partly to the remote future, *as to attainment.*

An objective must be more than merely possible. There must be some present grounds for thinking that it is probably attainable in the future, immediate or remote. If from our knowledge of the past and our acquaintance with existing realities we cannot foresee any definite probability of its accomplishment, then neither can we see how to plan, how to take steps now, toward achieving it. Such an objective is not practicable *now*—not even in the incomplete sense proper to remote goals.

As far as peace is concerned, the realist makes the more serious error. Even when he does not deny the possibility of peace, he fails to see the practical significance of its probability within a future that is really short, but too long for him because it goes beyond our lifetime. He erroneously supposes that practical thinking, planning and action, should restrict itself to goals that are attainable within the lifetime of the planners and agents, or at least during the lifetime of all the generations now alive.

Unless we rectify this error, unless we see that we have two goals, not one, we are likely to postpone the coming of peace by our failure to act now. We can also fail to postpone the next war by neglecting the truce that must be made, not for its own sake, but for the sake of peace.

5

Postponing the next war and securing perpetual peace are not incompatible goals to work for at the same time. On the contrary, prolonging the truce is not only an immediate goal, but it is also itself one of the *means* to the remote goal—peace. Postponing the next war—if this can be done by means which are essentially just as well as practically effective—may provide one of the conditions needed for the long-term project of gradually overcoming obstacles to those political institutions without which perpetual peace is impossible.

When two goals are related as immediate and remote, and the easier objective is itself a means to the more difficult one, two rules of practical wisdom should govern our conduct.

The first is: *never regard working for the remote end as something to put off until you have gained the easier objective.* This rule is violated by the man who knows that human happiness consists in more than the possession of *some* wealth but who, because wealth is one of the means to happiness, puts off the cultivation of his mind and virtues until he has first amassed a *large* fortune.

The second rule is: *employ only such means to a proximate objective which will not impede or defeat the attainment of the ultimate end in view.* This is violated by the man who indulges in a fraud to facilitate getting title to property before he dies, in order to bequeath it to his children, but which his children will lose as soon as the fraud is discovered, as it is likely to be.

CHAPTER 23

Means

THROUGHOUT THIS book we have been concerned with peace, with real peace, not the "peace in our time" which is nothing but a temporary truce. It would not have been necessary to argue at length the possibility of making another truce. They have always been made at the end of wars. They will be made again. Nor was it necessary to consider the probabilities concerning the next truce—whether it will last twenty years or fifty.

The means to prolonging the truce which will postpone the next world war do not need discussion here. Mr. Lippmann and others are right in thinking that the old game of power politics must be played again. There are, of course, various ways in which this can be done, some more likely to be effective than others, some calculated to serve the interests of one nation rather than another. But without passing judgment on the coalitions, treaties, or other policies which have been proposed, we can see that the standard of judgment must include two criteria. These are formulated by the following questions:

(1) Which is more likely to postpone the next war for the longest interval?

(2) Which is least detrimental to the cause of peace; or, to put it positively, which provides the conditions most favorable to its pursuit?

The measures taken in 1816 by the Congress of Vienna, for example, may have postponed a general European war until 1914; but because they involved an oppressive use of power for reactionary purposes, they also retarded the social and political reforms which might have operated to bring the whole world nearer to peace.

Since our dominant end is peace, we need consider the truce only as a means. We need consider the means for obtaining a "good" truce only to the extent that these means also affect the promotion of peace.

2

No schemes or projects which aim solely at trucemaking and exclude peacemaking from consideration can adequately solve the problem of means.

When planning for the next war—which, in truth, is all that any trucemaking plan is—dominates the scene, the nationalists in different countries can disagree. For some a system of alliances may seem most advantageous to the national interest. Independence of action and self-reliance may recommend itself to others. Furthermore, if the terms of the so-called "peace treaties" are manifestly unjust to any nation, whether among the vanquished or the victorious, then to the ardent nationalists of that country it may seem desirable to weaken whatever expedients would prolong the truce thus initiated.

But when the question of truce plans asks us to consider their contribution to the cause of peace, the divergence of national interests becomes irrelevant—at least for anyone who thinks that national interests must not be allowed to obstruct the path to peace. The man who thinks otherwise simply does not understand what peace is, and why it necessarily involves the subordination or sacrifice of partisan and divisive interests.

Since peace does not entail the betrayal of any interests which belong *commonly* to the peoples of all nations, disagreement about the means to peace will not follow national lines. There is as likely to be agreement among men of every nation as disagreement within each particular country. The same situation will prevail with respect to the conditions of a truce in so far as the truce is regarded as a means to peace.

3

In enumerating what I think to be the limiting conditions of a good truce—good for peace—I shall try to avoid the partisanship of a special pleader. I shall try to write as a philosopher who happens to be an American, not as an American who is willing to forget philosophy.

We are concerned only with the general criteria by which specific proposals must be judged. The specific terms cannot be formulated prior to the day the war ends, without irresponsible disregard for the unknown contingencies that will confront us on that day.

With respect to any plan proposed for maintaining "peace in our time," the following conditions should be satisfied:

1. That they commit no political or economic injustice, by way of inequitable distributions or unfair discriminations.

2. That they contemplate no alliance which will, directly or indirectly, preserve a *status quo* built upon already existing injustices.

3. That they use power, whether or not through the methods of coalition, to support international good faith, not to supplant it; to safeguard freedom, not to suppress it.

4. That they anticipate the direction of social, economic, and political changes so that no measures positively taken will operate as impediments to progress anywhere in the world, and so that some positive measures be taken to facilitate it.

5. That they permit, encourage, and even perhaps institute international agencies, such as the League of Nations and the World Court, not because such institutions can by

themselves postpone the next war, much less perpetuate peace, but because such institutions provide men with the image of an international community, and with the political experience needed for the formations of the future.

6. That they multiply such agencies as the International Labor Office which deal with problems common to all nations from the point of view of a common good that transcends national interests; and, in this connection, that they create an International Office of Education for the purpose of equalizing educational opportunity throughout the world at the highest level, and in order to guide education everywhere in the training of citizens.

These six conditions do not determine the precise way in which power shall be organized in a world of independent nations. But they do recognize that no international agency can yet be formed which transgresses the external sovereignty of states.

They do not decide whether a coalition of great powers is for or against the national interest of any state. But they do help a people to decide whether its attitude toward any proposed coalition springs exclusively from partisan interests or whether it also takes a larger common good into account.

These conditions do not measure the efficacy of any plan as a device for postponing or controlling the next war. Rather they require a balance to be struck between efficiency in prolonging the truce and efficiency in promoting conditions favorable to the future of peace. The difficulty of that requirement should prepare us to expect partial failure in either direction.

The pessimist or realist is likely to say that these conditions are utopian. He should be reminded that they have a practical bearing on the immediate as well as upon the remote future. In whatever degree we fail to make the truce good *by these criteria,* we shall fail to postpone the next war as well as to hasten peace.

Throughout, these conditions observe the distinction between *making* peace and *promoting* peace. Only the latter can be done in our day.

4

Since the probabilities make perpetual peace a remote objective, plans for world federation or blueprints for world government do not rightly solve the problem of means.

Our task is to find the means best suited to our day. They will be steps we can take now while the end is still remote. That is what makes them the proper means for us to employ during our lifetime—proper because they are as remote from the goal as the goal is remote from us.

We cannot make peace, but we can promote it, by action along the following lines:

1. A JUST AND EQUITABLE TRUCE
   Every citizen who has a voice in the matter (in any country where men are citizens) should support a settlement of this war which tends to facilitate, not merely the postponement of the next war, but the advent of peace. He should oppose any arrangements by treaty or alliance which, through their intrinsic injustice, impede the world's progress toward peace.
   The general criteria for making such a judgment about specific proposals have already been set forth.

2. INTERNATIONAL AGENCIES
   The citizen, through the exercise of his suffrage or otherwise, should try to form a governmental policy which actively favors and supports all international agencies that can function to good purpose, without now requiring the abolition of sovereignty.
   The experience gained from participation in international transactions will contribute toward overcoming

unlimited nationalism and toward transcending the limited internationalism that results from it.

3. A WORLD CONSTITUTIONAL CONVENTION

Citizens should urge upon their governments the formation of a *permanent* peace conference which will continue to operate during all the years of the truce and which, except for the interruption that may be occasioned by the next world war, will continue to function until peace is finally made.

This peace conference should be sharply distinguished from the diplomatic assembly whose sole purpose is to conclude the terms of a truce. It should perform the work of a constitutional convention, drafting the articles for the constitution of world government, and considering the steps that must be taken to procure its ratification by the nations to be federated.

4. REFORM AND REVOLUTION

Men everywhere (whether leaders or followers) must exercise their freedom to participate in and accelerate all social, economic, and political reforms, which aim to enact in practice the democratic principles enshrined in constitutions.

Where constitutions exist, this can be accomplished by their amendment or through due process of law. Where no constitutions exist, the natural right of rebellion against every form of injustice remains the inalienable prerogative of man. Justified rebellions in any part of the world should enlist the sympathies, and even the active support, of peace-seeking men elsewhere, whether or not the declared policy of their own governments is that of nonintervention.

5. EDUCATION

All those who are in any way responsible for the education of others should employ education as a prime instrumentality for effecting the mental, moral, and cultural changes prerequisite to peace.

They should recognize that education can function in many ways: through enabling men to become citizens in fact as well as in right, thereby exercising an intelligent voice in their own affairs; through equalizing the races of men by remedying the accidentally conditioned or artificially induced immaturity of the so-called backward or primitive peoples; and, above all, through instructing men about the possibility and probability of a durable world-wide peace, the conditions of its attainability, and the rewards of its attainment.

These five suggestions describe steps which can be taken *now* and which, in the course of time, can be augmented by others, or enlarged in their own effectiveness.

They are addressed to any man who has some opportunity to follow one or more of these lines of action. They do not promise him the achievement of the remote goal. But they do seek to enlist his individual effort on the ground that thereby he can contribute his iota of impulse to a great historic motion that will finally reach its goal through the accumulated efforts and the patient collaboration of a vast multitude—including many generations of men as yet unborn.

These suggestions will have no appeal to the impatient, nor to men who cannot bring themselves to want peace *for their posterity.*

5

If it be asked where the plans and blueprints for world federation enter into this formulation of the means now available for peace, the answer is simple.

In the future, such plans will direct the actual making of peace.

For the present, they belong to the educational part of the enterprise which can promote, though it cannot make, peace.

The circulation and attention which schemes for world government have recently enjoyed are but the beginning of a great educational work which must be augmented and spread in ever-widening circles.

It is of the utmost importance not to discuss these plans as if they were proposals for immediate execution. That detracts from their sanity and merits their dismissal. Rather they should be examined for their implicit principles. These, when fully explicated in the light of history and political theory, provide the evidence and reasons for believing in the possibility and probability of peace.

CHAPTER 24

The Long Run

GRANTED, SAYS the practical man, that perpetual peace is possible. Granted that it is highly probable—in the long run! The trouble with the long run is that it has a way of stretching out into infinity. Meanwhile there are things right at hand crying to be done.

Reason can prove that there is a middle ground between to-morrow and infinity. Reason can prove that goals beyond our lifetime do have practical significance for us. But the passions are impetuous. Desires naturally seek quick satisfactions. We find it difficult to sustain long-range policies with emotional zest. The fact is that men are temperamentally averse to the long run.

This fact dominates all discussion about war and peace. Whoever addresses himself to his fellow men on this subject—writer or orator or leader—suffers from the subconscious awareness that the most winged words or the most rational counsels will lack appeal unless they promise an early consummation of desires.

The proponents of perpetual peace seldom restrain the rhetorical impulse to advance their plans *as if* they were capable of realization in the present. The proponents of "peace in our time" tend, for the same reason, to conceal or soft-pedal the fact that what their plans offer is not peace, but a temporary truce.

Can we appeal to reason against temperament and still win our fellow men over to the hard and long pursuit of perpetual peace? Can we move the practical man by showing him that his rejection of the remote goal condemns his posterity to the plight in which he finds himself?

Perpetual peace may look far off, but how far off it is depends, in some part, on what we do. If most men in this generation, or the next and the next, refuse to lift a finger to hasten the day, then we ought to become pessimistic about the long run. Instead of bringing the day nearer, we ourselves will have put it off almost to eternity.

2

In the individual life, remote goals frequently compete with, and even dominate, immediate interests. Fortunately for the human race, a large majority of men willingly devote their daily energies to gain results that are postponed for years.

Were this not so, most of the things which enrich a human life would never be achieved. Health in maturity must be safeguarded by care in youth. Freedom from penury in old age must be planned for and worked for at the same time one is acquiring the goods to be consumed each day. What is true of health and wealth is even more true of knowledge and virtue, friendship and the blessings of a good society. Only the pleasures of the passing moment are as immediate as they are evanescent.

In the individual life, planning is the very essence of prudence. Planning consists in making today's activities and choices fit into the larger scheme of one's whole life. It requires us to count on chickens that are not yet hatched, to think of the two birds in the bush as well as the one in the hand. Above all, it requires us to project our whole life imaginatively, in order to make a proper estimate of what must be done now for the sake of the future. The unexamined life, it has been said, is not worth living. The unplanned life will, at its end, not be worth examining.

Prudence needs help, for it must work against the natural tendency of the emotions toward present pleasures and immediate goods. Help comes through the virtues of temperance and fortitude. Temperance is the habit of foregoing immediate pleasures and profits for the sake of a greater good in the future. Fortitude consists in suffering present pains and hardships for the sake of a greater, yet remote, good.

Any man who succeeds in enriching his life by the attainment of difficult goods, which at one time may have seemed remote, possesses these virtues in some degree.

3

It will be said that this proves nothing. The individual who acts on hope deferred nevertheless expects the fruits within his lifetime. The virtues may be able to redirect the emotions, and even to sustain an emotional interest in delayed rewards; but the virtues normally operate within the scope of a single lifetime.

Fortunately, again, for the human race, the facts are otherwise. I am not thinking of the obvious fact that in all religious traditions men have, with undivided emotions, sought a promised land that is not on earth. I am thinking of the equally obvious fact that most men do make plans for their posterity. Cherishing their children as their alter egos, the begotten image of themselves, men identify their own happiness with a happiness they wish for others.

It is fruitless to debate whether such devotion represents selfishness or altruism. The point is that men are so made that their own happiness includes the happiness of others—their children, or their friends and neighbors in every sort of community.

Men are emotionally inclined to work for the welfare of their children even if they may not live to see the full fruition. They are emotionally inclined to work for the good of their compatriots even though they can hardly participate intimately in the lives of all concerned.

Why, then, should it be so difficult to make these drives and virtues operate in the cause of peace? The answer, I think, lies in some failure of imagination and in some lack of thought.

4

The failure of imagination is natural enough. Men find it easier to project themselves into the lives of their own children and the grandchildren they have enjoyed knowing than to identify themselves with the fortunes of their more remote and distant heirs. Yet the difference is only one of degree.

When the pessimist talks about postponing the next world war, he asks us to think of more than our own lives. He asks us to consider our children and even, perhaps, our grandchildren.

The man who aims at perpetual peace goes a little further. He must ask us to consider the grandchildren of our grandchildren. They, too, will be flesh of our flesh. The trouble is that our imagination fails here. If we could but imagine them concretely as belonging to us, we might feel as deeply about their welfare.

The same failure of imagination occurs with respect to our neighbors. We feel the person across the street to be our fellow man. We can even manage to use our imagination to make the common good of the larger community a concrete reality. But when, as in the case of world peace, the common good belongs to the whole human race, our imagination fails us woefully. We may be able to think of this good abstractly, as we say, but our imagination does not intercede to make it concretely touch our hearts.

Our imaginations need to be amplified. For that, an amplified experience is needed. The world would be nearer peace than it now is if most men had the experience that a few have had—the experience of the world's physical unity, and of its potentialities for social and political unity. Mr. Wendell Willkie has done us all a service by enabling us to participate vicariously in his own vivid experience of these realities.

But the firsthand experience will not be widely possessed for another century or two. In the meantime, in order to extend our imaginations, we must try to make up by thought for our lack of experience.

5

All of us recognize the difference between individual and social problems—the latter requiring us to co-operate with others in an effort to solve them. But for the most part we do not understand clearly enough that some social problems demand, not merely the co-operation of men who are contemporaries in a single community, but also the collaboration of many generations of men the world over. Such pre-eminently is the problem of peace.

It will remain unsolved until men have understood it well enough to adjust their thinking to its demands. Unlike the problem of trucemaking, it will not yet yield to temporizing efforts or hasty improvisations. The practical man must come to see the two fundamental prerequisites for its solution: first, the ordering of the gradual steps by which a remote goal can be approached; and second, the co-operation of successive generations in the discharge of obligations suited to their time and competence.

The men who wrote the Declaration of Independence and the Constitution of the United States were animated by such far-sighted conceptions of their task. They did not lightly use the word "posterity" in those great documents. They knew that they were beginning what they themselves could not complete. The amplitude of their purpose not only involved preserving to posterity the blessings they intended; it also involved calling posterity to the task of enlarging that endowment.

The building of democracy in the new world, like the building of Gothic cathedrals in the old, followed a plan which took for granted that no single generation could raise the structure from foundation to spire. Employed at the level and in the offices which time assigned, each generation gained impetus for its own labors from the labor already done; each took pleasure in the contribution of its hands; each expected the succeeding generations to enhance the whole. They did not ask for more. They did not refuse to work because an accident of birth placed them in a generation too early to see the work finished.

Some of the Gothic cathedrals took three hundred years to build. But they were used for worship before they were completed. Democracy in America has taken almost two centuries to develop. It still remains to be rounded out, but men have already begun to prosper under its auspices. In the execution of time-spanning projects, projects which dedicate the efforts of many generations to a remote posterity, the generations which come before the ultima Thule have, nevertheless, their own rewards.

Perpetual peace will never be made unless the work is begun and carried on by generations of men who will not live to see it accomplished. To be satisfied with the tasks and rewards which time has allotted to them, they need only understand the character of the problem they are trying to solve. Then they will know why they should not do less than they can do, or expect more than they can get.

Once this is understood, membership in the human race should be enough to bring their virtues into play and to overcome their indifference to the long run.

BIBLIOGRAPHY
OF QUOTED MATTER

*Note: The following citations refer to authors and **books** or periodicals quoted, arranged according to the chapters and pages where reference to them occurred. Dates of publication are given, and wherever copyright material is involved, the publisher's name is included. I wish to thank authors and publishers of these copyrighted works for their kind permission to reprint the quotations incorporated in the text.*

M. J. A.

Chapter 2

PAGE

12 WALTER LIPPMANN, *Some Notes on War and Peace*, Macmillan, New York, 1940: pp. 14-17.

12 *Ibid.*, pp. 13-14.

13 WALTER LIPPMANN, *U. S. Foreign Policy*, Little, Brown and Co., Boston, 1943: pp. 166-68.

13 fn. HERBERT HOOVER, in an address delivered before the Kansas City Chamber of Commerce, as reported in *The New York Times*, October 29, 1943.

15 MICHAEL STRAIGHT, *Make This the Last War*, Harcourt, Brace and Co., Inc., New York, 1943: pp. 283-84.

15 *Ibid.*, pp. 392-93.

17 JOHN FOSTER DULLES, in an address reported in *The New York Times*, September 25, 1943.

18 TALK OF THE TOWN, in *The New Yorker*, May 15, 1943.

19 BACKGROUND FOR PEACE, in *Time*, Sept. 13, 1943.

20 TALK OF THE TOWN, in *The New Yorker*, July 10, 1943.

Chapter 4

40 JEAN-JACQUES ROUSSEAU, *A Lasting Peace* and *The State of War* (c. 1756). trans. by C. E. Vaughan, London, 1917: p. 127.

Chapter 5

PAGE

44   THOMAS HOBBES, *Leviathan* (1651): Part I, Ch. 13.

44   JEAN-JACQUES ROUSSEAU, *op. cit.*, pp. 121-22.

44   J. A. HOBSON, *Towards International Government*, Macmillan, N. Y., and Allen & Unwin, Ltd., London, 1915: p. 180.

44   THORSTEIN VEBLEN, *An Inquiry into the Nature of Peace and the Terms of Its Perpetuation*, Macmillan, New York, 1917: p. 4.

47   EMERY REVES, *A Democratic Manifesto*, Random House, Inc., New York, 1942: p. 64.

47   TALK OF THE TOWN, in *The New Yorker*, May 6, 1943.

48   WALTER LIPPMANN, *Some Notes on War and Peace:* pp. 10-11.

49   ST. AUGUSTINE, *City of God* (413-26): Book 19, Ch. 13.

Chapter 6

55   THOMAS HOBBES, *op. cit.*, Part I, Ch. 14.

57 fn. ALEXANDER HAMILTON, *The Federalist Papers*, No. 6.

63   ALEXANDER HAMILTON, *Federalist Papers*, No. 6, No. 51, February 8, 1788, and No. 15, November 19, 1787.

67   MARCUS TULLIUS CICERO, *De Officiis* (45-44 B.C.): Book I, Ch. 11.

Chapter 7

76   KARL VON CLAUSEWITZ, *On War* (1832), trans. by O. J. Matthijs Jolles, Modern Library, New York, 1943: Book I, Ch. 1, p. 16.

79   WALTER LIPPMANN, *Some Notes on War and Peace:* pp. 20-21.

80   EMERY REVES, *op. cit.*, p. 78.

83   THUCYDIDES, *History of the Peloponnesian War* (431-411 B.C.): Book II, Ch. 1.

Chapter 8

94   BACKGROUND FOR PEACE, in *Time*, September 13, 1943.

96   THOMAS HOBBES, *op. cit.*, Part I, Ch. 13.

PAGE

96 JOHN LOCKE, *Of Civil Government* (2nd Essay, 1690): Ch. 2, ¶ 14.

97 *Ibid.,* Ch. 19, ¶ 219 and 232.

97 JEAN-JACQUES ROUSSEAU, *op. cit.,* p. 47 and pp. 86-87.

97 IMMANUEL KANT, *Perpetual Peace* (1795), reprinted by the Columbia University Press, New York, 1939: pp. 10-20.

98 *Ibid.,* pp. 21-23.

99 GEORG WILHELM FRIEDRICH HEGEL, *Philosophy of Right* (1833), trans. by T. M. Knox, Oxford, 1942: Part III, Third Section, B, ¶ 330-34.

99 JOHANN GOTTLIEB FICHTE, *Lectures to the German Nation* (1807) .

Chapter 9

102 fn. EDITORIAL in *The Commonweal,* October 8, 1943.

105 JOHN CHAMBERLAIN, in a review of *Germany's Master Plan,* in *The New York Times,* Jan. 30, 1943: p. 13.

105 PLATO, *Republic,* Book IX.

106 ALEXANDER HAMILTON, *The Federalist Papers,* No. 6.

Chapter 10

110 D. G. RITCHIE, *Studies in Political and Social Ethics:* p. 169.

Chapter 11

114 HANS KELSEN, *Law and Peace in International Relations,* Harvard University Press, Cambridge, 1942: p. 112.

Chapter 12

142 fn. JOHN K. JESSUP, "Our Foreign Policy," in *Life,* Sept. 20, 1943; and Background for Peace in *Time,* Sept. 13, 1943.

149 TALK OF THE TOWN, in *The New Yorker,* May 8, 1943.

PAGE

150 ISOCRATES, *Panegyricus*, 1, 172.

150 THORSTEIN VEBLEN, *op. cit.*, p. 7.

Chapter 13

159 HANS KELSEN, *op. cit.*, pp. 150-51.

160 fn. MR. JUSTICE ROBERTS, Address before The American Society of International Law, reported in *The New York Times*, May 2, 1943.

160 WALTER LIPPMANN, *U. S. Foreign Policy:* pp. 133-35.

Chapter 14

169 ARNOLD TOYNBEE, *A Study of History*, Oxford, London, 1939: Preface to Parts IV and V.

Chapter 16

192 ARISTOTLE, *Politics*, Book I, Ch. 1, 2.

196 THUCYDIDES, *History of the Peloponnesian War*, Book I, Ch. 1.

206 J. A. HOBSON, *op. cit.*, p. 192.

207 GEORGE BURTON ADAMS, *Civilization During the Middle Ages*, New York, 1894: pp. 187-88, and fn. 1 on p. 222.

Chapter 17

214 JOHN STUART MILL, *Of Representative Government* (1861): Ch. 1.

216 JEREMY BENTHAM, *Plan for An Universal and Perpetual Peace* (1786), Essay IV in *Principles of International Law,* in *Works,* ed. by John Bowring, Edinburgh, 1843: p. 546.

216 IMMANUEL KANT, *op. cit.*, pp. 24-25.

Chapter 18

222 PLATO, *Republic*, Book II.

226 fn. JOHN FOSTER DULLES, "Toward World Order," in *A Basis for the Peace to*

PAGE

Come, published by Abingdon-Cokesbury Press, New York, 1942: pp. 45-46, 49.

227 J. A. HOBSON, *op. cit.*, p. 180.

227 HARRY SCHERMAN, "The Last Best Hope of Earth," in the *Atlantic Monthly*, November, 1941: p. 576. Also published in book form, Random House (1941).

229 EMERY REVES, *op. cit.*, pp. 124-25.

Chapter 19

237 JACQUES MARITAIN, "Europe and the Federal Idea," in *The Commonweal*, April 19, 1940: p. 545.

246 WILLIAM PENN, *An Essay Towards the Present and Future Peace of Europe* (1693); Everyman's Library, pp. 14-15.

247 WALTER LIPPMANN, *U. S. Foreign Policy*, pp. 105-06.

247 fn. BACKGROUND FOR PEACE, in *Time*, September 13, 1943.

249 EMERY REVES, *op. cit.*, p. 42.

249 THORSTEIN VEBLEN, *op. cit.*, pp. 31, 38, 78.

251 EDITORIAL, *Detroit Free Press*, Jan. 17, 1943.

251 ROANE WARING, Address in San Francisco, Aug. 16, 1943; as reported in *The New York Times*, Aug. 17, 1943.

Chapter 20

254 JEAN-JACQUES ROUSSEAU, *op. cit.*, p. 72.

255 *Ibid.*, p. 91.

262 R. H. TAWNEY, *The Acquisitive Society*, Harcourt, Brace, New York, 1920: p. 179.

Chapter 21

270 EMERY REVES, *op. cit.*, pp. 99-100.

273-4 EDWARD J. BYNG, *A Five Year Peace Plan*, Coward-McCann, Inc., New York, 1943: pp. 5, 29.